Youth Culture and the Post-War British Novel

Youth Culture and the Post-War British Novel

From Teddy Boys to *Trainspotting*

Stephen Ross

BLOOMSBURY ACADEMIC
LONDON • NEW YORK • OXFORD • NEW DELHI • SYDNEY

BLOOMSBURY ACADEMIC
Bloomsbury Publishing Plc
50 Bedford Square, London, WC1B 3DP, UK
1385 Broadway, New York, NY 10018, USA

BLOOMSBURY, BLOOMSBURY ACADEMIC and the Diana logo are trademarks of
Bloomsbury Publishing Plc

First published in Great Britain 2019

Cover design by Eleanor Rose
Cover image: Teddy Boys in Gateshead, Tyne and Wear, England, Circa 1965 © Mirrorpix

A catalogue record for this book is available from the British Library.

Library of Congress Cataloging-in-Publication Data
Names: Ross, Stephen, 1970– author.
Title: Youth culture and the post-war British novel :
from Teddy Boys to Trainspotting / Stephen Ross.
Description: London : Bloomsbury Academic, 2018. |
Includes bibliographical references and index.
Identifiers: LCCN 2018003583 (print) | LCCN 2018025701 (ebook) |
ISBN 9781350067875 (ePUB) | ISBN 9781350067882 (ePDF) |
ISBN 9781350067851 (pbk.) | ISBN 9781350067868 (harback)
Subjects: LCSH: English fiction–20th century–History and criticism. |
Youth in literature. | Masculinity in literature. | Conflict of generations in literature.
Classification: LCC PR888.Y69 (ebook) | LCC PR888.Y69 R67 2018 (print) |
DDC 823/.9109352421–dc23
LC record available at https://lccn.loc.gov/2018003583

ISBN: HB: 978-1-3500-6786-8
PB: 978-1-3500-6785-1
ePDF: 978-1-3500-6788-2
eBook: 978-1-3500-6787-5

Typeset by Newgen KnowledgeWorks Pvt. Ltd., Chennai, India
Printed and bound in Great Britain

To find out more about our authors and books visit www.bloomsbury.com
and sign up for our newsletters.

To my mother, who absolutely is a baby boomer,
no matter what she says.

CONTENTS

FIGURES

ACKNOWLEDGEMENTS

My first and most resounding thanks go to my wife, Stephanie Novak, and my kids, Adam and Kathleen Ross. They put up with me and this project, sometimes even with good humour, for longer than any of us thought they'd have to. Their support and understanding can't be overstated. Likewise, I would like to thank my mom for her support my entire life and assert once and for all in print that she absolutely *is* a baby boomer. I have benefitted beyond merit from many conversations with my colleagues at the University of Victoria, chiefly Christopher Douglas, Allan Mitchell, Nicholas Bradley, Erin Ellerbeck, Matthew Huculak, Shamma Boyarin, Adrienne Williams-Boyarin, G. Kim Blank, Emile Fromet de Rosnay, Magda Kay, Elizabeth Grove-White and Gary Kuchar. It really does take a village, I suppose. I'd also like especially to thank the various graduate students in our department who became stalwarts of Write Club, during which the entire first draft of this book and most of its revisions were completed: Emily Arvay, Amy Tang, Tiffany Chan, Tiffany Parks, Denae Dyck, Samantha MacFarlane, Katie Tanigawa and Jana Millar Usiskin. Amy Tang whipped the manuscript into shape with such speed and accuracy that she made me question the space–time continuum, for which cosmic gratitude. The students, both undergraduate and graduate, who enrolled in the classes where I worked out much of this book also deserve thanks: you are too many to enumerate, but you played an important role. The University of Victoria Speakers Bureau, under whose aegis I had the chance to present my research to the broader community in Victoria, provided a sorely needed chance to test-drive ideas and language, and – fortuitously – to speak to some veterans of the original Teddy boy, Teddy girl, mod and rocker groups. Thanks in particular to Mandy Crocker for facilitating those talks.

Further afield, I would like to thank Angeliki Spiropolou for inviting me to present part of this research at the Institute of Advanced Study of the University of London; Vassiliki Kolocotroni and Nigel Leask for hosting me in a similar vein at the University of Glasgow; Christine Reynier and Jean-Michel Ganteau for the kind invitation to speak and stay in residence at the Université Paul Valéry Montpellier III; and Derek James Ryan at the University of Kent for invitations, hosting and general conviviality. Likewise, David Avital and Clara Herberg at Bloomsbury have been simply wonderful: David for being willing to listen to a pitch for something other than a traditional scholarly monograph and Clara for her superhuman patience and organizational abilities. I'm so grateful that they've given this Misfit Toy a home. The anonymous readers provided valuable feedback and invaluable encouragement. Such work is all too often thankless, so, since *you* at least know who you are: thank you.

Finally, this whole thing began with Evelyn Cobley, my then-department chair, coming by my office in 2003 to tell me that she'd assigned me to teach post-war British fiction – about which I knew pretty much zilch. Thanks, Evelyn. It worked out in the end.

Introduction

What this book is

The foundation for *Youth Culture and the Post-War British Novel* was laid way back in 2003 when the chair of my department came to my office door and informed me that I had been assigned to teach a course on British fiction from the Second World War to the present. I demurred: I was then (and, really, remain) a specialist of pre-Second World War literature and culture. She insisted: I *would* teach the course. 'What on earth', I thought in something of a panic, 'am I going to put on the course?' I quickly made a list of the post-Second World War novels I knew well enough even to have a stab at teaching. The list was pretty broad, including *The Satanic Verses, Saturday Night and Sunday Morning, The Infernal Desire Machines of Dr. Hoffmann, The Bluest Flower, The Golden Notebook, Trainspotting, Molloy, The Buddha of Suburbia* and several more besides. Casting about for a thread linking some subset of these works, something that could hold them together as a course rather than as a random sampling of post-Second World War British and Irish fiction, I hit upon their engagement with youth culture. Having, in my time, played at being a punk, a skater and a new romantic myself, I was especially smitten with this confluence and set about exploring its parameters and potentials. What I found was both fascinating and alarming.

First, the fascinating. There is indeed a whole suite of post-Second World War British novels that continue to capture the imaginations and allegiances of readers twenty, forty, even sixty years after they appeared. In some cases, as with *Saturday Night and Sunday Morning*, readers coming to the novel for the first time may well be repeating the discoveries and intense identifications of not just their parents, but also their grandparents. As Jon Savage and Nick Bentley have outlined in great detail, the advent of the category of the teenager in the decade after the end of the war both responded to and perpetuated a set of anxieties around identity formation, masculinity, history and generational progress/tension that resonated in surprisingly durable terms. So much so that multiple generations have, for example, seen themselves in *Saturday Night*'s Teddy boy protagonist Arthur Seaton, with his anarchistic, at times nihilistic, ethos. What's more, even people with no apparent interest in post-Second World War British fiction at least know of some of these novels: They have public recognition that is, often, far in excess of their literary merit. *The Golden Notebook* is superior to *A Clockwork Orange* as a novel, but the latter has far greater public recognition. No doubt this is in large part due to the controversial film version of Burgess's novel, while Lessing's has gone un-adapted. But I think there is more to it than just this. Part of what has made both the film and the novel versions of *A Clockwork Orange* so enduringly popular is precisely that they captured the public imagination: They provoked outrage, spawned copy-cat crimes, challenged readers with their difficult language and still – over fifty years after the novel was published and over thirty years after the film was released – inspire countless Halloween costumes. 'Something interesting', I thought to myself, 'is going on here. Something linking together these novels and keeping them relevant to new and seasoned readers alike, for decades after they first appear.'

So much for the fascinating – which, to be honest, will preoccupy us for the next couple of hundred pages, so we can safely park it for the moment. Before we carry on with that, though, we have to deal with the alarming. Though a wide range of youth cultures are represented in these novels, and issues of race, class, sexuality and nationality are all in play, the perceptive reader will already have noticed that they are all written by men and that they all feature male protagonists. They are uniformly preoccupied with masculinity, obsessed with it even. This is alarming for obvious reasons: Women were full participants in youth culture, women write plenty of novels and women are traditionally under-represented in scholarly work as it is. Keenly aware of this as a significant potential problem from the outset, I spent several years in vain attempts to discover and integrate women writers – or at least female protagonists – into the fold.

To this end, I experimented with a range of novels by women. Muriel Spark provided perhaps the most promising possibilities. Her astonishing output, including *The Ballad of Peckham Rye* (1960), *The Prime of Miss Jean Brodie* (1961) and *Girls of Slender Means* (1963), outshines the work of most male post-war writers in terms of literary merit, and deals extensively with the challenges of young women coming of age in the post-war. Antonia White's *Frost in May* trilogy of the 1950s similarly looks promising, providing a sustained examination of female post-war *Bildung*. But this book is not about youth progressing to maturity, nor about the trials of simply being young, adolescent or pre-adult. It is about popular youth-cultural formations that were clearly identified as such, given widely accepted names and understood in terms of explicit stylistic and attitude identities. Spark's and White's novels certainly address the cultures of young women, but they do not do so in terms of contemporary mass youth cultures. The girls of slender means do not find the meaning of their lives in youth-cultural affiliations, roaming the streets to establish and reinforce their identities or pack allegiances. As they navigate the shoals of young adulthood, they do not become Teddy girls and do not actively set themselves in rebellious attitudes towards the parental generation. Instead, they get on with it and just grow up. Perhaps sadly, this places them in a whole separate league from virtually all the young men in novels such as *A Clockwork Orange*. Though they were not actively writing about youth culture, writers such as Spark, Emma Tennant, Iris Murdoch and Angela Carter were clearly participating in some of its impulses, moving away from fictions of authenticity and settled traditional or received historical wisdom and towards performance, speculation and play. Likewise, they continued the post-war project of recovering women's experience, both historical and contemporary, and bringing it into the open.

Carter's *Infernal Desire Machines* merits a further note in this regard, since it is among the handful of candidate novels I experimented with and ultimately had to leave out of this study. That novel explicitly invokes Dr. Albert Hofmann, the man who first synthesized LSD and thus provided psychedelic hippiedom with its signature drug. It also features a wide-open field of desire, sex and sexuality, and a speculative approach to history that conforms well to the patterns that we see in *The Rachel Papers* and *The Buddha of Suburbia*. It follows a mixed picaresque/Bildungsroman narrative arc, like so many of the novels discussed here, and revives the surrealist faith in the utopian potential of dreams. Above all, its main characters are young people trying to find their way in a world apparently gone mad. But, as I've found out, there is a big difference between the culture of young people – adolescence, youth, even delinquency – and youth cultures proper. *Infernal Desire Machines* absolutely belongs in a study of the cultures of youth, but it presents too little for inclusion in a study of youth cultures: Though the link between Dr. Hofmann and hippies is certainly *there*, it's not enough to hang an entire youth culture on. It's a tough loss to take.

Though such novels concern themselves with young people, as many thousands of novels do, they do not think with and about youth cultures per se. They are not engaged directly with the contemporaneous subcultures of the young that were having such an outsized impact on the world around them. I will want to come back to this, and offer something by way of a speculative account of why this might be so shortly, when we talk about why both youth cultures and novelistic representations of them appeared when they did. For now, though, perhaps it will suffice to say that my sense of the reason for this gap between male and female representational strategies is quite simply that women had better things to do. To be sure, they participated as fully in the same youth cultures as did young men (and they still do), but women writers seem to have had other fish to fry, and men writers seem to have been characteristically preoccupied with what was emerging in the post-Second World War decades as a near-existential crisis of masculinity. Like the titular Rachel of Martin Amis's *The Rachel Papers*, women appear to have been busy getting on in the world, discovering their potential and charting new territory in the worlds of work, pleasure and culture, while some men – like the narrator-protagonist of Amis's novel, Charles Highway – were doing a lot of navel-gazing, trying out various forms of masculinity and maturity and writing it all down for posterity. More on both of these anon.

As I taught this material again and again, it gradually assumed the shape of a coherent study. So, one day, against my better judgement and all warnings to the contrary, I decided to try writing it. Taking this decision meant reading a lot of sociology and cultural history, along with literary criticism and literary history, and talking to anyone who would listen (see the acknowledgements page for a list of those I badgered most persistently). I tested out ideas, asked for recommendations and spent a lot of time thinking about why there weren't more novels written by women about women, or by men about women. In the end, I simply had to overcome my scruples about writing a book that was just about men writing about men (a man writing about men writing about men – just what we need!) and face the music. 'Damn the torpedoes', I thought, 'full speed ahead! Something undeniably interesting is going on in these novels, and I want to know what it is.'

What this book is about

This book is about how a suite of iconic post-Second World War British novels think both *with and about* youth cultures. It has three main objectives:

1. It aims to animate those novels for readers coming to them for the first time or seeking a way into the much larger field of post-Second World War British fiction.
2. It hopes to reanimate those works for non-specialist readers who may think they already know them.
3. It advances new interpretations of works by both well-known and emerging writers alike.

To these ends, it

1. briefly outlines in broad strokes the incredibly complex social, political and historical contexts in which both the youth cultures emerged and the novels were written. It summarizes rather than detailing these contexts, attempting to create high-level overviews that allow me to characterize the sorts of tensions and anxieties driving youth cultures and how they are represented. It thus

takes us from the devastation and plight of displaced persons in the immediate aftermath of the war through the Suez Crisis, the Profumo Affair and England's massively symbolic World Cup win in 1966, to the resurgent Troubles in Northern Ireland, the Energy Crisis and labour troubles of the 1970s, Thatcherism and the rise of neoliberalism, and wraps up with the heroin crisis of the 1990s and the political/cultural rebranding of the UK in terms of 'Cool Britannia'.

2. introduces key aspects of the succession of youth cultures that punctuated the last half of the twentieth century, beginning with the Teddy boys of the 1950s; and moving on to the mods, rockers and hippies of the 1960s; the glam rockers and punks of the 1970s; the new romantics, soulsters, rude bwais and Rastafarians of the 1980s; and wrapping up with the ravers and heroin chic devotees of the 1990s.

3. pairs each of these contexts and youth cultures with one or more novels: *Saturday Night and Sunday Morning, Absolute Beginners, A Clockwork Orange, The Rachel Papers, The Buddha of Suburbia, Brixton Rock, East of Acre Lane* and *Trainspotting*.

As I hope is abundantly clear by now, my primary focus is on these novels. This is first, last and throughout a study of literary works in their contexts, rather than a study of those contexts per se (more about what this book is not about later in this chapter). I have chosen these novels for inclusion because they actively represent the youth cultures of, or very close to, the decades in which they were written. They are explicitly about those youth cultures at the same time as they use them as handy metaphors for engaging with larger sets of concerns. That is, as the vast body of sociological and cultural-historical work on these youth cultures has shown in enormous detail, the youth cultures themselves arise out of felt tensions and anxieties in the shifting realities of the post-Second World War world. As such, they furnish writers with ready-made figures for further exploring those very same tensions and anxieties. For the youth cultures themselves, these dynamics are often unconscious, blind and fumbling, and not infrequently productive of violent outbursts. The writers who represent these figures and the complex situations they both express and inhabit, by contrast, can expose those unconscious investments and anxieties. Uncovering the unconscious ways youth cultures engage with problems of race, class, gender and sexuality and expanding upon them through representations of youth culture both accord the successive youth cultures of the post-war period their proper due as legitimate forms of cultural expression and negotiation, and provide new perspectives on problematics that have been around much longer than the teenager. Teddy boy, mod, rocker, skinhead, glam rocker, punk, raver, heroin addict, rude boy or perpetual outsider barred even from access to these designated 'outsider' groups, the characters in these novels present semiotic knots to untangle. Doing so will, I hope, help us understand both how the British post-war period was marked by a new kind of generational conflict and how that conflict helped shape some of the most influential literature of the second half of the twentieth century. Chief among the concerns *Youth Culture and the Post-War British Novel* traces in this suite of novels are crises of masculinity, race and ethnicity, generational relationships and history itself in the wake of the Holocaust. It aims to shed new light on how they are embedded in, and responded to, their cultural moments. Likewise, it illustrates how these novels embed such concerns in plot, characterization, narrative detail and style.

Naturally, as mass media expand and youth cultures both innovate and persist, the representations shift dramatically as well. Authors increasingly come to understand youth cultures as representational regimes in themselves, as much products of media-savvy self-fashioning as expressions of (a longing for) authentic identity. As *Youth Culture and the Post-War British Novel* progresses, then, my treatment of the novels also gets more complex. Self-awareness is both the blessing and the curse of adolescence, as it is equally for novels about youth cultures. The increasing self-referentiality of both the youth cultures and the novels about them, particularly from about 1970 onwards, means that representations proliferate and authenticity becomes at once more precious and more elusive. Much of the discussion in the second half of this book, therefore, concentrates on an additional crisis on top of those already enumerated: That of identity itself, not in terms of discovering who one is (What is my core identity?) but in terms of whether identity itself is even possible (Is it a coherent category at all, or is everything just a matter of performance?). This crisis culminates, as does this book and, I contend, the post-Second World War current of youth-cultural experimentation, with the triumph of chemical dependency in the heroin chic aesthetic of *Trainspotting*. There, the problem of authentic identity is not so much resolved as finally deferred and evaded. The physical dependency produced by addiction displaces questions of what's authentic and real versus what's inauthentic or fake. Necessity displaces truth, and the deeper engagements of previous youth cultures are effaced by the 'honest' need produced by heroin. The result in terms of youth culture is pastiche, as *Trainspotting* freely deploys aspects of virtually all the previous youth-cultural stylistic ensembles and pillages the music, art, language and ethos of the preceding fifty years of experimentation. Even the novel's conclusion, as we will see, presents nothing like progress so much as the promise of backsliding and further futile entrapment. It's not exactly a chipper ending to the story – either the story of Mark Renton or the story of post-Second World War novels about youth cultures – but it's where we end up: Like Begbie's father, making jokes to a son he doesn't even recognize about trainspotting in the disused Leith Central train station.

What this book is not – I: sociology

Youth Culture and the Post-War British Novel is emphatically not a study of
post-war youth cultures in any sociological or cultural-historical sense. There
is an entire field of scholarship that approaches youth cultures, subcultures,
underground cultures, club cultures, deviance, criminality and so on from a
sociological perspective. At least since G. Stanley Hall's initial identification
of adolescence as a developmental category back in 1904, people have been
studying the young we have come to think of loosely as teenagers. This
book contributes to our understanding of particular subgroups of that much
larger category by analysing how they are represented in the novels of their
day. It draws upon sociological and cultural-historical studies to sketch in
broad strokes the styles and attitudes of punks, skinheads, mods and so on.
But it does not undertake the sort of archival or field work required to add
materially to our understanding of how such groups formed, operated and
understood themselves either in the immediate moment of their flourishing
or in the latter-day reconstructions and re-animations to which they seem
perpetually given.

Readers who are interested in pursuing the line of sociological and
cultural-historical research should likely begin with Hall's establishment
of adolescence as a distinct developmental stage, just to get a sense of the
root configuration of the category that would eventually become that of
the teenager. Howard S. Becker's *Outsiders: Studies in the Sociology of
Deviance* (1963) is among the first and most important works to approach
the problem of youth subcultures in the context of deviance and criminality,
two features that were popularly aligned with groups such as the Teddy
boys, mods and rockers. On the tension between popular conceptions of
these movements and their actual dimensions, Stanley Cohen's landmark
Folk Devils and Moral Panics (1972) is perhaps the *locus classicus* and
an important precursor to the later studies to follow. The advent of the
Birmingham Centre for Contemporary Cultural Studies (BCCCS) in 1964
coalesced growing interest in cultural history under the rubric of Cultural
Studies and spawned many of the most influential and insightful studies
of youth cultures to emerge in the second half of the twentieth century.
It includes path-breaking – and enduringly useful – studies such as Stuart
Hall and Tony Jefferson's *Resistance Through Rituals* (1975) and Dick
Hebdige's *Subculture: The Meaning of Style* (1979), both of which collect
papers previously circulated in mimeograph within the BCCCS. Angela
McRobbie's work is of paramount importance in the literature on post-
Second World War youth cultures, especially because it focuses on young
women, feminism, and gender and sexuality. Her 'Shut Up and Dance: Youth
Culture and Changing Modes of Femininity' (1993) and 'Top Girls? Young
Women and the Post-Feminist Sexual Contract' (2007) represent just the
tip of the iceberg. A large portion of her most significant work appears

in 'Jackie': An Ideology of Adolescent Femininity (1978), Zoot-Suits and Second-Hand Dresses (1988) and Feminism and Youth Culture (2000). The turn of the millennium produced a flurry of excellent studies such as Mike Storry and Peter Childs's British Cultural Identities (1997); Hans-Jürgen Diller, Erwin Otto and Gerd Stratmann's Youth Identities: Teens and Tweens in British Culture (1999); Chris Jenks's Subculture: The Fragmentation of the Social (2005); Jon Savage's Teenage: The Creation of Youth Culture (2007) and England's Dreaming (2002); Steve Redhead's The Clubcultures Reader (1998); and Simon Reynolds's Generation Ecstasy: Into the World of Techno and Rave Culture (1999). The tradition of such study is strong and deep, and continues today with new publications every year dedicated to illuminating and analysing the particularities of youth cultures as they continue to evolve. As we introduce specific youth cultures in each chapter, we'll indicate some more specific resources for those interested in learning about their particulars from a sociological perspective.

What this book is not – II: a scholarly intervention in the field of post-Second World War British fiction

Youth Culture and the Post-War British Novel makes no pretence to being a significant scholarly intervention in the field of post-Second World War British fiction. That field is vast, and Youth Culture and the Post-War British Novel covers only a very narrow slice of it. It makes no attempt to upend the scholarly consensus with its insights, though I do hope that it will bring something new to those working on the specific novels treated here. In this respect, my intention in writing this book has been different than that of a traditional literary-critical monograph. Rather than attempting to move the field itself in a new direction, Youth Culture and the Post-War British Novel aims to bring new readers into it via an engaging treatment of some key works, as well as to reinvigorate the interest of readers who may already be familiar with some or all of the works it analyses. It advances new readings and suggests that these novels are properly understood through their engagements with contemporary youth cultures, but it tries to avoid becoming technical or arcane in its handling of those readings. It depends upon the wider body of scholarship in the field, to be sure, but engages with it using a light touch, deferring more in-depth scholarly engagement for another time, another opportunity. So, while Youth Culture and the Post-War British Novel is indeed literary criticism, and I fondly hope that even experts in the field will find something of value in my readings, it should be clear from the outset that it is not the sort of book that is aimed at causing a stir among scholars much more firmly grounded – and with much greater stakes – in the field than I.

My hope is, rather, that *Youth Culture and the Post-War British Novel* will serve as a work of popular literary criticism, after the models of popular history, popular science and even popular religious studies. Such works are written for general readers with some grounding in the subject matter and an interest in learning more about it. They presume readers both interested and educated enough to make sense of the narratives they spin, and inherently interested in – or at least potentially interested in – the material. Though there is precious little precedent for such work in the field of literary studies, my sincere wish is that this book will find such an audience. Just as there are readers interested enough to read a popular history of Rome, or a popular account of evolutionary theory, even to tackle so unassumingly difficult a book as Stephen Hawking's *Brief History of Time* (1988), so, I hope, there will be readers sufficiently interested in these iconic novels and/or the youth cultures they represent to make their way through the remainder of this book.

Readers seeking broader overviews of the field of post-Second World War British fiction and/or who are more interested in its larger contours could do significantly worse than to follow the work of David James. James's critical monograph *Legacies of Modernism* (2011) is among the best treatments of the post-Second World War literary scene as anchored in the pre-Second World War tradition and yet striking out in new directions. It ranks with Thomas S. Davis's *The Extinct Scene* (2016), Marina McKay's *Modernism and World War II* (2003) and *British Fiction After Modernism* (co-edited with Lyndsey Stonebridge 2007), Steven Connor's *The English Novel in History 1950–1995* (1996) and Andrzej Gasiorek's *Post-War British Fiction* (1995) as key points of orientation for understanding the scholarly state of play in the field. Readers interested in really delving into the contemporary scholarly context will find more than enough material in the bibliographies of these works to keep them going for a good long time.

Along the same lines as James's and McKay and Stonebridge's collections are the terrific overview collections provided by Robert L. Caserio's *The Cambridge Companion to the Twentieth-Century English Novel* (2009), James Acheson's *The British and Irish Novel since 1960* (1991), Brian Shaffer's *A Companion to The British and Irish Novel 1945–2000* (2005) and Randall Stevenson's *The Oxford English Literary History*. Vol. 12, *1960–2000: The Last of England?* (2004). Finally, readers with a penchant for the contemporary in a slightly narrower frame might do well to begin with James F. English's *A Concise Companion to Contemporary British Fiction* (2006), Dominic Head's *The State of the Novel: Britain and Beyond* (2008) and Zachary Leader's *On Modern British Fiction* (2002). As these few touchstones indicate, the field is incredibly vibrant, wide ranging and deep. *Youth Culture and the Post-War British Novel* presumes only to have a small but acute impact on the field. Perhaps a slight stinging sensation will be felt on its outermost layers, but if it reaches the kind of readers it hopes most ardently to reach, then with luck it will incite them to read more, to research further and to advance their own interventions down the road.

That said . . .

That said ... *Youth Culture and the Post-War British Novel* does offer something genuinely new in the field, even if it does not advance that new offering in the traditional terms of scholarly intervention. As I indicated earlier, the youth cultures in play here have been subject to intensive and extensive sociological and cultural-historical study. And yet, it remains true, as Nick Bentley wrote in 2010, that 'there has been relatively little research done on the way those subcultures were represented in contemporary fiction' (16). Some of the novels under consideration here – *Saturday Night and Sunday Morning, A Clockwork Orange, Trainspotting* – have generated a significant amount of criticism and research. Oddly, though, they have rarely been treated in terms of the youth cultures they represent. With the odd exception here and there, most critical explorations of these novels ignore or too easily dismiss the question of youth culture. At best, they subsume it into other considerations. Such is the case with the insightful contributions of Alice Ferrebe's *Masculinity in Male-Authored Fiction 1950–2000* (2005). Ferrebe's book takes up what I consider to be perhaps the signal preoccupation of male writers in the latter half of the twentieth century. It illuminates in much broader terms than *Youth Culture and the Post-War British Novel* how male writers in the post-Second World War era have understood, represented and contributed to popular configurations of masculinity. It even explores some aspects of youth-cultural representation in contemporary literature. It does so, though, only in passing, en route to other topics. Peter Hughes Jachimiak's ' "Putting the Boot in": *The Commitments*, Post-'69 Youth Culture and the Onset of Late Modernity' (2008), Beryl Schlossman's 'Burgess/Kubrick/*The Commitments* (twenty-to-one)' (2008) and Berkem Gurenci Saglam's 'Rocking London: Youth Culture as Commodity in *The Buddha of Suburbia*' (2014) likewise contribute to the study of representations of post-war youth cultures in British and Irish fiction. Such articles provide excellent elucidations of the key concerns and conventional readings of these novels. As they do this, though, they too often take the novels' authors at their word. In doing so, they forego the challenge of reading these works for how they might articulate viewpoints that run counter to the surface narrative – or even that outright contradict the author's statements. As we will see in the brief overviews of the critical reception of the novels discussed in the chapters that follow, such critics have often been too ready simply to repeat and amplify Anthony Burgess's patently untrue claims that *A Clockwork Orange* argues that free will is a fundamental aspect of human existence. Likewise, they read *Saturday Night and Sunday Morning* as gritty, quasi-documentary, realism when in fact it erases tens of thousands of West Indian and African immigrants from the city of Nottingham. *Youth Culture and the Post-War British Novel* aims at once to build upon and complicate these contributions. Doing so, I hope, will ignite interest in the study of how British cultural production understood the often-befuddling explosion of youth cultures in the post-war decades.

What's their problem?

A series of post-war crises – of masculinity, of institutional authority (church, school, politics, law), of history and of narrative itself – structure these novels. These crises are directly related to the historical break experienced by young and old alike after the war. A host of changing social and political conditions, starkly offset by the discovery of the true nature and extent of the Holocaust, produced a widespread sense of a rupture between the past and the present, with the future become radically unpredictable. Think only of how the advent of the atomic bomb affected people's ability to think of the future as continuous with the past. Long traditions, bound up with a national and imperial history, seemed to have made themselves obsolete with the end of the Second World War, producing a dual sense of discontinuity on the grand scale of history itself and on the generational scale of parents and children. Historical discontinuity and generational conflict are twin aspects of the same phenomenon, and each often articulates the other in the minor key, as it were. Expressions of historical discontinuity in these novels frequently find articulation in terms of tensions between the young and the old(er). Expressions of generational conflict, likewise, frequently find articulation in terms of historical discontinuity. These mutual expressions inevitably involve reworking and distortion. These distortions are the focus of my analyses, since they provide the most interesting insights into how youth cultures were thought in the literary imagination and how they were mobilized to think through related – often unprecedented – other matters.

The generational conflicts that drove and shaped youth cultures in the post-war period clearly resonate on several scales. They are at once deeply personal (one's conflict with one's parents) and much broader (youth's conflict with the 'parent culture'). They derive from a sense of historical discontinuity that extends to a break with traditional forms of history and narrative themselves. They confront a new world order in which the powers of good would appear – at least according to the official narrative – to have overcome the forces of evil. And though rationing would continue in the UK until 1955, an era of unprecedented prosperity was clearly in the offing, bringing with it hitherto unimaginable freedoms. The persistence of pre-war legislative categories meant that those freedoms came with very little in the way of responsibilities. The accompanying lack of guaranteed rights was a small enough price to pay for many young people, given that much of what they wanted to do was a matter of privilege rather than legal right anyway: Smoke, drink, move freely about the city, have sex, mingle with people of other classes and races, fight, steal and enjoy themselves. Some members of the first generations of youth cultures – the Teddy boys, mods, and rockers – had grown up during the austere years of the war and immediate post-war. Some of them even fell under the requirements of the National Service. For them in particular, the ready access to money and mobility, combined with suspicion and resentment towards the pre-war generation, generated a sense of unofficial rights and responsibilities, underwritten by the privilege of youth. Indeed, it was the assertion of these 'rights' that generated much of the generational conflict in the first place, as young people found themselves resented for enjoying precisely what their parents had fought to provide for them:

> It was primarily the urban freedoms enjoyed by the young, according to 20 teenage interviewees of the *Daily Mirror* in 1956, which underlay the adult hatred of Teddy Boys and Girls. According to Mark, a nineteen-year-old labourer, 'I think the older generation have got the needle. They're always saying they worked for the younger generation to have better times than they had in their young days. Well, we've got that better time and they've go[t] the needle because we are happy.' Sixteen-year-old Jane, a dress-factory machinist, echoed this, commenting, 'Women say, "When I was young, I couldn't do this or that, and I hadn't your money." *They're jealous.*' (Qtd. in Bell 10)

If the war had made possible a new world, and a new world order was clearly coming into existence with the decline of the Empire, the onset of the Cold War and the advent of the atomic age, then it belonged to the young to shape themselves in response to it. They were the first aliens in a world created by the parental generation: 'we found that no one couldn't sit on our faces any more because we'd loot to spend at last, and our world was to be our world, the one we wanted and not standing on the doorstep of somebody else's waiting for honey, perhaps' (MacInnes 12). The world they faced was new to them and to their parents, but they lacked the shackles of convention and historical fatigue that constrained their parents' ability to adapt. Instead, they made themselves new in response, even as they sought out sites of stability and authenticity and navigated shifting realities in which performance and self-fashioning increasingly threatened even the conceptual coherence of 'authenticity' at all.

From Teddy boys to *Trainspotting*

Post-war British society was marked by a rapid succession of high-profile youth subcultures: Teddy boys, mods, rockers and so on. The end of the war and its accompanying sense of historical transition seem to have created the ideal conditions for pronounced generational divergence expressed in starkly visible terms. The combination of money, time and mobility saw youth cultures emerge as market demographics in unprecedented ways. In

FIGURE 0.1 *This punk's jacket features standard punk iconography: the Union Jack paired with the Nazi swastika, the circle-A sign for anarchy at the bottom and the title of the Sex Pistols' hit 'God Save the Queen' at the top. The chains and pins, along with the hand-drawn lettering, illustrate the DIY ethos that animated and expressed punk's rage. (Photo by Chris Moorhouse/Getty Images.)*

rapid succession, youth cultures succeeded one another as styles rapidly shifted – though by and large the attitudes, values and concerns underwriting those styles remain remarkably constant. The 1940s gave us skiffle kids and blitz babies, the 1950s Teddy boys, the 1950s and 1960s mods and rockers, the 1960s saw the emergence of skinheads and hippies, while the 1970s yielded first glam and then punk, and the 1980s produced new wave/new romantics and rave culture, before everything seems to have culminated in 1990s heroin chic.

The progression was not simply serial, though. It was also syncretic, so that even as each youth culture was superseded by the next, it never fully died out. The Teddy boys who terrorized the 1950s did not disappear as mods and rockers took over in the 1960s, but persisted alongside them, though in a reduced importance. Rearguard groups of Teddy boys held on to their style as they aged, and new Teddy boys continued to emerge well into the 1980s, whose 'Teddy-boy resurgence' stands as testament to the enduring appeal of this particular stylistic ensemble. The youth-cultural landscape thus got increasingly crowded and less identifiably *young* as the decades went by. As mods morphed into either skinheads or hippies, both they and rockers also persisted, now alongside Teds and the emerging groups. When glam and glitter emerged in the early 1970s, skinheads, Teds, mods and rockers were also on the scene. The tensions, affinities and conflicts among the groups got correspondingly complicated, though it is true that pretty much everyone took offence at punk (and punk took offence at everyone else). Even so, punk persisted long after its brief glorious flare-up in 1976–1977, and even experienced a resurgence at the same time as the Teddy boy resurgence in the 1980s, when hardcore caught fire in the United States. And so on: new wave and new romantic styles shouldered their way in alongside die-hard adherents of all the previous styles, even as young white Britons discovered the long-standing West Indian tradition of occupying warehouses for all-night DJ (or 'sound system')-driven dances, rechristened them 'raves' and transformed immigrant-based rude boy or bad bwai culture into a neon-highlighted, Ecstasy-fuelled, locus of hedonism (peaking in the so-called second Summer of Love on the Spanish Island of Ibiza in 1987).

Starting with skiffle, youth cultures had always borrowed what they could from other styles, making do and fabricating what could neither be begged, borrowed nor stolen. By the 1990s, though, youth culture seems to have reached a level of saturation where such borrowing simply became an aesthetic in itself. Heroin chic makes borrowing and irony key elements of its style, even as it defines a new level of lean, stripped-down, gaunt, self-presentation. Combining elements of Teddy boy criminality with mod dedication to a particular substance (for the mods it was speed), glam emaciation, rave trance or house musical style and punk nihilism, heroin chic marks the culmination of white British youth culture. Both die-hard and newly minted adherents of all of the above-listed youth cultures, and more besides, can be found today around the world.

Equally, literary treatments of these youth cultures become more complex, self-aware and crowded as the decades go by. Where Alan Sillitoe's 1958 *Saturday Night and Sunday Morning* presents us with a relatively isolated Teddy boy in Arthur Seaton, Colin MacInnes's 1958 *Absolute Beginners* treats its 'Ed the Ted' as a figure of (menacing) fun and charts the early emergence of mods. The overlap starts, that is, in the same year that rock 'n' roll produces its first home-grown hit in Cliff Richard's 1958 single 'Move It'. The early 1960s battles between the mods and rockers are recast in *A Clockwork Orange* even as Burgess anticipates the emergence of the skinhead and the drug-addled psychedelia of late-hippie and early glam cultures. Amis's *The Rachel Papers* includes representatives of all of these youth cultures, more or less gently mocking them, fully exploiting the comedic potential of hippies in particular. *The Buddha of Suburbia* likewise includes a host of youth cultures and follows Charlie Hero as he morphs from hippie to glam to punk and finally new wave over the course of the 1970s and early 1980s. The novel's protagonist, Karim, watches from the sidelines and anchors these metamorphoses from his perch as a racialized young man permanently unable authentically to adopt any of them. The racial script that has quietly undergirded most of the novels thus far gets flipped when we turn to Wheatle's *Brixton Rock* and *East of Acre Lane*, where the mods, Teds, skinheads, hippies and punks finally play second fiddle to the open tensions between Rastafarians and rude bwais. Our tour concludes with *Trainspotting*, in which every single youth culture from 1950 on makes an appearance in a flattened cultural landscape where they all co-exist simultaneously. History itself is levelled here, with individuals stylistically agile enough to shift from one youth-cultural identity to another almost from day to day. Just as youth cultures have been multiple, overlapping, syncretic and complicated from the very moment of their emergence in the aftermath of the Second World War, so also have fictional representations of them.

Where *you* from, then?

Immigrant youth cultures follow a slightly different trajectory, but as Dick Hebdige has pointed out in his seminal *Subculture: The Meaning of Style*, they underwrite virtually all of the white youth cultures indicated earlier. Their influence initially comes via American GIs stationed in the UK during and especially after the Second World War. With the British Nationality Act of 1948 opening the UK's doors to all members of the global British Commonwealth, black immigrants began to exert ever-stronger influence on the development of white youth cultures. This influence was deeply fraught, however; though many – if not all – white youth cultures borrowed from African-American and West Indian immigrant cultures, an equal number of them were openly racist, and frequently violently so. Teddy boys, for example, are notorious for their love of black music, and yet for playing a leading role in attacking West Indian immigrants, most notoriously in the 1958 race riots (which I discuss in Chapter two). Thus, at the same time as they provided models of cool for young white Britons, black immigrant youth pursued their own lines of development, though with much less obvious variation than their white counterparts. Beginning with African-American GIs' importation of soul and blues music, and Zoot suit styles in the 1940s, young black Britons added in Jamaican rude boy and bad bwai sensibilities to form distinctive youth-cultural aesthetics that articulated the tensions, crises and opportunities specific to their status in the UK. With the rise of reggae music in the 1960s, beginning in Jamaica but quickly moving around the world, black British youth culture rediscovered Rastafarianism, and an alternative to the bad bwai mode of being in the world. Tension between rasta and rude boy cultures persists through the end of the century, often intersecting and overlapping with specific white youth cultures (see, e.g. Hebdige on the links between reggae and punk).

Indian and Pakistani cultures had a far less significant impact on youth culture in the UK, perhaps because the assimilationist impulse was so much more fully established in this context. With a century of British-designed Indian education behind them, Indian and Pakistani immigrants often appeared to be even more British than native Britons. And though they encountered just as much racism and discrimination as West Indian immigrants, East Indian immigrants seem to have responded with further attempts to assimilate and/or to conform to persistent British Orientalist fantasies. As we will see in our reading of *The Buddha of Suburbia* in Chapter four, East Indian youth simultaneously felt that youth-cultural experimentation was unavailable to them (it was the privilege of whiteness), and yet failed to develop distinctive youth-cultural styles of their own. If the fictional record is any indicator, the simple problem of being Indian or Pakistani was enough, and there appears to have been little appetite to stand out even more from the dominant white culture. The protagonist of Hanif Kureishi's *The Buddha of Suburbia*, Karim, ambivalently records this sense by locating himself in a group of 'two hippies and a Paki' without specifying whether he's one of the 'hippies' or the 'Paki' (75). Of course, in large part thanks to the Beatles' experiments with the Maharishi Mahesh Yogi, Indian culture achieved a level of hipness that had previously evaded it in the 1970s. That relevance was largely confined to hippie appropriations of 'Eastern' traditions, though and – as *The Buddha of Suburbia* charts with such humour – depended fully upon white Orientalist fantasies more than elevating immigrant or immigrant-descended youth to youth-cultural coolness. Equally, East Indian influences such as bhangra music and dance finally penetrated into mainstream British culture in the 1980s, but in ways that were not youth-culturally specific; they certainly do not form the basis of any extended literary treatment, as do virtually all of the other youth cultures I've mentioned so far.

Both West and East Indian immigrant youth cultures got a late start in England, in large part due to their arrival after the war. Moreover, they have fundamentally different orientations towards the parent culture than white youth cultures. As cultures colonized by Britain for hundreds of years, they appear on the landscape already marked as others, for whom rebellion against the parent culture is nowhere near as simple or direct as it is for white British youth.

Historical conditions

The conditions for the emergence of these youth cultures, and their chief characteristics or formal features, remain remarkably consistent, despite the tremendous variety of musical, sartorial and chemical styles through which they manifest. Inescapably, the war itself looms at least through the 1980s as an immediately present feature of the mainstream culture against which and in dialogue with youth cultures defined themselves. As late as the 1971 release of the film version of *A Clockwork Orange*, the Second World

War iconography features prominently to define young Alex and his droogs' youth culture: Their rival gang led by Billy-boy appears in the film clad in *Wehrmacht* regalia, the minister in the prison chapel wears a toothbrush moustache and mimics the Nazi salute in his sermon and so on.

My treatment of the literary representations of post-war British youth culture depends upon linking youth-cultural developments to the political and cultural contexts in which they take place. Like the youth cultures of the post-war period, these contexts are cumulative, most of them extending back to the 1910s. Notably, the first really significant post-war youth culture, the Teddy boys, are so named because they dress in a style expressly intended to mimic the style of the Edwardian period before the First World War. The Great War and the Great Depression are fully as present in the political and cultural contexts of post-war youth cultures as is the Second World War, at times even more fully thanks to the added heft of cumulative impact. One key element is the loss of innocence that begins in August 1914 and continues through the Depression of the 1930s and the horrors of the Holocaust. This loss of innocence does not occur all at once and takes a long time to work its way through the cultural consciousness, tracking the decline of the British Empire but also the decline of faith in high culture, education, church and patriarchy more broadly. The realities of the Holocaust became increasingly apparent in the late 1940s and into the 1950s, via the series of trials beginning with the Nuremberg Trials in 1945–1946 through the end of the Majdanek trials in 1981. Hand in hand with the loss of faith accumulating through the recent history of the horrors of gas, aerial warfare, total war and mechanized slaughter in the Great War; the epidemic of the Spanish Flu, mass unemployment, widespread starvation and malnutrition at home, the rise of fascism and the slaughter of civilian populations culminating with the *Wehrmacht's* bombing of Guernica; and the twin shocks of the Holocaust and nuclear weapons – with the extension of the latter in the Cold War arms race's official doctrine of Mutually Assured Destruction – came a steep loss of faith in many of the time-honoured institutions that had held together the social fabric for hundreds of years. The Church, education, the Law and political institutions, once sources of security and certainty – or at least of a sense of continuity – are abandoned as, at best, belonging to a previous order and, at worst, having been exposed as the causes of the present crises. Over and over in literary representations of the post-war decades, we find depictions of empty or derelict churches, schools and government offices. Class is among the most suspect of these previous long-standing institutions to come under attack, and many of the youth cultures that emerge in the post-war years articulate clear confrontations with class distinctions.

Horrifying wars, genocides, economic crashes and epidemics of illness have all occurred before the twentieth century, though perhaps not on the scales made possible by modernity. What gives them the sort of traction and reach necessary to influence widespread youth-cultural innovations, though, is the rise of mass media in the mid-century. The expansive reach of broadcast radio, the newsreel, the daily newspaper, telephone, increasingly reliable portable photography and of course television – especially television news, but also such mainstream shows as the mod vehicle *Ready, Steady, Go!* – made these factors simultaneously known and relevant to larger populations than had ever before been possible. Cinematic representations in particular quickly mediatized and represented particularly sensational versions of history – the history of the present – to audiences who as often as not came to understand their current circumstances with reference to fictionalized accounts. That is, the rapid iterability effect produced by mass media closed the gap between historic-political events and their consumable forms. As such, they provided a ready context in which youth cultures could simultaneously invent themselves and imagine themselves as mediatized representations. This mechanism is perhaps the signal difference between pre-war youth cultures such as the Swing Kids of 1930s Germany and the post-war youth cultures, enabling the latter to spread rhizomatically, seemingly springing up simultaneously across the country and thus taking on both the utopian prospect and the moral panic of a shared youth consciousness.

The age of majority in England remained at 21 until 1970, though all young men were liable to conscription (during the Second World War) and then mandatory National Service from the age of 18 (until 1960, with final demobilization in 1963). What this meant for all young people was that they had neither rights nor responsibilities until at least age 18; for women it was at least age 21. For young men, it meant that though they could be conscripted into the army and required to perform military service at 18 years of age, they could not vote until 21. The result might have seemed to be disempowering, and no doubt it was in many key respects – not being able to vote for the government for which you may be required to fight seemed to many to be profoundly unjust. Certainly, characters such as Arthur Seaton in Alan Sillitoe's *Saturday Night and Sunday Morning* experience the National Service as an insulting imposition and dream only of using their military abilities to attack the government that imposes it. At the same time, as the Teenager in *Absolute Beginners* makes abundantly clear, the relative lack of status accorded to young people in the post-war years provided a great deal of opportunity. Young people, young men in particular, found ready work in the aftermath of the war, and were paid exceptionally well, especially when compared to what their fathers and mothers could earn. Continued rationing into the 1950s meant that mothers and fathers continued to struggle to provide for their families, often on pre-war wage levels, while young men and women earned post-war wages and had to provide for no one but themselves (though many, of course, contributed to their parents' households). The regular hours and predictable work-weeks also meant that there were regular and relatively abundant periods of leisure time. Nor were these periods of downtime like those of the pre-war years, when there was no money to spend and little to do for entertainment. The 'dirty 30s' were long over, and a young person in possession of disposable income could look forward to having a good time with few or no cares in the world. The work was steady, goods – though rationed – could be had for the right price on the thriving black market and the lifting of curfews and the end of fears of bombing meant a greater sense of mobility and freedom than most young people had *ever* experienced. It was a heady combination that appears to have more than compensated for the lack of legal status attendant upon being labelled technically a child until one's late teens or early twenties.

And, though certain problematics are fairly specific – such as problems of high unemployment and emerging neoconservatism, devolutionary politics in Scotland and Ireland, and the heroin epidemic of the 1990s – others persist across the decades and give shape to my analysis.

Masculinity on trial

Perhaps chief among these persistent problematics is a crisis of masculinity. The crisis of masculinity is central to post-war representations of youth cultures, and indeed arguably central to the youth cultures themselves. With a few exceptions such as the mods and infrequent but sensational reports of Teddy girl gangs, post-war British youth cultures are highly masculine affairs. With all due deference to the important work of scholars such as Angela McRobbie establishing that female youth cultures were and are every bit as complex and prevalent as male youth cultures, I have been unable to locate novels about those youth cultures per se. To be sure, there are novels that deal with young women and their particular concerns, but I have not yet come across such a work that deals with the situation of young women expressly in terms of their participation in specific youth cultures. It is true that every youth culture featured a young women's auxiliary, and no doubt necessarily so; the crisis of masculinity would surely only be exacerbated if the youth cultures engaging with it were exclusively homosocial. At the same time, the fact is that despite the anti-feminist backlash of the 1950s, women's situation was generally improving in the post-war. More opportunities in the workforce combined with shifting morals and gender norms to make 'women's liberation' a rallying banner under which greater freedom and agency could be exercised. The introduction of the birth control pill in the 1960s decisively transformed women's social role and upended centuries of gender normativity, freeing women from such traditions – or at least making freedom from those traditions seem possible.

For men, freedom from tradition was precisely the problem. The crisis of masculinity after the war comes down in effect to the existential challenge of discovering that, as a 'man' (whatever that might mean now), one was, in Sartre's words, utterly free, responsible and alone. Precedent could no longer provide a clear, unmarked path to manhood through military achievement, hard work or providing for a family. The generation of young men coming of age after the Second World War were the first in 65 years to have to achieve mature masculinity in the absence of a war by which to define manhood. With the advent of atomic weapons, conventional warfare with its soldierly models of bravery under fire and chivalrous self-sacrifice was shoved aside: The next conflict, many felt, would be over before it started in a matter of a few flashes of light. Moreover, women's increasing sexual liberation challenged gender norms that gave men privilege in terms of pursuing, initiating, enjoying and benefiting from sex, while women assumed the lion's share of the risk. As reproductive technology improved, and women could take greater ownership of their sexuality, this ground of male privilege – and of masculine identity – shrank: If women also liked and pursued sexual relationships for pleasure alone, that is, if women were just like men in that regard, then what made men, men? Finally, if women were increasingly entering and staying in the workforce, earning their own money and thus relying less and less on men to support them, allowing them to put off marriage and child-bearing if they wished, where did that leave men in terms of identifying masculinity with the power to provide for one's family? Indeed, where did it leave men in terms of having families at all? The result is a crisis of masculinity characterized by what we might call an overall decline in paternal prestige. Over and over again in post-war British novels that engage with youth culture we find young men struggling to discover what it can possibly mean to be a man in a world where traditional roles are shifting or disappearing altogether. Some of them indulge in pseudo-martial conflict via gang wars (e.g. Alex in *A Clockwork Orange*), others in sexual conquest (e.g. Charles in *The Rachel Papers*) and still others in a last grasp at traditional gender and class values (e.g. Arthur in *Saturday Night and Sunday Morning*). Not one of them has a viable father figure to emulate, and all suffer mightily from this absence. Virtually all the fathers in the novels under discussion here are ineffective, self-absorbed or absent altogether. They provide no viable models of masculinity for their sons and delineate the absolute separation between the pre-war and post-war generations.

Identity crisis

Following on from the crisis of masculinity is a crisis of identity, accompanied by an overwhelming obsession with authenticity. The enabling condition of youth-cultural self-fashioning such as we see explode in the post-war decades is a sense that identity is either something that must be discovered through trial and error or (increasingly, as the century wears on) that identity is a matter of choice, construction and performance. Going hand in hand with this liberating – and anxiety-inducing – new understanding of identity is a powerful urge towards authenticity. Where the open-endedness of identity presents endless freedom to be who or what one wishes, it also provokes a tremendous urge to locate stability, to be certain that one is who one thinks one is. Every one of the novels I take up here deals with this challenge, as members of disparate youth cultures all struggle to discover whom they ought to be, whom they prefer to be and whom they are perhaps even meant to be. They try on different identities, explore alternative morality, experiment with drugs and alcohol, rebel and do their best to outrage their parents. At the same time, they almost uniformly seek the authentic, a way of life that will feel 'right' to them, that will confirm their identity and grant them a transcendental sanction for being as they do in the world. For some it is racial identification, for others it is identification with their desire and for a surprising number it is simply adulthood. That site of inauthenticity, the mainstream source against which youthful rebellion takes up its implacable opposition, becomes the locus of true identity in the end far more frequently than one might think. Indeed, as I will argue in the chapters that follow, many of these novels are ultimately quite pessimistic about the potential for youth-cultural change, and re-contain the rebellious energies they appear to unleash so optimistically in their incipits.

The end of history?

These microcosmic crises find a macrocosmic counterpart in a general crisis of history. Though the Allied Powers had indeed won the war, and the war before that one, the victory was undercut by the twin emerging recognitions that Britain's status on the world stage was in steep decline, and the ideology of progress and moral superiority behind that empire was more and more transparently a sham. With the United States and Soviet Union emerging as superpowers, and the Cold War swinging into high gear, British influence on the world stage was palpably reduced. The empire, already crumbling before the war thanks to widespread decolonization movements, continued to come apart at the seams. Though fantasies of British importance continued to be articulated via, for example, the James Bond novels and film franchise, it was clear to all that the age when Britannia ruled the waves was clearly drawing to a close.

For many, this inevitability was accompanied by a dawning sense of discomfort about the moral authority that had underwritten the empire, and that appeared to ratify the victory in the war. Much of that moral authority was bound up with the Arnoldian notion of high culture as morally improving, as evidence of the superiority of cultured Europeans over 'barbarians', be they Africans, Aborigines or Germans. Of course, up until at least the Great War, the British had recognized the Germans as their cultural counterparts, equally civilized and cultivated. The brutality of the Great War, and the necessary vilification of the Germans in British propaganda, downplayed that concord but the fact remained that much of what counted as the greatest music, art and literature in the Western world was German, and that Germans had every bit as highly cultivated a sense of appreciation for it as did the British. Even Hitler's philistinism with regard to modern art found echoes in British attitudes towards the avant-garde, as it did likewise across the Atlantic in the United States. Faith in the morally improving value of art became a reversible syllogism: If you appreciate high art, you must not be a bad sort, since only good sorts (the cultured) can appreciate high art. This snobbery was sharply challenged in the immediate post-war revelations about concentration camp commandants listening to Bach, Beethoven and Mozart; creating orchestras of highly trained musicians in their camps; collecting masterpieces of painting and sculpture; and then turning on the gas chambers and ovens to exterminate millions of people. You could hardly ask for a starker rebuttal to the notion that 'music hath charms to soothe the savage breast', or to the notion that history was the story of progress, of the gradual advance of enlightenment and morality over savagery and benightedness. Of course, the accelerating decolonization movements supplemented this revelation by exposing the brutality with which the British Empire had been established and maintained over centuries as well. Add in Britain's persistent anti-Semitism, and its lingering fascism – a fascism that would flare up glaringly as immigration to England exceeds expectations and overwhelms British hospitality – and you have a recipe for disillusionment. Try as they might to smooth over these unsettling insights, official accounts of the Empire and its triumph in the war could not keep them from the public awareness. Max Horkheimer and Theodor Adorno's *Dialectic of Enlightenment* (1948) is only one of the works that charted this failure of the Enlightenment and articulated its descent into disrepute. Increasingly, as news of Western industrial interests' collaboration with the Nazi regime, links among British royals and the Nazis (Edward VII and Wallace Simpson were welcome guests of Hitler's), and far-reaching sympathy with Nazi anti-Semitism spread, many young Britons experienced a crisis of history. Having been raised to believe that history is progressive, and that Britain was a leading light in bringing about the gradual improvement of humanity under the banner of civilization, culture and good government, they had to face the brutal underbelly. Walter Benjamin's statement that 'there is no document of civilization which is not at the same time a document of barbarism' voiced this emerging sense powerfully (256). It gave rise to precisely the sort of suspicion about official history that made George Orwell's *1984* so resonant and gives such heft to many of the youth-cultural rebellions against the 'parent culture'. Young people after the war are not merely rebelling against their parents; they are rebelling against an entire history which culminates in the war and from which the war provides sufficient distance to view critically.

This crisis of history ultimately came down to a crisis of who had the right to write history and of who controlled the narrative. It quickly generated simply a crisis of narrative per se. As with the other crises so far enumerated, the crisis of narrative was rather a continuation than a clear break. There is an important shift, though. Where modernist experimentation had toyed with narrative form and raised the unreliable narrator to an art form, the post-war narratives under discussion here – and many more besides – problematized their own status as narratives. Frequently, they foreground their status as narratives, with narrators referring to themselves as such (e.g. Alex in *A Clockwork Orange*), narratives that themselves recount the process of arranging material to create a narrative (*The Rachel Papers*) and narratives that are explicitly about performance and self-fashioning (*The Buddha of Suburbia*).

At stake here is a widespread, and increasingly normalized, sense that narrative itself is a function of power, that it is all ideological and at least tendentially arbitrary. Seizing control of the narrative is part and parcel of adopting a style that allows individual young people not to express their inner selves, but to fashion personae for circulation in the world. The crisis of faith in institutions such as the church, school, law and government – all producers of powerful *grands recits*, as Jean-François Lyotard had it in his 1979 – joins with a crisis of history itself in the very period when historical catastrophe seems to have been averted in the Allied victory. History is less and less understood as a factual record of events, or even of the lives of great men, and more and more as a narrative produced by people in power to advance particular structures of domination and subordination. The generational logic detectable here, where the 'parent culture' dictates the frame in which youth-cultural rebellion and achievement takes place and is measured, depends upon a positivist understanding of narrative. One of the ways these novels think through this crisis of narrative, then, is both by attempting to understand how youth cultures are troubling and appropriating narrative strategies and also using youth cultures to think through the post-modern turn in narrative.

How this is going to go down

Each chapter of *Youth Culture and the Post-War British Novel* deals more or less with a single decade. For the most part, they feature some form of broad strokes introduction to the youth-cultural and broader historical contexts for the novels under consideration. They also mostly confine themselves to novels written in the decades they are about, though there are significant deviations from this scheme as well. As the circumstances dictate, the main novel or novels under discussion may be supplemented with some treatment of popular music, pulp fiction that represents the same youth cultures or concrete historical realities that impinge upon the social worlds the novels represent. Chapter four, for example, begins with a brief discussion of the historical and cultural conditions under which youth culture becomes aware of itself *as a cultural phenomenon*, to set the context for the following treatment of *The Rachel Papers* and *The Buddha of Suburbia*. Chapter six outlines the politics of Scottish parliamentary devolution and the neoliberal politics of Thatcherism to help contextualize *Trainspotting*'s descent into the culture of heroin chic.

The rest of this Introduction features brief abstracts of the chapters, so readers may select where they would like to begin, figure out which chapters are most interesting to them or simply discern the overall pattern before reading from start to finish.

Chapter One – Angry(-ish) Young(-ish) Men: *Saturday Night and Sunday Morning* and *Absolute Beginners*

This chapter contrasts how Sillitoe's and MacInnes's novels handle elements of youth culture, racial politics, masculinity and violence. It illuminates surprisingly disparate attitudes and charts two very different views of youth culture and its potential. I argue that Sillitoe's novel erases the black immigrants who had been arriving in Nottingham by the thousands since 1950, presenting a strangely time-warped narrative in which pre-war Nottingham is presented as the post-war reality. By contrast, MacInnes's novel appears obsessed with race in London and seeks to align the youth-cultural promise of the Teenager with the vibrant energy of immigrant cultures. It, too, however, ends on a regressive note that undercuts its comparatively progressive racial politics. Problems of masculinity are similarly prominent. For Sillitoe, racial tensions culminate in sexually charged domestic violence, while MacInnes's Teenager reverts to a strikingly conservative vision of gender roles.

Chapter Two – How Did Burgess Invent the Skinhead? *A Clockwork Orange*

This chapter argues that Burgess outstrips even the violence of the Teds and the mods/rockers by inventing the skinhead – five years before the first real-life specimen appeared in the streets of London. I argue that Burgess predicts the evolution of youth culture in a violent direction that is tightly bound up with a masculinist backlash against the feminizing influence of soft mod style and a post-war world in which everything was too easy.

Strikingly, this remains true even though the novel is primarily concerned with the bankrupt flaccidity of the parental generation in the face of the young protagonist's hard masculine freedom. And yet, *A Clockwork Orange* is ultimately not so different from its precursors. Like *Saturday Night and Sunday Morning* and *Absolute Beginners*, *A Clockwork Orange* ultimately reaffirms a conservative world view in which the revolutionary energy of youth is scattered, overcome by the passage of time.

Chapter Three – Youth Culture Goes Metastatic: *The Rachel Papers* and *The Buddha of Suburbia*

Martin Amis's *The Rachel Papers* and Hanif Kureishi's *The Buddha of Suburbia* mark a new stage in the development of post-war youth cultures: A crisis of authenticity that produces a range of responses. Amis's protagonist openly makes the narrative a problem of mature masculinity by establishing the time of the narration as the last day before he turns twenty and must become a man. For Kureishi, the entire narrative is framed as a coming-of-age tale in which the protagonist Karim matures alongside his father Harry, sampling and rejecting or adopting parts of various models of masculinity along the way. Taken together, these novels constitute something of a requiem for the first stage of youth culture, a stage during which authenticity functioned as both an ideal and an unmarked background, an assumption upon which one could proceed as one experimented with styles of being in the world.

Chapter Four – Sojourn in Babylon: *Brixton Rock* and *East of Acre Lane*

This chapter places race at centre stage in its exploration of Alex Wheatle's *Brixton Rock* and *East of Acre Lane*. For Wheatle's working-class Brixtonians, class affiliation – still marginal, oppressed, hopeless – outweighs race or ethnicity as a key factor in their youth-cultural affiliations. Both novels portray a world in which father figures are virtually absent, leaving the young men at their centres to divine acceptable patterns of masculinity for themselves. This reality is compromised even further by the powerful roles assigned to women, and the ease with which they assume the social, familial and cultural space once reserved to mature masculinity. I conclude by arguing that the 1980s present us with novels that seem to accept youth culture as something stuck in the present, pressed on one side by an idealized distant past of authenticity and on the other by a series of insuperable obstacles to progress.

Chapter Five – Rave and
Heroin: *Trainspotting*

Trainspotting marks a terminal point for post-war youth culture in the UK, by shifting away from an aesthetics of rebellion, utopian projection and independence towards what I call an *anaesthetic* youth culture. The youth cultures represented in *Trainspotting* represent themselves through numbness, evacuation of the self and retreat from the social and political. This shift away from engagement with the outside world manifests in rave and heroin subcultures. Once again, issues of masculinity loom large, as models of masculinity veer crazily between the 'hard-man' and the emasculated junkie. Drugs and sterility plague efforts to chart a future that can evade the cycle of violence, withdrawal and futile repetition.

1

Angry(-ish) Young(-ish) Men: *Saturday Night and Sunday Morning* and *Absolute Beginners*

The year 1958 was pivotal in the development of British youth culture and in post-war writing about it. In addition to the publication of *Saturday Night and Sunday Morning*, 1958 saw the appearance of Keith Waterhouse's hugely popular *Billy Liar* (made into a film starring Tom Courtenay and Julie Christie a scarce five years later) and Ernest Ryman's sensational novel *Teddy Boy*, which contrasted the rehabilitative effects of a reform school on juvenile delinquents with the downward spiral into deviance and violent criminality of the Teddy boy living outside the reform system. The year also yielded the first bona fide rock 'n' roll hit song to come out of the UK, in Cliff Richard's 'Move It', and the dance craze/song 'The Stroll' – which would already belong to the distant past by 1971 when Led Zeppelin sang that 'It's been a long time / Since I did the Stroll.' It's the year during which Colin MacInnes' *Absolute Beginners* was written and in which it was set, though the book itself did not appear until the following year. Finally, and perhaps most importantly of all, 1958 is the year of the first post-war race riots in England, starting in Nottingham and the Notting Hill and Notting Dale sections of London at the very end of August.

In this chapter, we will see how Sillitoe and MacInnes think *about* the emergent fact of truly distinct youth cultures. We'll also see how they use those cultures to think *with*, approaching a heady mix of issues including masculinity, sex and sexuality, class, violence, the legacy of the war and above all race. Along the way, we'll encounter the first true post-war youth-cultural group, the Teddy boys, along with early prototypes of the mods and rockers who will usurp the Teds' status as folk devils du jour as the 1950s give way to the 1960s. Contrasting how these two near-contemporaneous novels handle these youth cultures illuminates surprisingly disparate attitudes and sets the stage for the next chapter's consideration of perhaps the most self-contradictory post-war novel of all, *A Clockwork Orange*. Ultimately, though, we will see how profoundly conservative both *Saturday Night and Sunday Morning* and *Absolute Beginners* end up being – again, in anticipation of Burgess's arch-conservative novel.

One of the key differences between the two novels is their temporal orientation: *Saturday Night and Sunday Morning* faces backwards, presenting a 1958 that is still well and truly in the clutches of the 1930s, while *Absolute Beginners* gives us a 1958 that is in a desperate rush to leave the past behind and to arrive in the future now, if not sooner. They present complex temporalities that overlap, conflict and shift arbitrarily depending on which aspect we focus on. The novels' divergent treatment of Teddy boys illustrates this divergence in temporal orientation.

That divergence has its origins in Teddy boys themselves. As 'Britain's first youth subculture' (Bell 3), Teddy boys articulated a complicated cultural moment. For many members of the British public, the Teds presented a menacing view of the future arriving just a bit too early for comfort. Life had just begun to return to normal after the end of rationing in 1954 and here already were people chafing under that normalcy. Refusing to go back to pre-war social distinctions, the Teds mobilized their unprecedented prosperity – achieved through full employment, but also through black market economies trading on goods 'liberated' from American PX stores still in England – to challenge the old social hierarchies. They took advantage of relaxed curfew laws and increased urban mobility to assert their agency in the streets, flaunted their affluence and embraced aspects of American culture such as African-American music (though preferably played by whites). 'Usurping the Savile Row-sponsored neo-Edwardian style of young aristocrats in the late 1940s, "Teddy" style also combined the fashion of wartime "make-do-and-mend" customization, "spiv" gangsters, American "zoot" and East End "cosh boy" youth gangs' (Bell 3). They seemed harbingers of a brave new world, one marked by swagger, brash confidence and a determination to take full advantage of the privileges won for them in the war.

And yet the Teds were not by any means only a forward-looking group. The moral panic they provoked had as much to do with their invocation of a past that was gone for good as it did with a heady vision of the future. The two are but sides of the same coin, to be sure: The edgy threat of Teddy boy futurity gains heft in its contrast with an idyllic past that can never again be. On this point, Bell goes on to note that the Teddy boys' 'complex postwar reaction to austerity, rationing and National Service' was 'measured against a nostalgic vision of the English past' (3). This 'nostalgic vision' is key; the Teds sought not only to assert their agency against a bewilderingly changed world, but also to anchor their identities in pre-First World War certainties. The 'Edwardian' aspect of their dress did not just assert affluence in its use of extravagant quantities of fabric and its flamboyant colours;

it also anchored the Teds in the warm glow of Britain's last time of self-assurance – the summer of 1914. Sartorially at least, the Teds rejected both world wars, the 'roaring twenties' and the 'dirty thirties', reaching back to the days of their grandparents' youth for an historical correlative to their sense of present possibility. Contrary to what many thought at the time, and what most commentators since have continued to assert, the Teds sought not only to break with the past, but also to anchor their claims to authenticity in a nostalgic vision of the summer of 1914. In doing so, the Teds introduced the problems that would dog youth cultures for the rest of the century: Crises of masculinity, class and national identity provoked by Britain's changing place on the world stage; shifts in women's status and rights; massive immigration; post-war prosperity; and the horrors of the Holocaust. By asserting allegiance to Edwardian values in their choice of clothes, Teddy boys also declared a clear, elemental model of masculinity and national identity.

The Teddy boy phenomenon was far from exclusively masculine, though its afterlife in fiction and mass media alike might well lead one to think so. As with all the youth-cultural groups of the 1950s and 1960s, the male core was attended by a strong and vibrant female auxiliary. Teddy boys were joined by Teddy girls, or 'Judies', who ran their own gangs and indulged in the same vices and behaviours as their male counterparts. Ken Russell's series of photographs entitled 'The Last of the Teddy girls' provides the most vivid document of this group, recording these rebellious young women in poses of defiance, swagger and arrogance truly befitting the Teddy brand. As these images illustrate, Teddy girls dressed like Teddy boys, came from the same class background and neighbourhoods as Teddy boys and fought just as viciously as well. Though they ran in smaller numbers and provoked much less of a moral panic than Teddy boys, they were indeed a force to be reckoned with.

Tellingly, though, this clearest record is visual – it exists in a series of photographs and has no textual equivalent. Indeed, none of the women in *Saturday Night and Sunday Morning*, *Absolute Beginners* or even Ryman's *Teddy Boy* is presented as a Judy. Nor are there any readily identifiable female mods or rockers, even in MacInnes's cutting-edge depiction of English youth culture. As I discussed in the introduction, the problems surrounding women's exclusion from fictional representations of post-war youth cultures – at its most acute in the 1950s and 1960s – are complex. Simply put, in the 1950s, such subcultural young women seem not to have captured either the popular imagination or the writerly fancy as their male counterparts did: To put it colloquially, they were wild in the streets but nowhere in the sheets (of paper). Whatever the reasons for this disparity, the fact remains that while up-and-coming writers such as Sillitoe and MacInnes were thinking with and about the emergent youth cultures of their day, women writers such as Iris Murdoch, Doris Lessing and Muriel Spark were exploring different topics.

FIGURE 1.1 *Teddy boys and Teddy girls, or 'Judies', 1955. (Photo by Popperfoto/ Getty Images.)*

These historical and cultural complexities mean that the Teddy boy functions as a much more complex figure than most critics have thus far allowed. Not simply the product of relatively lawless childhoods during which they 'had spent the most important years of their childhood during the war, with fathers away in the Forces and mothers often out on war work' (Elloway in Waterhouse 204–5), nor simply thuggish young men with money, time, mobility and a heady sense of agency marauding the streets, the Teds in fact articulated a dense knot of conflicted temporalities with complicated ideological significations. The differences in how contemporary writers such as Sillitoe and MacInnes think with and about this figure are thus profoundly interesting.

On one side of the divide is *Saturday Night and Sunday Morning*. Sillitoe's novel articulates a vision of the Teddy boy as an authentic representative of traditional English masculinity, individualism and agency. The novel appears in 1958, but presents a vision of life in industrial Nottingham that is riven with nostalgic disjunctions, glaring blindspots and a profoundly conservative outlook. It is nostalgic about the war years, and grudgingly optimistic about post-war prosperity (as measured against the terrible years of the 1930s), but ultimately uninvested in the revolutionary potential of youth culture despite having a Teddy boy as its main character. Sillitoe teases the liberatory anarchic potential of the Teddy boy, only to yank away any promise it may hold at the first sign of trouble. Most crucially, the novel presents a vision of post-war Nottingham that nourishes a National Front fantasy of the harmonious working-class city: Sillitoe's 1950s Nottingham has virtually no black people in it, despite the fact that tens of thousands of West Indian immigrants had been arriving in England throughout the 1950s.

Let's begin with Arthur Seaton, Sillitoe's Teddy boy protagonist. Thus far, critics have either ignored Arthur's Ted credibility or else vacillated about its authenticity. Of the very few critics who have considered Arthur's nomination as a Teddy boy worthy of critical commentary, Ian Brookes is exemplary, insisting that 'Arthur is not a Teddy Boy but he is twice identified as one' (Brookes 21). He offers no justification for his reading. Nick Bentley ultimately withholds his verdict. Likewise insisting that Arthur cannot 'be said to be part of a subculture such as the Teddy boys' (Bentley 2010, 24) and that 'Arthur is not a Teddy boy in the sense of his belonging to a subculture' (25), Bentley allows that 'Arthur Seaton's relationship with his clothing matches [that of ...] Teddy boy subculture' (26) and 'the suits Arthur owns are of the style worn by the Teddy boys' (26). The logic behind these repudiations eludes me, I confess. Brookes and Bentley both seem to be marking a distinction without a difference.

That Arthur does not run with a gang of other Teds seems a wholly inadequate reason to discount the fact that he is explicitly presented as a Teddy boy. He is repeatedly called a Teddy boy, first by the woman he throws up on in the novel's famous opening scene ('"Looks like one of them Teddy boys, allus making trouble"' [16]) and then by a sergeant-major during his two weeks' national service ('"You're a soldier now, not a Teddy-boy"' [138]). His clothing is uniformly characterized as being in the Teddy boy style, from the 'teddy-suit' he prefers 'for going out in at night' (Sillitoe 28), to the closet full of flashy, expensive items in which he has invested a huge amount of money:

> [He] selected a suit from a line of hangers. Brown paper protected them from dust, and he stood for some minutes in the cold, digging his hands into pockets and turning back lapels, sampling the good hundred pounds' worth of property hanging from an iron-bar. These were his riches, and he told himself that money paid-out on clothes was a sensible investment because it made him feel good as well as look good. (66)

Later still, he surveys 'his row of suits, trousers, sports jackets, shirts, all suspended in colorful drapes and designs, good-quality tailor-mades, a couple of hundred quids' worth, a fabulous wardrobe of which he was proud because it had cost him so much labour' (Sillitoe 169). Even his girlfriend

Doreen takes note, in tones of admiration and suspicion alike (is this the kind of man you marry?):

> 'Are all them clo'es yourn?'
>
> 'Just a few rags', he said.
>
> She sat up straight, hands in her lap. 'They look better than rags to me. They must have cost you a pretty penny.' (185)

Even Arthur's footwear fits the Teddy boy mould, corresponding to the crepe-soled 'brothel-creepers' favoured for dances, fights and loitering in the streets (66). Moreover, Arthur wears his 'fair hair short on top and weighed-down with undue length at the back[, sending] out a whiff of hair cream' (66), in the signature Teddy boy style of the quiff up front and the duck's arse or duck-tail in back. If Arthur is not a Teddy boy, he sure as hell looks like one.

And yet, Bentley is not entirely wrong to suspect that there is something missing – something inauthentic – in Arthur's Teddy boy credentials. He lacks some key features of Teddy boy comportment: He is not gratuitously violent, he does not loiter in the streets, he carries no weapons, and he does not participate in any criminal activity – at least not of the sort typically associated with Teds (e.g. black marketeering and theft). We know nothing at all of his musical preferences, let alone whether they are consistent with the Ted affection for 'black gospel and blues [...] fused with white country and western' (Hebdige 49), whether he dances the Teddy boy signature dance, 'The Creep' or whether he shares the growing Teddy boy antipathy towards the flood of immigrants entering the UK in the 1950s. But absence of evidence is not evidence of absence, and it may even be the case that it's the Teddy boy's ambiguity, his unknown quantity and the new possibilities he embodies that make him such a flexible figure for Sillitoe to use in his navigation of emerging realities after the war. In what follows, I show that Sillitoe recognized these possibilities in both cultural and narrative terms, and seized his chance to use the Teddy boy as a figure for working through a range of anxieties about masculinity and race.

The question of Arthur's attitudes toward race is especially poignant, since it points to Sillitoe's particular take on the Teddy boy, and thus to the novel's larger politics. In particular, the novel's racial politics are critical to any understanding of it as a key cultural document of 1950s England. To get there, though, we must first lay the groundwork of understanding Arthur's masculinity and his politics. Put simply, Arthur is very clearly an 'angry young man', with a distinct impulse towards violence. He is an open misogynist and latently violent anarchist, though only in a vulgar sense: He lacks the coherent political or ideological awareness of the genuine anarchist. In both his misogyny and his anarchy, Arthur betrays *Saturday Night and Sunday Morning*'s temporal displacement from its contemporary moment in the 1950s, anchoring Sillitoe's view of youth culture in a profoundly conservative direction.

Arthur's masculinity is of central importance. Sillitoe uses the figure of the anarchic, virile, swaggering Teddy boy to interrogate some of the institutions associated with traditional British culture, perhaps chief among them marriage. The figure of the Teddy boy articulated a whole range of possibilities, particularly with regard to sexual liberty and sexual relationships. In its capacity as a folk devil, the Ted presented a clear and present danger to the social norms embodied in institutions such as marriage. Sillitoe capitalizes on this by pitting Arthur's cavalier sexual adventurousness against the domesticated, worn down, parental masculinity of the war generation. What he discovers or shows is that the Teddy boys' youth-cultural masculinity and bravado is far more fragile than first appearance and that long-standing institutions of domesticated masculinity are more durable than one might think.

At first glance Arthur's conception of masculinity seems relatively straightforward. He claims that all he wants is 'plenty of work and plenty of booze and a piece of skirt every month till I'm ninety' (183) to be comfortable in life. This view itself is articulated to perform a strong, clear, decisive masculinity, one that Arthur desperately wants to affirm and with which he longs to be content. And yet, a powerful sense of resentment and aggression undergirds it. Though he certainly enjoys his time with Brenda, Winnie and Doreen, Arthur simultaneously hates them for being available to him and hates their husbands for their wives' availability:

> He had no pity for a 'slow' husband. There was something lacking in them, not like a man with one leg that could in no way be put right, but something that they, the slow husbands, could easily rectify if they became less selfish, brightened up their ideas, and looked after their wives a bit better. For Arthur, in his more tolerant moments, said that women were more than ornaments and skivvies: they were warm and wonderful creatures that needed and deserved to be looked after, requiring all the attention a man could give, certainly more than the man's work and a man's own pleasure. (Sillitoe 44)

Lest there be any confusion on the point, the narrator confirms for us that the central problem with the '"slow" husband' is masculinity: 'Arthur thought again about Jack, this time with a feeling of irritation that he should be so weak as to allow his wife to go off with other men. It was funny how often you felt guilty at taking weak men's wives: with the strong men's you have too much to fear, he reasoned' (Sillitoe 53). For Arthur, to be a strong man is to be able to keep a woman, perhaps through care and attentiveness (when he's 'in his more tolerant moments'), but ultimately through violence or the threat of it:

If ever I get married, he thought, and have a wife that carries on like Brenda and Winnie carry on, I'll give her the biggest pasting any woman ever had. I'd kill her. My wife'll have to look after any kids I fill er with, keep the house spotless. And if she's good at that, I might let her go to the pictures now and again or take her out for a drink on Saturday. But if I thought she was carrying on behind my back she'd be sent back to her mother with two black eyes before she knew what's happening. (Sillitoe 146)

In his less 'tolerant moments', Arthur conceives of masculinity as the power violently to assert one's will and authority over one's wife. Consistent with the 1950s backlash against women's advances during the war, Arthur articulates a violent fantasy of oppression that would enforce traditional roles for women: cooking, cleaning, child-rearing and sexual availability. Against the threat of physical violence for failing to comply – 'I'd kill her' – Arthur imagines a grudging generosity in which he might – just *might* – *let* her go to the pictures or take her out with him. The irony is patent, of course, since the emblems of the misbehaving wife Arthur imagines himself beating up are the very women he is currently sleeping with: Brenda and Winnie.

The crisis in Arthur's masculinity thus stands starkly exposed, as he blames anyone but himself for behaviour he finds enjoyable and which he sees as essential to his long-term satisfaction. He both wants sexual liberty and hates those who make it possible. His status as a Ted already reveals Arthur as participating in a post-war crisis of masculinity. Deprived of the sorts of violent struggle that provided the testing ground for their parents' and grandparents' mature masculinity, the Teds sought domestic fora for asserting their masculinity: 'With the disappearance of more conventional methods of establishing one's masculinity, such as the performance of courage and physical strength through wartime action, and struggling and starving while looking for employment', the Teds had to explore other means of asserting their manhood (Lewis 94). Moreover, for Arthur, the assertion of masculinity through violence is incompatible with the assertion of violence through sex – to have an affair with a married woman means he has greater sexual prowess than the 'slow' husband, but he only has sex with wives of 'slow' husbands because he is scared of the 'strong men' whose wives he sees as not worth the risk. Notably, he prefers not to fight the swaddies who chase him down for his affair with Winnie and only turns to face them when they trap him outside a pub.

Tellingly, Arthur compensates for this gap in his narcissistic fantasy of masculinity by finding an outlet for violence in his relationships with women. While he congratulates himself for the reasonable stance that avoids potential confrontations with 'strong men', and for preferring not to use his fists if he doesn't have to – 'Only the stupid fought with their fists' (100) – Arthur not only fantasizes about beating his future wife, but hurts the women he is dating as well. First, when Brenda tells him that Jack may come to check on her story that she is part of the darts team, and thus discover their affair, Arthur changes plans and they head into the woods for a quickie. Though Brenda goes along willingly, Arthur takes out his frustration and aggression upon her:

> He knew he was hurting her, squeezing her wrists as he led her deeper into the wood, but it did not occur to him to relax his hold. Trees and bushes crowding around in the darkness made him melancholy. One minute he thought he was holding her wrist so tightly because he was in a hurry to find out a good dry place; then he felt it was because there was something about her and the whole situation that made him want to hurt her, something to do with the way she was deceiving Jack. Even though he, now leading her to a spot that suddenly came into his mind, would soon be enjoying it, he thought: 'Women are all the same. If they do it to their husbands they would do it to you if you gave them half the chance.' He trod on a twig that sent a cracking sound circling the osier-lined indistinct banks of dark water below. Brenda gasped as some bush-leaves swept by her face; he had not bothered to warn her. (Sillitoe 51)

Fully aware that he is hurting Brenda, Arthur reasons that she deserves it for being an adulteress in the first place. More to the point, Arthur is responding violently to Brenda's information because it threatens his conception of his own masculinity: It potentially forces his Teddy boy fantasy of masculine prowess to confront some harsh reality.

The seismic shift in his self-conception and behaviour after the swaddies beat him senseless backs up this reading. When Arthur is finally confronted by just the sort of man he hopes to be – the sort of man who would beat his wife for carrying on and then seek out and beat up her lover as well – his fantasy of potent masculinity must be revised. Arthur's anarchic youth-cultural masculinity is literally disciplined by representatives of the war generation, embodied in the two swaddies who beat him up. It is no accident that it's two members of the military who beat Arthur up, nor that his beating quickly leads to his decision to pursue a traditional marital relationship with Doreen. And though Arthur keeps up his bravado after this episode, the quiet power of long-standing social norms ultimately wins out, as he ceases his affairs with both Brenda and Winnie, and charts a new course for a rather safer harbour – discretion being the better part of honour and all.

This last act of the novel is perhaps Exhibit A in my argument that it adopts a conservative, even regressive, attitude towards the youth-cultural potential of the post-war. Larding the final pages of the novel with references to T. S. Eliot's *The Waste Land*, Sillitoe makes it clear that the explosive energies of youth-cultural sexual exploration and freedom can only lead to physical, emotional and psychological damage. Instead, the image of

Arthur/the fisher-king fishing on the banks of the 'dull canal' assumes centre stage. In a neat reversal, Sillitoe presents us with an Arthur who is both a fair-minded fisherman – releasing the first fish he catches – and himself ready to be caught: 'It meant death for a fish, but for a man it might not be so bad' (217). His future is clear, traditional and bereft of the sort of anarchic energy both he and the Teds in general embodied. It culminates not in an affirmation of life, energy and utopian potential – as MacInnes struggles to propose at the conclusion of *Absolute Beginners* – but of death even in the midst of passion. When he and Doreen at last have sex, it is hardly joyous: 'They followed his short cut towards home, and came to the loneliest place of the afternoon where, drawn by a deathly and irresistible passion, they lay down together in the bottom of a hedge' (Sillitoe 207). Arthur and Doreen finally consummate their relationship, but it is hard indeed to imagine a less enthusiastic depiction, one less full of hope for the future. 'Deathly and irresistible', their sex seems robotic and inevitable, rather than spontaneous and loving.

I have used the term 'anarchic' to describe Arthur's energy and want now to turn to its real political valence in the novel as a counterpart to his incoherent masculinity.[1] Arthur's politics, such as they are, emerge in a realm of unprecedented prosperity and individual rights, and indeed, Arthur appreciates his privileged status, knowing full well that he's better off than his parents ever were in terms of money and job security: 'The difference between before the war and after the war didn't bear thinking about. War was a marvellous thing in many ways, when you thought about how happy it had made so many people in England' (Sillitoe 27). Another Arthur, this time cultural historian Arthur Marwick, backs this sentiment up with some figures: 'Between 1951 and 1961 average weekly earnings of men over 21 almost doubled from £8.30 per week to £15.35 per week. Television sets had still been a rarity in the early 1950s, but by 1961, 75 percent of families had one' (n.p.). And though Arthur Seaton (back to the novel now) appreciates the stability of his role in the factory, he both resents paying the income tax that underwrites the improved social conditions in post-war England and longs to blow up the factory along with everyone in it:

> If they said: 'Look, Arthur, here's a hundredweight of dynamite and a brand-new plunger, now blow up the factory', then I'd do it, because that'd be something worth doing. Action. I'd bale-out for Russia or the North Pole where I'd sit and laugh like a horse over what I'd done, at the wonderful sight of gaffers and machines and shining bikes going sky-high one wonderful moonlit night. Not that I've got owt against 'em, but that's just how I feel now and again. Me, I couldn't care less if the world did blow up by tomorrow, as long as I'm blown up with it. (Sillitoe 40)

Perhaps even more of a nihilist than he is an anarchist, Arthur imagines himself here as a saboteur, an *agent provocateur* committing just the sort of destruction that the country has just spent the better part of a decade trying to stave off. Factories were, of course, among the chief targets of German bombing runs, and even though victory in the war is directly responsible for the level of prosperity he now enjoys, Arthur remains in thrall to an outdated political consciousness that can only ever understand the employer as the enemy. It's a heady fantasy, one that delivers a rush to Arthur's youthful appetite for 'action' regardless of its consequences.

But it's not only that. Instead, it fits into a much larger sense of youth-cultural rejection of parent-cultural bromides. Though he benefits directly and enduringly from the new age of post-war prosperity, Arthur nonetheless sees in its ornaments a plot to deprive people like him of their autonomy:

> What did they take us for? Bloody fools, but one of these days they'd be wrong. They think they've settled our hashes with their insurance cards and television sets, but I'll be one of them to turn round on 'em and let them see how wrong they are. When I'm on my fifteen-days' training and I lay on my guts behind a sandbag shooting at a target board I know whose faces I've got in my sights every time the new rifle cracks off. Yes. The bastards that put the gun into my hands. I make up a quick picture of their stupid four-eyed faces that blink as they read big books and papers on how to get blokes into khaki and fight battles in a war that they'll never be in – and then I let fly at them. Crack-crack-crack-crack-crack-crack. Other faces as well: the snot-gobbling gett that teks my income tax, the swivel-eyed swine that collects our rent, the big-headed bastard that gets my goat when he asks me to go to union meetings or sign a paper against what's happening in Kenya. As if I cared! (132)

With near total indiscrimination, Arthur gives free rein to this Billy Liar-esque scenario, violently repudiating anything that smacks of collectivity. He rejects not only the rent collector, but income tax, the military, the union representative and the humanitarian. What's striking here is less that Arthur would reject the call to yet more sacrifice in the name of the collective – many in England felt the same after having suppressed their individual ambitions in the name of national solidarity during the war – than the persistence of 1930s political concerns. Arthur understands himself as an individual fighting against oppression not only in terms of economics and opportunity, but also in terms of militarization and yet another war. In this respect, he remains mired in pre-war political views that even extend to the fantasy of raising a domestic army out of the factory's employees (recalling the fears about an 'army of the unemployed' that circulated in the 1930s). Observing the men and women streaming into work, Arthur wonders 'how many columns of soldiers could be gathered from these crowds for use in a rebellion' (Sillitoe 165). I do not wish to overstate my case, since certainly there was great continuity, especially for the working class, of political concerns from the pre-war to the post-war years, but I think it is undeniable that Arthur's politics betray a greater familiarity with the past than with the present – and certainly lack any real consideration of the future. In terms of youth culture, *Saturday Night and Sunday Morning*'s politics remain oriented towards an earlier time, one in which the full potential of what the Teddy boy signified simply could not be recognized. Indeed, this political rear-view may explain why critics have been so reluctant to recognize that Arthur is in fact a Teddy boy – he just thinks too much like an old man.

Much the same dynamic we saw in the novel's treatment of masculinity also obtains in its treatment of race, which is likewise focalized through the figure of the Teddy boy. In both instances Sillitoe simultaneously thinks about emergent youth culture in the figure of the Teddy boy and thinks with the Teddy boy as he explores apparently new possibilities and conflicts with long-standing models of social normativity. As Dick Hebdige has demonstrated conclusively, post-war British youth cultures were inextricable from the influence of both African-American music and style, largely as imported by American GIs stationed in England, and – crucially – West Indian and African immigrants to Britain after the war. The 1948 British Nationality Act (BNA) granted full citizenship to all members of the Commonwealth. Predictably, almost immediately when the Act went into effect in 1949 a flood of immigrants – known now as the Windrush Generation – coming 'home' to the mother country was unleashed. Tens of thousands of immigrants, largely from the West Indies, entered England in the first half of the 1950s, catching both the authorities and the general population off guard. The result was increased pressure on food supplies (rationing remained in effect until 1954), housing, jobs and social services. This pressure was registered immediately and loudly across public discourses, finding its way into novels within a matter of two or three years. As early as 1956, Samuel Selvon could write:

> And this sort of thing was happening at a time when the English people starting to make rab about how too much West Indians coming to the country: this was a time, when any corner you turn, it ten to one you bound to bounce up a spade. In fact, the boys all over London, it ain't have a place where you wouldn't find them, and a big discussion going on in Parliament about the situation, though the old Brit'n too diplomatic to clamp down on the boys or to do anything drastic like stop them from coming to the Mother Country. But big headlines in the papers every day, and whatever the newspaper and the radio say in this country, that is the people Bible. (Selvon 2)

By 1958, the pressures had gotten bad enough that race riots broke out in Nottingham (the setting for *Saturday Night and Sunday Morning*), Notting Hill and Notting Gate in London. Importantly, much of the violence was caused by Teddy boys: 'teds were frequently involved in unprovoked attacks on West Indians and figured prominently in the 1958 race riots' (Hebdige

51). Having earned notoriety as violent thugs in the first half of the decade, especially following the sensational Teddy boy murder of 1953,[2] the Teds cemented the image of themselves as defenders of a retrograde, white, British, working-class masculinity with the 1958 riots. Racial tensions had been building with the successive waves of immigration from 1949 to 1958, such that the eruption of violence came to seem almost inevitable at the time. Recognizing the scope of the problem, British authorities began scaling back the provisions of the BNA, until it was decisively rewritten in 1981.

It comes as something of a shock, then, to discover that race is virtually absent from *Saturday Night and Sunday Morning*, a novel celebrated from the moment of its publication up until today for its gritty social realism. There are three non-white characters in the novel: Chumley, Doddoe and Sam. The first two are imperial flotsam, washed up on the shores of England singly and taking up with widowed Englishwomen only to be silenced or browbeaten into near-total insignificance. Readers could be forgiven for forgetting they appear at all. Sam is even more fully integrated into the imperial framework: He visits Nottingham after having made friends with one of Arthur's cousins during the war. He represents precisely the Commonwealth contribution to the British war effort which the 1948 BNA was intended to recognize. Crucially, he is merely visiting and has no wish to remain in England – he can in no way be confused with the immigration problem that *Saturday Night and Sunday Morning*'s first readers would have had at front of mind.

Sam's visit is fascinating for two reasons. First, Sam is presented as a complete novelty to the other characters. Second, Sam's presence may be the cause of a vicious act of domestic violence between Arthur's sister Jane and her husband Jim. First, when the 'tribe' are expecting Sam, Arthur is sent out to see if he's gotten lost on his way from the station to Aunt Ada's house; he is supposed to be impossible to miss because he will be the only black man in the city: '"You wain't be able to miss him though. All you have to do is look for a black head wrapped up in a kakhi coat"' (Sillitoe 191). Arthur's cousins run through any number of racist stereotypes both before Sam arrives and during his visit, even though Sam appears to be at least as used to the accoutrements of Western civilization as they are. Bert, in particular, seems unable to come to terms with what Sillitoe presents as a wholly novel experience: '"He thinks all telegrams are sent by tom-tom,"' 'Of course, Bert said in a loud whisper, he misses the tom-toms'; 'Is [your girlfriend] as black as the ace of spades'; when Arthur declares that Sam need not contribute to the beer fund because he is a guest, '"It's just as well," Bert remarked. "He'd on'y pay in beads,"'; 'Bert accounting for [Sam's skill at darts] as a legacy left over from throwing assegais' (Sillitoe 191-193). Dave pretends 'to jump with surprise on seeing for the first time in his life a Negro sitting in the living-room' (Sillitoe 191), and even the next morning Bert still jokes, '"Hey, mam, there's a Zulu in my room"' (Sillitoe 197). For Sillitoe's characters, living in Nottingham in the mid-1950s, the sight of a black man is profoundly out of the ordinary, if not totally unprecedented, despite the near impossibility of this being so in any documentary sense.

The strain behind this presentation presents an enigma with wide-reaching implications. First, it suggests that Sillitoe simply did not know about the immigration to Nottingham in the first half of the decade. Though he settled in Majorca soon after being demobilized, Sillitoe worked briefly in Nottingham before doing so (Marwick n.p.). Though he wrote the novel in Majorca, and claimed that he had not even been in a factory for at least ten years before that (Sillitoe 5), it seems impossible that he did not know about the changing racial complexion of the city, the truly disruptive capacities of the young and the racial/generational tensions brewing as a result of these two shifts.

So where are all the black people? You're not going to like the answer. *Sillitoe erases an entire population from the city.* He simply could not *not* have known about the changes taking place in Nottingham and across the UK, but he specifically creates a novel almost totally devoid of black people. What's more, he does it in the name of an authentic mode of reportage, supposedly telling it like it is. A powerful impulse to disavowal is at work here, one that knows very well the historical truth, and yet refuses to represent it. As I argue just below, this is a profoundly troubling move, one that plays into a narrative of white supremacy.

The ongoing reception of the novel as authentic, true, gritty, realistic and so on only spreads the problem all the wider. I have not yet come across a single review or piece of criticism that even notices this erasure, much less takes issue with it. From its first reviews to its periodic revivals today, *Saturday Night and Sunday Morning* is uniformly praised for its documentary realism. To call this novel 'that rarest of all finds: a genuine no-punches-pulled, romanticised working-class novel' and Sillitoe himself 'a born writer, who knows his milieu and describes it with vivid, loving precision' (*Daily Telegraph*, qtd. on back cover) is to partake of its massive (self-)deception. Such evaluations guarantee the authenticity of the works they assess; they back up those works' claims to documentary truth. And, they do so by appealing to a profound, if quietly ubiquitous, racism.

This glaring problem finds elucidation in the second reason Sam's visit to the Seaton household is so fascinating: the domestic violence with which it concludes. Sally Minogue and Andrew Palmer refer to this simply as 'a curious argument between Jane and her husband' (138), but it seems far more significant than that. Through the gaiety of the first full day the family spends celebrating Christmas, an undertone of tension gradually grows. Sexual innuendo accompanies racial unease, as both Bert and Arthur take note of their young cousins' blossoming sexuality (Sillitoe 200) and Bert uses the mistletoe to attempt to coerce his cousin Alma into kissing Sam (she runs from the house rather than submit) (200). At exactly that moment, violence – though as yet only verbal – erupts: 'Above the uproar Jane's voice was heard saying to Jim: "I don't believe it. It ain't true. You want to mind what you're saying you dirty bleeder" – in a voice of hard belligerence' (200). The moment passes without note, however, as the next line returns to Bert's (now successful) efforts to get Sam kissed: 'Bert succeeded in getting Annie and Bertha kissed by Sam under the mistletoe' (200). This context is vital, as it places Jane's hard, angry outburst in immediate reference to the carnivalesque license of the mistletoe. It also implies that whatever Jim has said has sexual implications and that Jane finds it deeply offensive. Shortly after, Ada tells Sam a story and then 'kissed him beneath the mistletoe' as well, prompting Betty to name the source of growing tension in the room: '"Well, that's not the first time she's bin kissed by a black man, I'll bet"' (200). At last, Jane speaks to Sam directly, though in a context suggestive of a strategy to provoke Jim's jealousy: '"Do you like England then?" Jane asked Sam. She had been out of the room for a few minutes. "I like it very much," Sam stammered. She threw her arms around him and kissed him, turning her back on the rabid face of her husband near the door' (200–201). All the cards are now on the table, and when Sam stands up to head off to bed,

> The room went suddenly quiet. Jane was standing up, staring at Jim with tight, angry lips. 'You aren't going to say that about me', she cried loudly. Arthur saw a beer-glass in her hand. 'What did he say, then?' Ada asked of everybody. Jane did not reply, but struck her husband on his forehead with the glass, leaving a deep half-inch split in his skin. Blood oozed and fell down his face, gathering speed until it dropped onto the rug. He stood like a statue and made no sound. The glass fell from her hand. 'You aren't going to accuse me of that', she said again, her lips trembling. (201)

For his part, Jim seems completely bewildered by Jane's violence – he asks again and again what he said or did to provoke her. Jane declines to explain.

In a final turn of the screw, Sillitoe makes this event the occasion for Arthur's return to form after a long funk following his beating by the swaddies:

> He pressed the cold wet handkerchief to Jim's head, feeling strangely and joyfully alive, as if he had been living in a soulless vacuum since his fight with the swaddies. He told himself that he had been without life since then, that now he was awake once more, ready to tackle all obstacles, to break any man, or woman, that came for him, to turn on the whole world if it bothered him too much, and blow it to pieces. The crack of the glass on Jim's forehead echoed and re-echoed through his mind. (201)

What are we to make of this? It is Christmas, the family are all together, they have a welcome visitor, there is much jollity and goodwill. On one view, it's a sentimental vision of working-class authenticity and belonging. At the same time, race and sex are increasingly bound up together in a rising tension that culminates in two violent eruptions as Jane first yells at Jim and then hits him with a beer glass. And yet these eruptions pass almost without comment, the second one even provoking an epiphanic release for Arthur.

This episode is in fact the heart of the novel, the place where its repression of race and dismissal of youth culture's explosive potential return from repression. Put simply, Arthur is a Teddy boy. He is rejuvenated not just by violence, but by racially motivated violence, by the fusion of race, class, sex and youth in an apparently random explosion of rage. In this he is no different from the Teds who were at the forefront of attacks on immigrants in the 1958 riots in Nottingham. Though he does not directly participate in the violence, and though he appears not to have any personal issue with Sam, even when Sam kisses his cousins and aunt, Arthur is inexplicably re-animated by the violence caused by Sam's presence and the threat of miscegenation systematically ramped up by Bert's use of the mistletoe and Jane's efforts to get back at Jim. Captured in this tableau is precisely the violent return of England's repressed racism that the novel tries so hard to avoid, even as the historical context makes it more and more obvious.

That virtually every reviewer and critic of the novel thus far has (wilfully?) ignored this aspect of the novel is thus all the more troubling. Not only is the novel dishonest in its depiction of post-war Nottingham, so is the *un*-critical reception of it as social realism. Far from being a gritty, unromanticized portrait of working-class authenticity in the post-war years, *Saturday Night and Sunday Morning* instead promulgates a profoundly racist understanding of England and Englishness as inherently white at precisely the historical moment when such an ideology was about to explode in real violence on the streets. The novel rejects the future and even tries to repress the present, far preferring a conservative view of history that sees tradition restored, cycles repeated and England unchanged. Dick Hebdige has argued that 'the potentially explosive equation of "Negro" and "youth" had [...] served as the nucleus for the teddy boy style' by the mid-1950s (49–50). This equation is the backbone of the novel's refusal to engage seriously with youth culture and its culture-changing potential. It is also why the novel achieved such popularity among white readers when it was published in 1958. It is why it is still celebrated today.

If youth and blackness are violently separated in *Saturday Night and Sunday Morning*, with one neutered by the novel's end and the other sent back to Africa so that its factual presence in England can continue to be ignored, they are openly engaged and even celebrated in Colin MacInnes's *Absolute Beginners*. Written in the same year *Saturday Night and Sunday Morning* was published, and appearing only a few months after it, *Absolute Beginners* is directly concerned with issues of race, emerging white nationalism and the latent violence of an empire on the verge of collapse. It includes a much more varied and lively panoply of youth cultures and characters than *Saturday Night and Sunday Morning*. It both acknowledges the debt owed by emerging white youth cultures such as mods to African, West Indian and African-American influences and decisively aligns those youth cultures' utopian energies with the influx of new ideas, practices and aesthetics from the colonial margins. MacInnes is famously positive about teenagers, embracing their youthful idealism and celebrating their potential for overturning the chauvinism of the parent culture – especially as it is expressed through youth-cultural traitors such as the Teddy boys. And yet it would be a mistake to read *Absolute Beginners* as the progressive rejoinder to Sillitoe's regressions. As Paula Derdiger puts it, MacInnes's 'vision of a free world inhabited by a multiracial and sexually diverse group of squatters and hustlers was ultimately more wishful thinking than it was convincingly real and accurate' (65). Though *Absolute Beginners* is much more keenly aware of racial problems and possibilities than *Saturday Night and Sunday Morning*, it, too, ultimately reinforces traditional forms of masculinity and lapses into a passive, self-satisfied, racism.

But we've gotten ahead of ourselves. First, we should note that the youth-cultural landscape in *Absolute Beginners* is already more crowded than it was in *Saturday Night and Sunday Morning*. Let's begin where we left off with Sillitoe: with the Teddy boys. For MacInnes, the Teds had already become passé. They were outmoded by the mid-1950s and persisted only as ideological remnants of a wartime mentality that positively revelled in isolation, exclusion, vulgarity and Little England ideologies. Though they are not by any means class warriors, MacInnes's Teds belong firmly to the working class, remaining defiantly inarticulate, loutish and violent. MacInnes caricatures them through the figure of Ed the Ted, whose very appellation already signals his comic-book-villain characterization. Ed first appears on the scene menacing the narrator with a key-ring on a chain and 'panting like a hippo' (MacInnes 42). The narrator immediately stereotypes Ed, by remarking on the fact that he is out of 'uniform' and not armed with the typical Teddy boy arsenal:

> 'What, Ed?' I said. 'No bike-chain? No flick-knife? No iron bar?' And, as a matter of fact, he wasn't wearing his full Teddy uniform either: no velvet-lined frock-coat, no bootlace tie, no four-inch solid corridor-creepers – only that insanitary hair-do, creamy curls falling all over his one-inch forehead, and his drainpipes that last saw the inside of a cleaner's in the Attlee era. (MacInnes 42)

As the narrator makes clear, the Teddy boy had become so conventional that his style could easily be enumerated – and dismissed – by 1958. Ed, it turns out, has been ejected from the gang he used to belong to and has moved back in with his mother to lick his wounds. This does not, however, prevent him from continuing to manifest all the characteristics of what the narrator refers to as 'the full-fledged Teddy-boy condition – slit eyes, and cosh, and words of one syllable, and dirty finger-nails and all' (43). Though he is clearly a figure of fun for the narrator, Ed is also dangerous; though he hurts only himself with his keychain, smacking his knuckles when he tries to stop it spinning, he also hurts the narrator simply by slapping his back. Moreover, Ed rebounds from his humiliating ejection from his first gang by falling in with the sinister Flikker, whose gang is at least partly behind the racial violence with which the novel culminates. Though he is clearly a figure of fun, Ed the Ted is also dangerous and violent, as is the cultural current he represents – white British nationalism – as the teenage narrator learns to his dismay at the novel's end.

For MacInnes, the Teddy boys have betrayed the true revolutionary potential of post-war youth, so instead of lumping all youth cultures together under one banner, as Sillitoe appears prepared to do, he depicts a variety of alternatives. Attuned to the ferment of youth-cultural innovation at the end of the 1950s in a way Sillitoe was not, MacInnes depicts a youth-cultural moment in which what will be mods and rockers are taking shape, hipsters glide through the city and people of colour feature prominently as sources and guarantors of cool.

Much of this understanding is based upon a fundamentally future-oriented vision that directly contrasts with Sillitoe's nostalgia; it coalesces around class in the first instance. Where Sillitoe's Arthur Seaton is cemented into a role as exemplar of the newly prosperous working class, MacInnes's teenager rejects class affiliation wholesale, in favour of a utopian present/future characterized by jazz clubs:

> the great thing about the jazz world, and all the kids that enter into it, is that no one, not a soul, cares what your class is, or what your race is, or what your income, or if you're a boy, or girl, or bent, or versatile, or what you are – so long as you dig the scene and can behave yourself, and have left all that crap behind you, too, when you come in the jazz club door. (MacInnes 61)

The teenager's view of the jazz world, naive though it is – and he will soon learn how naive it is – is nonetheless utopian and full of potential. Class, race, income level, sex, gender, sexuality: All are irrelevant if you enjoy jazz and are willing to follow suit by leaving your other affiliations at the door. Needless to say, someone like Ed would not be welcome with his prejudices, though arguably if he were to abandon his politics (if we can call them that) and simply enter into the spirit of enjoying the jazz, even he would be welcome.

As evidence of this catholicism in the jazz scene – and thus by extension his own self-congratulation for being so tolerant – the teenager presents us with several alternatives to the Teddy boy's chauvinism. There's the flamboyantly gay Fabulous Hoplite, the butch dyke ponce Big Jill, the preternaturally hip black man Mr. Cool and so on. Each of these depictions now appears clearly to us as verging on stereotype itself – the gay man is flamboyant, slight, elfin; Big Jill is large, loud, vulgar; Mr. Cool is black, ergo cool and so on.[3] But at least they are present; in Sillitoe's world none of these characters is even possible, much less presented in a positive light.

In terms of how MacInnes thinks *about* youth culture, the most fully drawn characters are Dean Swift, the Misery Kid and the Wizard. Let's take the last of these first, as evidence both that MacInnes was well aware of the variety of possible trajectories for youth-cultural revolutionary energy and that he knew it would not necessarily take a positive shape. The Wizard starts out as a close friend of the narrator's, if he can be said to be anyone's friend. He is an edgy, petulant young man with a penchant for picking arguments with grown-ups, then playing the youthful innocent card to get his way. He does not understand the narrator's hopeful view of teenagers and views the entire phenomenon as a situation of mutual exploitation:

> It's been a two-way twist, this teenage party. Exploitation of the kiddos by the conscripts, and exploitation of themselves by the crafty little absolute beginners. (…) I tell you. As things are, I won't regret it when the teenage label's torn off the arse pockets of my drip-dry sky-blue jeans. (MacInnes 12)

Despite this bitterness, the Wiz still holds teenagers above all others: 'the Wiz has for all oldies just the same kind of hatred psychos have for Jews or foreigners or coloureds, that is, he hates everyone who's not a teenager' (13). In fact, the Wiz turns out to be precisely the same as the 'psychos' who hate Jews, foreigners and coloureds, joining a fascist rally in the midst of the race riots with which the novel culminates:

> Then I looked at the Wizard. And on my friend's face, as he stared up at this orator, I saw an expression that made me shiver. Because the little Wiz, so tight and sharp and trim and dangerous, had on a little smile, that showed his teeth a bit, and his wiry little body was all clenched, and something was staring through his eyes that came from God knows where, and he raised on his toes, and shot up his arms all rigid, and he cried out, shrill like a final cry, 'Keep England white!' (191)

It's a climax that immediately excludes the Wiz from the utopian vision of the jazz clubs articulated earlier. It recognizes the potential for youthful revolutionary energy to go awry, not ushering in a better world, but lapsing into the vicious paranoia of fascism. Crucially, the narrator – the most teenaged of the teenagers in the book – responds by striking the Wiz in the face and heading back into the fray of the riots in quest of a more positive possibility.

The positivity upon which he bets his life manifests in two much more authentic teenage specimens, Dean Swift and the Misery Kid, 'the Dean being a sharp modern jazz creation, and the Kid just a skiffle survival, with horrible leanings to the trad. thing' (62). The mod/rocker clashes that will become fodder for moral panic in the next decade have not yet solidified, but already MacInnes can show us the emerging tension: 'If you know the contemporary scene, you could tell them apart at once, just like you could a soldier or a sailor, with their separate uniforms' (62). The military reference is vital here, both for how it links post-war youth cultures to the long shadow of the Second World War and for how it anticipates the street violence of the riots that consume the last third of the novel and the future battles between mods and rockers. Let's

> take first the Misery Kid and his trad. drag. Long, brushless hair, white stiff-starched collar (rather grubby), striped shirt, tie of all one colour (red today, but it could have been royal-blue or navy), short jacket but an old one (somebody's riding tweed, most likely), very, very, tight, tight, trousers with wide stripe, no sox, short *boots*. (62)

Our narrator clearly does not approve of the Misery Kid's musical tastes, his clothing style or his way of being in the world – 'still living like a bum and a bohemian, skint and possibly even hungry' (63) – but he respects him and even calls him 'heroic' (63). He works with the Misery Kid in his photo shoots and recognizes his stoical ethics: 'to argue when the dirt dropped down on your head was contrary to his whole trad. ideology' (64). In a few years' time, the Misery Kid will have morphed into a rocker, more fully than ever invested in the emerging sounds of rock 'n' roll, rockabilly and the remnants of skiffle, along with traditional jazz (hence the moniker 'trad.'). With more money and a more clearly defined stylistic ensemble, including motorcycles, leather jackets and a clarified group belonging, the Misery-Kid-as-rocker will have gone from pitiable to problematic in the perpetual dialectic of youth-cultural innovation and its regressive undertows. MacInnes even previews this deplorable development for us, as the Misery Kid departs the cafe past Dean Swift: 'As Misery Kid passed by the Dean on his way out, Dean Swift looked up and hissed at him. "Fascist!" which the Kid ignored. These modern jazz boys certainly do feel strongly about the trad. reaction' (64). Mods and trads, mods and rockers, skinheads and punks, skinheads and hippies, sharks and jets – *plus ça change*. On the other side of the barricade (still, admittedly, under construction) is

> the Dean in the modernist number's version. College-boy smooth crop hair with burned-in parting, neat white Italian rounded-collared shirt, short Roman jacket *very* tailored (two little vents, three buttons), no-turn-up narrow trousers with 17-inch bottoms absolute maximum, pointed-toe shoes and a white mac lying folded by his side, compared with Misery's sausage-rolled umbrella. (62)

Dean Swift belongs to what is by far the most significant youth culture depicted in *Absolute Beginners*: the mods. The narrator is an incipient mod, and though it is anachronistic to think of them as full-blown instances of the

FIGURE 1.2 *31 December 1965, 'The Who' appear on 'Ready Steady Go' for a special new year edition. (Photo by Bentley Archive/Popperfoto/Getty Images.)*

mod subculture that would not flourish for another few years (in the early 1960s), they represent a stunningly well-attuned version of what will become perhaps the most enduringly influential of all post-war British youth cultures.

The term 'mod' derives from the use of the term 'modernist' to describe aficionados of modern jazz in the late 1950s. As the 1950s turned into the 1960s, 'modernist' was shortened simply to 'mod', many of the stylistic predilections of the group sharpened into a clear sartorial, musical, vehicular, stimulant and linguistic ensemble. In keeping with their anti-Ted aesthetic, the mods opted for Italian-styled shoes and clothes – fitted, stylish, elegant – jazz music, motor scooters (Vespas for preference) for transportation, amphetamines rather than alcohol as the stimulant of choice and a patois that fused the black argot of the jazz world with the stutter characteristic of amphetamine users. By far their most well-known avatars are The Who, whose early stylings are quintessentially mod, right down to the stuttered lyrics in 'My Generation'. They are also the first youth subculture to enter the popular imagination as both potentially dangerous and yet also assimilable. Because they dress stylishly, though perhaps a bit *too* stylishly for some tastes, the mods are the first – perhaps the only – youth culture whose members can go to work in their weekend kit. Savvy about their self-presentation in a way that the Teds were not, the mods manage to convey through their stylistic ensemble both respectability and menace, flamboyance and elegance. Their media savvy generated a new pinnacle of youth-cultural influence when they became the only youth group to have a popular prime-time television show dedicated to them: *Ready, Steady, Go!* It is no accident that the teenage narrator of *Absolute Beginners* is an amateur photographer who specializes in depicting fictional scenarios for the (sometimes perverse) appetites of his clients. Nor is it without significance that the Fabulous Hoplite finds his greatest success in front of television cameras, on a new show featuring the lovelorn.

Clearly, proto-mod culture is the most promising of the youth-cultural developments presented in *Absolute Beginners*, but it is important not to confuse mods with the larger utopian impetus MacInnes associates with teenagers *per se*. As with Ed the Ted's actual danger, despite his depiction as a clown, and as with the Misery Kid's redeeming stoicism, despite his deplorable trad. affiliations, so Dean Swift's hyper-cool modernism is undercut by the fact 'that he's a junkie' (64). This fact opens up a gulf between the narrator and Dean, compromising Dean's status as a figure of teenage optimism:

> If you have a friend who's a junkie, like I have the Dean, you soon discover there's no point whatever discussing his addiction. It's as senseless as discussing love, or religion, or things you only feel if you feel them, because the Dean and I suppose all his fellow junkies, is convinced that this is 'a mystic way of life' (the Dean's own words), and you and I, who don't jab hot needles in our arms, are just going through life missing absolutely everything worth while in it. The Dean always says, life's just kicks. Well, I agree with him, so it is, but personally it seems to me the big kick you should try to get by how you live it sober. But tell that to the Dean! (64)

Though he is enviable for his modernist cool, the Dean nonetheless cannot stand in for the teenage potentiality the narrator alone seems to embody: 'The Dean gazed round at the teenage products like a concentration camp exterminator. [...] I could see that now the Dean, as usual when skinned and vicious, was going to engage in his favourite theme, i.e., the horror of teenagers' (65). It's 1958. The horrors of the Holocaust have had scarcely more than a decade to be absorbed, and MacInnes compares the Dean's snobbery to that of a 'concentration camp exterminator' reviewing the people he will shortly eradicate. The effect even today is jarring, but for the novel's original readers in 1959 it must have struck a powerful chord. The first of the baby boomers could only just barely have become teenagers in time for the shocking announcement to be made about them. It's a subtle move, one that indicates that some teenagers – often those most readily identifiable by their stylistic affiliation with one or another identifiable subculture – are latent psychopaths. At the same time, it aligns the Dean with everyone who views teenagers as 'mindless butterflies' (66) as the worst of the worst: as Nazis. It's a move that asserts the utopian potentiality of teenagers by aligning them with the most oppressed people in recent memory – the Jews – but with a conservative rider. The revolutionary potential that MacInnes preserves in this move is shadowed by a rejection of substance-use. The narrator seems sincere in his rejection of any form of artificial intoxication: He only drinks twice, and never to intoxication. This move sanitizes the teenage potential MacInnes is so desperate to preserve, and yet avoids aligning that potential with any particular youth group or with the complacent parent culture against which it must be positioned.

Having shaded, nuanced and compromised various particular instantiations of the teenage revolutionary potential, MacInnes gives free rein to his fantasy ideal by linking it directly to the historical reality of the post-war. The vision of generational tension he develops is directly implicated in the movement of history – specifically in the decline of British might – and manifests in his relationship with his family. As the Teenager engages with his half-brother, his father and finally his mother, MacInnes pieces together a clichéd narrative of British history from the 1930s to the late 1950s, situating the Teenager as the harbinger of a new age. He represents a decisive break with a moribund past that has become degraded and self-indulgent in the post-war era. In each of these engagements, the Teenager meets his family's commitment to outworn narratives with scorn and derision, loudly declaring his exceptionalism.

The trouble begins when the Teenager visits his parents' home, itself already an allegory of British decline. The Teenager's mother runs a boarding house for Maltese and Cypriot immigrants. His hapless father and half-brother Vernon live there as well to lend a patina of respectability despite his mother's tendency to favour some of her lodgers with invitations to her bed. The paternal function here is defunct, as the Teenager's father has neither his wife's nor his stepson's respect or deference. As a figure for England, the house is bereft of any real claims to authenticity or respectability, and thus furnishes the ideal setting for the Teenager's multiple statements of his break with history. The tension circulates around the war and various perspectives on it, and is characterized by a series of reversals that show how truly non-conformist the Teenager's view of history is – and why MacInnes pins such enormous faith on its revolutionary potential.

The view of the 1930s on offer here comes via perhaps the most sympathetic character in the novel, his father. Almost immediately upon his introduction into the narrative, the Teenager's father strikes up his favourite tune: How much harder life was in the 1930s than it is in the 1950s:

'You've simply no idea what that pre-war period was like. Poverty, unemployment, fascism and disaster and, worst of all, no chance, no opportunity, no sunlight at the end of the corridor, just a lot of hard, frightened, rich old men sitting on top of a pile of dustbin lids to keep the muck from spilling over! [...] It was a terrible time for the young', he went on, grabbing me. 'Nobody would listen to you if you were less than thirty, nobody gave you money whatever you'd do for it, nobody let you *live* like you kids can do today.' (34)

This view of the 1930s, though largely accurate, has already hardened into a cliché for the Teenager. He simply doesn't care about his father's past struggles and, with the callowness of youth, responds only by asking why his father doesn't go out and enjoy himself if things are so much better now. The generational gap here widens into a chasm as the Teenager fails to comprehend how much one's youth remains an integral part of one's world outlook. His father can no more leave the 1930s behind than the Teenager will ultimately be able to leave the 1950s behind – as today's industry in baby boomer nostalgia illustrates.

As his father rushes 'out of the room, knocking things over' (36), the Teenager returns to his suspended argument with Vernon, wherein he outlines the teenage phenomenon in contradistinction to the war generation. Crucially, this contrast presents first and foremost in terms of clothing. The Teenager is wearing his 'full teenage drag', which is clearly proto-mod, though with some elements of Teddy boy flamboyance still in effect:

> The grey pointed alligator casuals, the pink neon pair of ankle crêpe nylon-stretch, my Cambridge blue glove-fit jeans, a vertical-striped happy shirt revealing my lucky neck-charm on its chain, and the Roman-cut short-arse jacket just referred to ... not to mention my wrist identity jewel, and my Spartan warrior hair-do. (MacInnes 32)

The Teenager's clothes are form-fitting, chic, colourful, and edgy – ultra-modern, in a word. As he himself notes, they are guaranteed to 'enrage' Vernon, who is wearing 'floppy dung-coloured garments' that appear to have been 'bought in a marked-down summer sale at the local casbah' (32). In fact, it's even worse: It's Vernon's demobilization suit. Not only is it ugly and indicative of an irretrievable lack of cool, it is directly linked to Vernon's age and military service.

As if his suit were not enough to mark him indelibly as 'square', Vernon makes it a point of pride, volleying the Teenager's scorn by parroting official Churchillian propaganda: ' "The war," said Vern, "was Britain's finest hour" ' (32). The Teenager responds insouciantly, baiting Vernon into asserting both the primacy of the Second World War and the Teenager's bad luck in not being able to remember it:

> 'What war? You mean Cyprus, boy? Or Suez? Or Korea?'
>   'No, stupid. I mean the *real* war, you don't remember.' (33)

This is the Teenager's opening. We've gone from a snobbish comparison of clothes to Vernon's insistence that his generation is superior because they not only remember the war, but lived it. He wagers the Churchillian myth of wartime authenticity against the Teenager's unearned privilege. It's a losing gambit, since as we've seen already, the Teenager is unable to relate to any moment before his own, and unashamedly prefers his open-ended futurity to any idealization of the past. Rather than bow his head in deference to the war generation, the Teenager insists that it is an 'old, old struggle' about which 'you pensioners' will not stop talking and for which they will not stop congratulating themselves (33). To Vernon's insistence that the Teenager will have to do his National Service just like everyone older than him, the Teenager takes a page from Arthur Seaton's book, declaring, 'no one is going to tell me to do anything I don't want to, no, or try to blackmail me with that crazy old mixture of threats and congratulations that a pronk like you falls for because you're a born form-filler, tax-payer, and cannon-fodder' (33). In one breath, the Teenager punctures the official myth of plucky Britain winning the war for all humankind and exempts himself from any implication in it. His simple refusal even to engage with his father's outraged nostalgia for the 1930s is compounded by his refusal to countenance any suggestion of the war generation's nobility.

A key part of Vernon's problem, according to the Teenager, is precisely what Vernon had implied was the Teenager's problem – he was born in the wrong historical moment. While Vernon means that the Teenager is unfortunate not to be able to remember the war, the Teenager means just the opposite: That Vernon was born late enough to miss active service, but not late enough to partake of the teenage phenomenon:

> The trouble about Vernon, really, as I've said, is that he's one of the last of the generations that grew up before teenagers existed: in fact, he never seems to have been an absolute beginner at any time at all. Even today, of course, there are some like him, i.e., kids of the right age, between fifteen or so and twenty, that I wouldn't myself describe as teenagers: I mean not kiddos who dig the teenage *thing*, or are it. But in poor Vernon's era, the sad slob, there just weren't *any*: can you believe it? Not any authentic teenagers at all. In those days, it seems, you were just an over-grown boy, or an under-grown man, life didn't seem to cater for anything whatever else between. (MacInnes 36)

Vernon is the Teenager's half-brother in more than just the familial sense; though they are quite close in age, they belong to different traditions, different paternities. To the Teenager, Vernon is not a beneficiary of history, but its casualty, a conscript without access to either the bragging rights of those who fought in the war or the pure freedom of the post-war generation. Like Arthur Seaton, Vernon is trapped in a time-warp, adhering to a set of values the Teenager and his ilk want nothing more than to get rid of. This is why his attack on his half-brother has such little effect.

Where the Teenager's father had simply given way to the Teenager's scorn, Vernon goes on offense on behalf of the war generation, determined at once to establish the superiority of that slightly older crowd and to cut the Teenager's sense of privilege off at the knees. He starts by criticizing the Teenager for having 'no social conscience' (37). He really means that the Teenager is inadequately grateful for how the post-war socialist administrations of Clement Attlee created the conditions of possibility for the emergence of teenagers. When the Teenager points out this fact, Vernon reacts paradoxically: He first says that it in no way means that he approves of the Teenagers, then claims that the benefits to teenagers were '"an unforeseen eventuality,"' before chiding the Teenager for not being grateful for them (37). It's the old broken kettle argument, where each subsequent position reveals the previous one to have been false. Vernon verges on incoherence here, and never really recovers his footing. When the Teenager affirms that he feels no gratitude for an accidental benefit, a side-effect of Vernon's 'pinko pals [doing] what they wanted to when they got in power' (37), Vernon immediately tries to revive the sacrosanct discourse of class consciousness: '"You're a traitor to the working-class!"' (37). As we have already seen, the Teenager's commitment to the utopian world of modern jazz means that he sees categories such as class to be outmoded and irrelevant: '"I'm just not interested in the whole class crap that seems to needle you and all the tax-payers"' (38). Vernon's final salvo is simply a charge of immorality, which the Teenager easily repudiates by pointing out that he and his cohort live more cleanly than Vernon does. The Teenager thus rejects more or less the entire social framework by which the parent generation parses value and asserts his utopian commitment to an unprecedented future.

Thus far, the Teenager has defined himself only in negative terms, but when he runs into the most formidable force in his family, his mother, he is at last forced to explain how he understands his generation's historicity. In the course of their argument, he articulates a broad generational resentment:

> 'You've too much spending money, that's your trouble!'
> 'That's just what's *not* my trouble, Ma.'
> 'All you teenagers have.'
> I said, 'I'm really getting tired of hearing this. All right, we kids have got too much loot to spend! Well, please tell me what you propose to do about it.'
> 'All that money', she said, looking at me as if I had pound notes falling out of my ears, and she could snatch them', and you're only minors! With no responsibilities to need all that spending money for.'
> 'Listen to me', I said, 'Who made us minors?'

'What?'

'You made us minors with your parliamentary whatsits', I told her patiently. 'You thought, "That'll keep the little bastards in their places, no legal rights, and so on," and you made us minors. Righty-o. That also freed us from responsibility, didn't it? Because how can you be responsible if you haven't any rights? And then came the gay-time boom and all the spending money, and suddenly you oldos found that though we minors had no rights, we'd got the money power. In other words – and *listen* to me, Ma – though it wasn't what you'd intended, admittedly, you gave us the money, and you took away our responsibility.' (39–40)[4]

This broadside expresses the Teenager's sense of resentment and entitlement, and a discourse of rights and responsibilities that goes to the heart of what the war generation imagined themselves to have been fighting for. As he did in his argument with Vernon, the Teenager points out that his mother's generation has created the conditions of possibility for the teenage revolution and that they regularly congratulate themselves on having done so. At the same time, he voices a distinct impatience with the parent culture's resentment of the very privilege for which they fought. Their children are doing much better than they did and have better prospects than perhaps any generation in history, and yet they are – at least from the Teenager's point of view – jealous of the fact.

Tellingly, the Teenager casts this in negative terms. He sees the relationship not as one in which his parents' generation fought for the freedoms he now carelessly enjoys, but as one in which his parents sought to limit his generation's rights, with the unintended consequence of simultaneously limiting their responsibilities. At stake here is a fundamental shift in the understanding of freedom, where the parent generation appears to have understood it in terms of taking on responsibilities in order to earn rights, while the Teenager's generation understands it in terms of having freedom from both, and thus operating outside the discourse of rights and responsibilities altogether. Just as he had earlier disavowed the entire discourse of class identity, the Teenager here disavows the discourse of liberal democracy in favour of a naive new utopian anarchism.

The proof of this disavowal lies in the novel's opening pages, where the parent generation is at once denigrated for having behaved out of historical necessity and resented for its efforts to undermine the teenage revolution. Both impulses appear in a single sentence:

This teenage ball had had a real splendour in the days when the kids discovered that, for the first time since centuries of kingdom-come, they'd money, which hitherto had always been denied to us at the best time in life to use it, namely, when you're young and strong, and also before the newspapers and telly got hold of this teenage fable and prostituted it as conscripts seem to do to everything they touch. (MacInnes 12)

Three aspects of this declaration need commentary. First is the historical slipperiness with which the Teenager manages to identify himself with all young people across the generations, as though his own status as a teenager were timeless and continuous with all previous teenagers. He refers to himself as a member of the 'us' to whom money had been denied in the past, making himself into a transcendental subject of adolescence. Second, he lays the blame for the failure of the teenage revolution at the feet of the parent generation, whose control of mass media has allowed them not only to appropriate the teenage phenomenon, but to 'prostitute' it as well. This brings us to the third, and possibly the most telling, aspect of the Teenager's rant: His use of the word 'conscript' to refer to members of the parental generation. In one sense, this simply refers to all those who were liable to conscription, beginning with the Military Training Act of 1939, which remained in effect until 1960 (though all those conscripted had been released from service by 1949) – that is to say, virtually all adults, though more men than women, living in the UK during the war. In another sense, though, it refers to the fact that conscripts are not volunteers; they are compelled to do their duty. For the Teenager and his friends, the term is a subtle put-down, since it indicates their belief that the parental generation is taking credit for making sacrifices they had no choice *but* to make. The term thus captures both (a) the contrast between the Teenager's sense of his generation's freedom versus his parents' generation's constraint and (b) the Teenager's generation's resentment of the parental generation's claim to moral superiority for having fought the war. The Teenager seems poised to lead a new generation into a wide open utopian future unbeholden to the sacrifices and constraints of the past.

The forceful logic behind the teenager's idealism is somewhat compromised, however, by his decidedly conservative notions of masculinity. The flipside of his rejection of the past is that he has no viable role models of mature masculinity: His father has been broken down by the one-two punch of the 1930s and his wife's infidelity, and Vernon is a lazy, quarrelsome oaf whom even their mother considers inadequate to lend an air of respectability as the official man of the house – hence her request that the Teenager move back in if his father should die. Partly as an accident of history and partly as a result of the inevitable anxiety of influence that so often drives a wedge between generations, the Teenager becomes the closest thing in his family to a traditional mature male: He is autonomous, independent, self-sufficient, strong of both mind and body, and morally pure. Ironically, his rejection of the 'dear old ancestral home' (29) leads him to embody many of the traditional masculine values he fancies himself to be breaking with – he will even take up arms in a just cause by the novel's end. Though *Absolute Beginners* would seem to be quite distinct from the masculinity on offer in *Saturday Night and Sunday Morning*, they actually converge on this point.

As the novel climaxes in an historic outbreak of violence that puts paid to the myth of British tolerance, the Teenager accedes to a new sort of masculine maturity. The novel directly ties this historical break to the Teenager's personal maturation into manhood as the Teenager leaves Suze (about whom more shortly) in his apartment and races through the riot-torn streets of London only to arrive too late to see his father one last time before he dies. Sure to be haunted by the fact that his father repeatedly asked for him in his dying moments – that is, to be haunted by a past he neither understood nor appreciated in his youth – the Teenager forcefully declines to return home to take his father's place. In this, he breaks with a certain notion of paternity and ancestral continuity that underwrites traditional British versions of manhood. This innovation is quickly undercut, however, by the Teenager's division of his inheritance with Vernon. Showing himself to be not all bad, Vernon keeps his word to the Teenager's father and gives the Teenager the manuscript of his father's 'History of Pimlico', along with 'four big envelopes' (199) filled with money. It's a poignant moment, one in which the Teenager's father has singled him out as his true heir. He leaves him an unfinished history (allegory alert!) and a small fortune that he has scraped together over the years as only a veteran of the 1930s and the war could have done. It is, as Vernon says, '"Your father's fortune"' (199). When Vernon points out that the money should properly go into the estate, he invokes British common law, with its firm anchor in paternity and inheritance. The Teenager rejects this move, though, breaking with the spirit of that law while finding a new way – a new male homosocial way – to honour its spirit. Instead of agreeing to put the money into the estate, the Teenager forges a new bond with Vernon by treating him as a full brother: He gives him half the money and both agree not to tell their mother. The Teenager's father's death thus serves as something of a break with traditional models of masculinity, even while it keeps their core homosociality – a circuit of support that explicitly excludes women – fully intact. Having lost his toehold in the 'dear old ancestral home' with his father's death, the Teenager abdicates his claim to the role of man of the house and anoints Vernon as his successor. Male privilege dies hard.

This tendency towards incremental change in traditional models repeats itself in the Teenager's relationship with Suze. Though the Teenager has gay friends, and appears to be at ease with a range of sexual proclivities, his affection for Suze is powerfully normative. The novel opens with the lovelorn Teenager puppyishly trying to win Suze's affections. Suze, however, enjoys her freedom and promiscuity, particularly when it comes to black immigrants in London. The Teenager's exchanges with Suze are always fraught with tension, as Suze insists on keeping her independence, while the Teenager by turns teases her about her promiscuity, physically crowds her and questions her about her love life. He focuses specifically on her proclivity for sex with black men: '"You ever think of marrying with one of them?" I asked her edgily, as usual slipping into that groove of nastiness that affects me whenever I talk to Suze of her love life' (18). Calling to mind Arthur Seaton's dangerous mix of violence with passion, the Teenager infuses his ongoing infatuation with Suze with an alarming degree of menace. When Suze reveals that she intends to make ' "a very *distinguished* marriage" ' (18) and has had the right sort of offer – though notably from her older, and gay, boss Henley – the Teenager shows his true stripes: ' "That horrible old poof!" I cried' (18). The Teenager's ensuing tantrum makes his emotional intensity for Suze indistinguishable from his homophobia and ageism. He shouts at and insults Suze (' "You're a secretary in that place, you're not even a glamorous model. Why should he want *you*, of all people, as his front woman alibi?" ' [18]) and finally gives voice to his misogyny: ' "You're marrying for loot," I shouted out. "With the Spades you were just a strumpet, now you're going to be a whore!" ' (18). It would seem that the rhetoric about the jazz world, where all such hang-ups must be left at the door (61), is only rhetoric – at least in this case.

Dismayingly, the novel plays directly into the Teenager's very conventional sense of masculinity, femininity and narrative closure – though with an odd twist. Suze ignores the Teenager's outrage and goes through with the marriage to Henley only to discover that life as an older gay man's 'beard' is distinctly unglamorous and unsatisfying. Rather than being celebrated for her unconventionality in the ostensible spirit of wide-open sexual, racial and interpersonal vistas the Teenager seems so desperate to link up with the teenage ethos, Suze is punished for her independence. In a scene that is almost directly out of a fairy tale, Suze is virtually imprisoned in a house in the country until the Teenager rescues her. He declares his undying passion, avows that he is waiting for her 'this evening, tomorrow, and every day until the day' he dies (158) and then runs off to finish saving his father, who has collapsed with – wait for it! – a *heart condition* while on a father–son bonding day-jaunt up the river. The dots scarcely need connecting from here on out, as the Teenager and Suze reconnect in the midst of the riots engulfing their neighbourhood, reconcile, make love (at last!) and engage to wed as the Teenager rushes out the door to try to see his dad before he finally passes away (196). All seems set for the pair: Suze must finalize her divorce from Henley, but that formality aside, they are committed and determined to live happily ever after as a married couple.

But here comes the twist, or rather, the twists. Even though he has both won the girl and consummated their relationship physically, he continues to insist upon physical and psychological domination. First, he cannot consider his victory complete until he displaces Henley: He 'grab[s] her hand and pull[s] off Henley's Bond street ring' then throws it out the window, followed up by a jaunty cry of ' "No reward for the finder" ' (196). What he perceives to be a romantic gesture is in fact rather violent, and a sign of more to come. He declares that he's ' "cutting out of Napoli" ' and that she is coming with him (196). When she demurs (' "I'm not leaving here," she said, with her pig-headed look returning, "until it's over" ' [196]), he physically intimidates her and infantilizes her in a single gesture: 'I grabbed her hair and wiggled her head about. "We'll talk about that," I told her, "a bit later" ' (197). Finally, as though to consolidate his newfound status as the alpha male, the Teenager rushes back one last time before he goes to attend his "dying father; he runs 'back and kisse[s] her till she struggle[d]' (197). The violence here is palpable, even if it does still wear the soothing disguise of youthful passion.

Second, the Teenager apparently forgets all about Suze and the honeymoon they are supposed to be leaving for that same day. Having won Suze once and for all, had sex with her and engaged to marry her, leaving only to attend to his dying father, the Teenager doesn't come back. Instead, he heads straight for the Air Terminal to leave it all behind! 'My present feeling was I'd leave Dad's body to Ma, and Suze to get over loving Spades, and me, I was going away for a while, and perhaps not coming back' (200). Having met all the requirements to become a man, the Teenager suddenly balks. As Arthur Seaton learned, becoming a man inevitably means leaving youth behind; it means no longer being a teenager; it means, in short, a narrowed horizon of possibilities, a future that is suddenly foreclosed in key ways. It means leaving the Empyrean heights of pure potential for the determinate plots of a given life, rather than Life itself.

The terror of this development leads the Teenager to shift gears rather suddenly, transferring the pure potentiality of youth onto a hybrid of youth and blackness embodied by a planeload of new arrivals to the country. Knowing full well that these new arrivals have landed in a country riven by violence over their predecessors, the Teenager nonetheless identifies them with a wide-open futurity. He knows all too well that they, like Mr. Cool before them, will be absorbed into the race politics of the country but desperately insists on identifying their exoticism with youth itself in the midst of a purifying rainstorm that will no doubt keep the rioters indoors and leave a cleansed metropolis for the utopian future in which MacInnes is so clearly invested:

> Out [from the plane] came a score or so of Spades from Africa, holding hand luggage over their heads against the rain. Some had on robes, and some had on tropical suits, and most of them were young like me, maybe kiddos coming here to study, and they came down grinning and chattering, and they all looked so dam pleased to be in England, at the end of their long journey, that I was heartbroken at all the disappointments that were there in store for them. And I ran up to them through the water, and shouted out above the engines, 'Welcome to London! Greetings from England! Meet your first teenager!' (203)

It's a powerful final moment of disavowal, not only of the violence that has just taken up the last third of the novel, but of the Teenager's own implication in the value systems and histories that led to it. It equates the novelty of new immigrants with the potentiality of youth and prompts us at last to turn our attention to the most striking difference between *Absolute Beginners* and *Saturday Night and Sunday Morning* – its handling of race and its willingness to engage with the violent political realities of it in the late 1950s.

First, the good news: Contra *Saturday Night and Sunday Morning*'s egregious erasure of virtually all people of colour, *Absolute Beginners* has plenty. It captures far more accurately than its overpraised counterpart both the sheer demographic pressure of immigration to England in the post-war years and the tensions – and ultimately violence – that came with that pressure. Where *Saturday Night and Sunday Morning* ignores the historical reality in favour of a sanitized vision of a still-white England, a fantasy of pre-war homogeneity leavened with post-war prosperity, *Absolute Beginners* virtually transcribes newspaper accounts of violent episodes that took place in the London streets in late August and early September 1958. It gives the race riots of that year their due and does not shie away from depicting their instigators as vicious racists. Its morality on the point seems clear, as the racists – the Wiz, Ed the Ted, Flikker – are clearly despicable, while those who admire the 'Spades' stand tall in opposition to the violence.

Naturally, however, there is also much more going on. The novel's depiction of the riots serves a less clear-cut narrative purpose, one that ultimately troubles any understanding of them as simply admirable. The novel works hard to equate generational tension with racial tension, and thus teenagerdom with blackness, all under the sign of *cool*. This equation is not without its problems, though, and while it is indeed both sincere and accurate (as Hebdige has shown, white British youth cultures were in fact almost uniformly shaped by black immigrant styles – of music, clothing, movement, drugs and so on), it is also shadowed by a residually imperialist mindset. This mindset identifies *cool* as part of black cultures precisely by exoticizing them and instrumentalizing them as a means to achieve teenage authenticity rather than as ends in themselves. As Bentley puts it, *Absolute Beginners* 'engages in a discourse of "reorientalizing" black identity through the process of exoticizing black individuals, revealing an ambivalent attitude to constructions of a black "other". In this sense, the text reinforces rather than challenges the Euro-centric cultural practice of projecting white exotic and erotic desire onto the imagined bodies of oriental and black individuals' (Bentley 2003/2004, 165). The Teenager himself, in his naive commitment to racial diversity, is the most overt agent of this problematic, as we will see.

The equation of the teenage vibe with black coolness appears most obviously in the parallels between the Teenager and Mr. Cool. In all key respects, Mr. Cool exemplifies the Teenager's self-conception and self-presentation, producing a chiasmus of sorts wherein the Teenager's approval gives Mr. Cool teenage cachet, and Mr. Cool gives the Teenager authentic black jazz cachet. The effect is something like a binary star system, in which two bodies revolve around each other, producing a greater effect than either could achieve on its own. The problem is that this reciprocity only works for the Teenager. Though Mr. Cool appears sympathetic to the Teenager, he is also aware of the greater seriousness of being a black man in England in the 1950s and, perhaps, recognizes as well that the Teenager's celebration of him is at least partly fuelled by racist exoticization.

The narrative, particularly as it is focalized through the Teenager's consciousness, works hard to establish a mutually affirming affinity between Mr. Cool and the Teenager. Mr. Cool is one of only three other tenants in his building that the Teenager deigns to sketch for us (the others being the Fabulous Hoplite and Big Jill) and he is drawn in terms of the Teenager's preferred set of characteristics: musical preferences, age, clothing style and non-conformist lifestyle. He 'listens to the MJQ' (i.e. the Modern Jazz Quartet), and thus belongs to the emerging mod scene (50). The Teenager tells us also that 'he's certainly younger than I am, but he makes me feel about nine or so he's do very poised and paternal', at once identifying him as a 'kiddo' and allowing the racist stereotype of the wise negro to seep into his admiration (50). Mr. Cool's clothing is identified as both elegant and yet limited by his relative poverty: 'the kid is always so skint, he's only one suit (a striped Italian black)' (50). Clothing-wise, he is up to date, and yet not so moneyed as to raise suspicion that he is inauthentic. In fact, the very mystery surrounding how he makes his money is part of what marks him out as cool: 'what the hell he does to keep himself in MJQ LPS I haven't an idea – I really haven't. I don't think it's anything illegal, which is what you might expect [...] either business, whatever it may be, is bad, or else, for reasons best known, he's covering up' (50). In all these respects, Mr. Cool reflects the Teenager's most dearly held ideas about himself: He belongs to the most cutting-edge age-group around, he is hip to the latest jazz scene, he dresses sharply though not extravagantly and his line of work is secretive, perhaps semi-legal.

The parallel is extended through a situational homology in Mr. Cool's and the Teenager's family status: They both have half-brothers with whom they have troubled relationships, and yet whose loyalty ultimately shines through. Both have mothers who have had children by two different men, though Mr. Cool's situation is further complicated by the fact that one of his parents is white while the other is black. We have already met the Teenager's half-brother Vernon. Mr. Cool's half-brother is Wilf. Though both he and Wilf are mixed-race, Mr. Cool is marked as black while Wilf can pass as white. He is a fascinating character, evidently struggling with his own racial identity. On the one hand, as Mr. Cool tells us, '"He doesn't like me much, and my friends he likes even less, specially my white ones"' (55). On the other hand, Wilf has come down to Napoli to warn Mr. Cool that '"there's trouble coming for the coloureds,"' a warning Mr. Cool takes seriously precisely because Wilf '"likes coming here so little it must be *something* that makes him feel he ought to"' (55). Nonetheless, Mr. Cool doubts Wilf's loyalty should the situation devolve into violence. When the Teenager asks him, '"And if anything should happen [...] whose side would your brother himself be on?"' Mr. Cool replies with a curt '"Not mine"' (55). The disjunction between Mr. Cool and Wilf mirrors the state of open hostility between Vernon and the Teenager, though it will also turn out to be just as shallow: Just as Vernon arrives in the midst of the riots to drag the Teenager back to his dying father, so Wilf makes a timely appearance during the riots to help defend his half-brother (185). Both teenage and black cool thus secure the status of a sort of loyal opposition to mainstream culture, fighting for difference from it, but ultimately protected by it at the same time. Of course, the stakes are drastically different in each case: The possibility of disinheritance for the Teenager, beating and even death for Mr. Cool.

The narrative engages with this disparity directly in its approach to the common fight against white racist Britons. For the Teenager, this fight manifests most immediately in the figure of Ed the Ted. Shortly before the riots erupt, Ed visits the Teenager, ostensibly to sell him some stolen LPs (including, ironically, the MJQ's recording of *Concorde* [133]) but really to deliver the message that '"Flikker wants Cool aht ov ear"' (132). The Teenager refuses to be intimidated, first rejecting Flikker's summons and then telling Ed to '"go and piss up [his] leg"' (132), apparently seizing control over the situation. The Teenager's victory here is quickly threatened, though, as Ed lets the insult go in his determination to rob the Teenager. The Teenager, who, like Arthur Seaton, 'hates fighting', not out of fear of injury so much as out of a distaste for the 'silly mess' it brings about if someone gets seriously hurt (132-133), handily disposes of Ed. He knocks him out and castigates him as he lies on the floor, '"You wasted mess of a treacherous bastard!"' (133). The line fuses the treachery of trying to rob someone you've known for years with the Teenager's pent-up rage over Ed's delivery of Flikker's message. As a young person, Ed ought, by the Teenager's logic, to be cool. He ought to see and respect the authentic value of modern jazz and its adherents like Mr. Cool. As a member of a violent racist gang of Teds who tries to rob his old acquaintance, Ed betrays both their personal and their generational relationships.

The Teenager's fervour seems to find ratification in Mr. Cool's arrival on the scene, and in the apparent meeting of minds it triggers. Having heard the '"turmoil"' in the Teenager's room, Mr. Cool has come to help. He takes in the situation at a glance and then offers to get rid of the unconscious Ed while the Teenager cleans himself up. When he returns, the Teenager appears to have earned his bona fides with Mr. Cool – the relationship appears to be approaching equal footing. When Mr. Cool returns from dropping Ed outside, he finds that the Teenager has put on the MJQ's recording of *Concorde*. He 'nodded at the music, said, "Nice," and asked if he could wash' (133–134). We appear to be on the cusp of the completed chiasmus, where the Teenager's cool will receive the benediction of black recognition, and Mr. Cool will align his racial authenticity with the Teenager's demonstrated commitment to equality. Mr. Cool, however, quickly puts that completion on hold.

The goodwill that had just manifest in their shared victory over Ed quickly disappears as the two share information: The Teenager tells Mr. Cool about

Flikker's message and Mr. Cool confirms that he's heard the same from Wilf, before recounting several episodes of violence he has already seen. The Teenager's self-delusion about the identification between himself and Mr. Cool echoes throughout: 'I didn't want to believe this whole thing at all' (134). Each time Mr. Cool relates an event, the Teenager questions it, until Mr. Cool finally glares at him and states plainly his sense of the unbridgeable gulf between them:

> A look had come into Cool's eyes, as he stared at me, just like the look he must have given those Teds. 'Don't glare at me like that man', I cried. 'I'm on your side.'
> 'You are?'
> 'Yes.'
> 'That's nice of you', said Cool, but I saw he didn't mean it, or believe me. (135)

The Teenager persists in refusing to believe that any violence will erupt, defending his sense of London, of England, of the British themselves as too decent, too cosmopolitan, even too lazy to undertake serious civil unrest. He peaks in a moment of incoherence that cuts against Mr. Cool in at least two directions: '"And Cool," I said. "You – you're one of us. You're not a Spade, exactly"' (136). A number of possible readings present themselves here. On the one hand, the Teenager may be trying to exempt Mr. Cool from the racial tension that is so demonstrably mounting: Mr. Cool is not really a black man because he is so much a member of the emerging mod youth culture. Or maybe he means that Mr. Cool is not really a black man because he was born and bred in England. On the other hand, the comment is chilling: Mr. Cool is not actually cool, not actually a representative member of the source culture for the white mod group to which the Teenager belongs. Or, again, perhaps his status as a member of that youth culture overrides his and his family's history, being erased by its absorption into the all-encompassing universalized white youth-cultural identity.

In any of these cases, the Teenager has just drastically withdrawn the very key characteristic with which Mr. Cool is identified: his authenticity. It's a Munchausen moment: The Teenager's white youth-cultural identification draws upon black style to consolidate its claims to cool, but in a moment of crisis the very authenticity of that style is disavowed, seemingly robbing the white youth culture of its very ground. It openly embraces Mr. Cool's white self while disavowing his black identity just as Mr. Cool expects will happen when the violence comes: '"If it comes to any trouble," he said, "I am [a Spade]. And the reason I am is that they've never questioned me, never refused me, always accepted me – you understand? Even though I am part white? But *your* people … No. The part of me that belongs to you, belongs to them"' (136). On that note, Mr. Cool leaves, not to reappear until the riots are well underway. Even then, though the Teenager and Mr. Cool seem to arrive at a new understanding based on their common enemy, they cannot stand together, their difference having been accepted rather than overcome (194-195).

Reasserting the importance of the 'teenage epic' over the problem of race, the narrative pivots away from Mr. Cool's experience to focus on the Teenager's reunion with Suze, who is herself deeply implicated in the novel's racial politics. Mr. Cool and the Teenager part ways after stepping together over Ed the Ted's bleeding body and only moments before the Teenager spots Suze in the fray: 'soon I got scooped into the thing, and I heard a cry, "Nigger's whore!", and through arms and bodies I saw Suze, and they'd got hold her, some chicks as well as animals, and were rubbing dirt all over her face, and screaming if that's the colour she wanted to be, she'd got it' (195). Sex, desire, race and generational loyalty are all forced into the foreground here, as Suze's well-known preference for sex with black men becomes the pretext for her humiliating assault. Notably, with the help of a 'Hooray Henry' and the ex-Deb of last year, the Teenager extricates Suze from the mob and takes her directly to his apartment where he cleans her up and claims her for his very own.

This sudden shift in the narrative is densely packed with significance, inasmuch as Suze particularly – and sex more broadly – is racially overcoded in the novel. Suze is initially presented to us in terms of a sexily exotic ethnic mixing: 'Suze is a sharp gal, and no doubt this is because she's not only English, but part Gibraltarian, partly Scotch and partly Jewish' (17). Throw in her predilection for black sexual partners and her unorthodox approach to marriage, and Suze may well have become the narrative's ultimate sign of a utopian future of racial diversity under the English banner. She could, ideally, be a harbinger of a browned future that would provide the phenotypical correlate to the teenage utopia. The Teenager's introduction to the jazz scene by which he takes his bearings would seem to advocate for such an outcome. The jazz ethos, remember, doesn't care if you are 'boy, or girl, or bent, or versatile, or what you are'. Sexual openness is inter-implicated with coolness, overtly presented to us in the figures of the Fabulous Hoplite and Big Jill the les., the Teenager's observation that Mr. Cool has 'kissable lips' and his comfort with Mickey Pandoroso's ambiguous sexuality.

Crucially, though, the sexual variety named in the jazz ethos and exemplified in the figures of Hoplite and Jill does *not* include racial intermixing. The Teenager seems not to mind that Suze sleeps with black men for preference, but the larger narrative won't have it. Suze is the love interest of the protagonist, and the novel is delineated as belonging to the 'epic' genre from its opening line: There will be no tragic outcome, but an historical narrative that sees our hero progress through difficulty to triumph. That triumph necessarily includes the love interest. And, though Suze is ethnically intermixed, she is so only to a very limited extent. That limit is phenotypical: Suze presents as white, regardless of her genetic make-up. She is English, Scottish, Gibraltarian and Jewish. The first three are clearly elements of white British imperial genealogy, while the fourth finds its anchor in the dynastic logic of the Teenager's Jewish friends, Mannie, Miriam and little Saul Katz (80–88). The Katzes represent a familial strength anchored in ethnic belonging whose pull the Teenager finds irresistible. Its strength warps the narrative itself against its own overt grain, as Suze's potential for production of a truly new future – something genuinely in line with the futurity the Teenager and MacInnes both associate with the teenage revolution – is cut off at the knees by narrative necessity.

Suze can *either* be the Teenager's bona fide love interest *or* she can represent a break with history in the name of a bold new British future, but she cannot be both. In view of the Teenager's narcissism and self-delusion, along with the repeated subordination of racial politics to the teenage ethos, the outcome seems to have been determined from the outset. Despite paying lip service to a vision of the future that literally does not look like the past, the narrative logic dictates an outcome that guarantees a phenotypically homogenous next generation. Keep Britain white, indeed.

The inter-implication of blackness and the teenage ethos under the sign of cool allows us to read the riots themselves as having at least as much to do with generational tension as with racial conflict. For MacInnes and the Teenager both, the riots are not just, or even mostly, an assault on blacks, but rather an outburst of oldster resistance to the future – a future that is teenaged first and racial only secondarily. Though MacInnes's novel is laudable for facing England's growing racial tension head-on, as against Sillitoe's near-total erasure of race from *Saturday Night and Sunday Morning*, it is anything but a straightforward rendering of the historical moment.

The riots in *Absolute Beginners* correspond directly to the race riots that plagued London in the late summer of 1958, but as with all representations of historical events, their specific articulation in the novel carries a powerful ideological undertow. MacInnes borrows from newspaper reports of events that took place during the riots for the action of his novel. Much of what the Teenager witnesses or hears about from other characters was reported in the daily papers at the time. In a sense, though, this does not really matter. Though the account thus gains an aura of authenticity, particularly for those who lived through the moment, that authenticity is not put in service of exposing Britain's racism or the political risks of unrestricted immigration. Instead, it is displaced onto the Teenager and his monomaniacal commitment to the teenage revolution. MacInnes does not repeat the news media's reporting to give longer life to the actual events, or to emphasize the human cost of the riots, but to reaffirm the authenticity of the Teenager's experience – and thus of his dedication to a permanent youth revolution as the answer. What's at stake for the Teenager is not so much racial tolerance or belonging, but an historical break – the advent of the 'teenage epic'. A hallmark of that break is indeed accommodation of immigrants and their cultures, not least because they furnish the requisite element of 'cool' that keeps the teenagers ahead of the parental curve. This reading is perhaps unnecessarily cynical, but it seems borne out by the Teenager's own callous instrumentalization of the riots. Racial emancipation and equality are harnessed to generational concerns – respect for immigrants is essential to the Teenager's ongoing status as cool and to sustaining his self-conception as cool.

The Teenager verges on a moment of awakening when he abandons his camera – symbolically opting for real experience rather than mediated images – but that quickly lapses in a riotous conclusion that sees all the key white characters, and the one black character with a name, safe and sound even as the riots continue to rage. The violence seems to happen *around* the white characters rather than *to* them. Even when Suze has mud smeared on her, the account minimizes what must have been a terrifying moment, and no one who matters in the narrative is ever seriously in danger, even when a fire-bomb is lobbed into a crowded basement club. The Teenager simply climbs out a window and makes good his escape; there is no panic or death. The Teenager flies through it all in a series of fortuitous rescues, near-misses, comical assaults and spirited fun. In other words, it's a romp rather than a riot, in which racial violence is reduced to a backdrop for the triumph of the teenage ethos over a regressive allegiance to the past that is most clearly anchored in the Teds. As one newspaper editorial in the novel puts it, 'it was only a minority – chiefly persons known by the name of "Teddy boys" – who had actually been guilty of a physical breach of the Queen's peace, and these youths should undoubtedly be restrained' (171). As we've seen, the Teddy boys are, for MacInnes and his Teenager, representative of precisely the backward, loutish, moronic little Englandism that teenage cool, abetted by immigrant style, wishes most fervently to break with in the name of a utopian future of perpetual youth and potential. The newspaper editorial wants to have its cake and eat it, too, undermining the teenage revolution by pitting one youth-cultural group against the rest and suggesting in the process that, deplorable though their actions are, the Teds are in fact on the right side of history and evolution in their defence of British civilization.

The editors need not have bothered, though.

The novel concludes by openly aligning the Teenager with British imperialism, suppressing race in favour of youth as the universalizing category – and thus emptying the riots that have dominated the last third of the novel of their true political significance. In its final moments, *Absolute Beginners* reasserts the universality of white youth culture by erasing the specificity of race and racialized experience under empire. Having missed the flight to Rio, and passing up the chance to board the plane to Oslo, the Teenager instead waits on the tarmac for a planeload of new arrivals, 'Spades from Africa' (203):

> Some had on robes, and some had on tropical suits, and most of them were young like me, maybe kiddos coming here to study, and they came down grinning and chattering, and they all looked so dam pleased to be

in England at the end of their long journey, that I was heartbroken at all the disappointments that were there in store for them. (203)

For Bentley, this ending 'anticipates later discourses of a "Cool Britannia" that appropriates youth and black subcultures in a vibrant and forward-looking construction of the nation' (2003/4, 160). He reads the new arrivals as 'full of hope and a reliance on the very English myths that the teenager has reproduced' (160). He may be right. But the Teenager's casual racism and instantaneous disregard for the realities these racialized newcomers are about to meet head-on provide a powerful counter to the optimism implicit in Bentley's reading.

The Teenager's reference to the newcomers as 'grinning and chattering' likens them to monkeys in time-honoured terms of racist denigration. His assertion of youth as the supreme identity category sidelines both race and the nation as equal, let alone overarching, constructions. As has been done throughout the novel, the category of youth overrides all other identities in a universalizing move that once again asserts the superiority of the white youth culture. The new arrivals' clothing, language and cultures are swept aside by the Teenager's certainty that 'most of them were young' and therefore 'like me.' As the epitome of youth, the Teenager becomes the standard by which all others are measured, and if these new arrivals are to be cool, they must necessarily embrace teenagedom – never mind the fact that if they have come to study they are likely carrying the hopes and investments of extended families, if not even larger social groupings.

As the rain pours down – a benediction, a baptism and a natural damper to the violence in the streets – the Teenager rushes the new arrivals: 'And I ran up to them through the water, and shouted out above the engines, "Welcome to London! Greetings from England! Meet your first teenager! We're all going up to Napoli to have a ball!"' (203). Arrogating to himself the role of civic and national representative, the Teenager simultaneously assumes that the new arrivals will never have met a teenager before and that it is an honour for them to do so now. Issuing an order, as he did earlier in his bullying of Suze, the Teenager informs the new arrivals of where they are going and drafts them into support of his project. His total failure to recognize that these new arrivals are not by any means the same as Mr. Cool or indeed as the West Indian immigrants who were by far the majority of black people in London at the time only highlights his blithe ignorance of race as a complex social reality. Apparently believing that all black people are the same – that is, cool – he whites out their difference from other black people and from himself with the sweeping generalization of youth.

The novel's last line ratifies this enormous arrogance with a trans-generational blessing: 'And I flung my arms round the first of them, who was a stout old number with a beard and a brief-case and a little bonnet, and they all paused and stared at me in amazement, until the old boy looked me in the face and said to me, "Greetings!" and he took me by the shoulder, and suddenly they all burst out laughing in the storm' (203). This reaction irrefutably links blackness and coolness: It can even overcome generational distance! This connection is then cancelled and preserved under the sign of the Teenager, who bleaches out the dimension of race by bringing everyone together under the big tent of white youth subculture. If they really do all head off up to Napoli, it will be to confirm publicly the Teenager's own self-conception, and thus the true power of the teenage revolution, rather than to reinforce the black population in its fight against racist violence.

Between them, *Saturday Night and Sunday Morning* and *Absolute Beginners* present divergent views of the first bona fide post-war British youth culture, the Teddy boys, and chart the advent of a new understanding of history. *Saturday Night and Sunday Morning* is hampered in its engagement with the emergence of youth culture as a potent force by its backwards-looking temporality. Though it is set in the mid- to late 1950s, Sillitoe's novel retains a pre-war sensibility that shines through most obviously in its ignorance of the mass immigration that had utterly transformed the urban landscape of Nottingham by 1958. *Absolute Beginners*, by contrast, is determinedly oriented towards the future, feeding all manner of social tension into the meat grinder of generational division so that the teenage revolution emerges as the master signifier of post-war potentiality. Even though it prominently displays the very racialized violence that *Saturday Night and Sunday Morning* so casually ignores, *Absolute Beginners* still perpetuates a fundamentally racist view of history in its appropriation of black culture – however it presents itself – into the project of specific white youth cultures. Were Arthur Seaton to wander into Napoli, he would no doubt be shocked at what he saw on all fronts, sneering at the Teenager even as he gawped at the masses of immigrants around him and – quite likely – clenched his fists at the insipid mass politics of Flikker and the Wiz. What emerges from these two very different visions of 1950s youth cultures in Britain is a powerful sense that youth is indeed a force to be reckoned with even when it does not know precisely what it wants and even if its urge to break decisively with the parent generation – or simply History – lapses into its reproduction as often as not. The mods and rockers who first appear in *Absolute Beginners* will soon enough throw mainstream British culture into its second youth-driven moral panic of the post-war years with their casual violence in the streets of London and, more famously still, on the beaches of Brighton. As we turn our attention to *A Clockwork Orange*, though, we encounter less a direct representation of those groups and their conflicts than a shockingly prescient vision of the Next Big Thing in violent youth culture: skinheads.

2

How Did Burgess Invent the Skinhead? *A Clockwork Orange*

At first glance, *A Clockwork Orange* appears to be a very different book from *Saturday Night and Sunday Morning* and *Absolute Beginners*. It is set in a dystopian near-future rather than contemporary England. Its young people are Nadsats and droogs rather than Teds and mods. It is permeated by a slang lexicon that corresponds to no historically existent youth patois. And its main character, Alex's, speech follows pseudo-Elizabethan rhythms and word orders. Burgess claimed that these were all strategies to provide an aesthetic shield against the pornographic violence depicted in the book. And there's plenty of that. *A Clockwork Orange* goes well beyond the fisticuffs of even the most heated riot scenes in *Absolute Beginners* to rape, savage beatings and even murder (twice). The vision of youth culture it presents is edgier, darker and more alienating than anything we've seen so far. In fact, it was edgier, darker and more alienating even than anything *anyone* had seen in post-war youth culture to that point. This novel doesn't reflect or even simply rework its cultural moment; instead, it senses certain undercurrents and fleshes them out into a vision of youth culture's next stage. I'm going to take a risk here and make a pretty bold claim on behalf of the novel: In it, Burgess actually invents the skinhead, a solid *five years before* the first skinheads appeared in the streets of London.

On the face of it, this might appear to be simple anachronism, but bear with me: Burgess purposely created a futuristic vision of British society, one in which the contemporary realities would have developed or atrophied to varying degrees. My reading takes that predictive impulse seriously and tests the speculative against actual historical development – with, I hope, some surprising results. The novel's strange predictive power presents a new twist on my overarching claim that writers such as Burgess think *with* and *about* youth cultures. In this case, to think *about* the youth culture is to invent a variation on preceding youth cultures that is equal parts accurate prediction and creation of a tool for thinking *with*. In *A Clockwork Orange*,

Burgess thinks about youth culture more broadly by identifying emergent strands of its current reality – that is, the reality in 1960–1962 of mods and rockers – and uses this invented youth culture to *think with*. Because of these complications, our approach here must be somewhat different from that in other chapters. Where I try to make the case that the other books I discuss think *about* youth cultures at the same time as they think *with* them, the case for *A Clockwork Orange* must be rather that it thinks *about* youth culture more generally and uses that generality to think through the post-war situation. In this vein, we will consider how the novel's prediction of skinhead culture is less about the specifics of that culture than a means of working through various problems – of masculinity, collapsing faith in public institutions, tradition, increasing violence and a creeping nihilism.

Burgess tried to give his narrative a grand theological–philosophical import by claiming that it was a meditation on the tensions between freewill and determination in which the very nature of humanity itself was up for debate. Far too many critics have fallen for this line, or else tried to anchor it in a critique of behaviourist psychology. The truth is that the novel is at best scarcely sophisticated enough to bear such weighty readings. Its rather pat and deflating ending makes these readings exercises in wilful ignorance. As I'll try to show, the novel is, instead, very much anchored in its contemporary moment. Virtually no one has yet read it this way, and certainly no one has yet read the novel as pertaining to skinheads (the movie is another thing altogether, as we'll see).[1] Allow me, then, to welcome you to a new reading, one which simply attends closely to the words on the page and aligns them with the cultural realities being forged in the streets of England's cities as the 1950s gave way to the decade of 'Swinging London'.

My reading involves two key claims. First, we'll see how strikingly Burgess predicts the advent of skinheads in terms of both style and ethos. He describes his droogs in terms that will find real-life expression only a few years after the book is published. He also anchors that emergent style in an ethos of regressive nihilism/anarchism based upon a fantasy of traditional masculinity (tough, violent, self-sufficient, loyal to pack/group). Burgess works mightily to think about this emergent youth-cultural reality in terms of authenticity, freedom and human essence – that is, to think about it in terms of utopian potentials. In the end, I think, he fails, which is where my second key claim comes in: The novel ultimately expresses a profoundly conservative – maybe even nihilistic – view. The revolutionary energy of youth – and the anarchic individualism with which Burgess associates it – is, by the novel's end, diffused and scattered, overcome simply by the passage of time. The famous (notorious?) twenty-first chapter sucks the oxygen right out of the youth-cultural optimism Burgess apparently wants to uphold. We'll explore these claims by simply turning our attention to the specifics of the novel's representations and resituating them in their cultural moment.

Burgess's prediction of skinheads involves another case of overlapping temporalities like that we saw in *Saturday Night and Sunday Morning*, though this time in a slightly different vein. In this case, the novel is not anchored in nostalgia for a fantasy past, but in a perverse utopianism. The cultural reality in England at the time was that of the moral panic over mods and rockers. But Burgess doesn't go there. Instead, he taps into the emergent elements of those youth cultures – and especially their violent crisis of masculinity – to prevision a new possibility. No one at the time could have recognized the novel as being about skinheads since there were no skinheads yet. When they did appear, in roughly 1967 or 1968, the novel had receded from view enough that the parallels were not immediately clear. Another move in this temporal game of Twister™ occurs with the release of Stanley Kubrick's film adaptation in 1971. At that point, the skinheads by now inescapably present in the streets recognized the film as being in some sense about them. So, a novel published in 1962 predicts the advent of a youth-cultural group in 1968, who then recognize themselves in an adaptation of the novel in 1971. Actual skinheads are bookended by fictional representations, one of which invents their style and ethos, the other of which arguably glamorizes them. We are in the presence of a complex cycle of invention, (mis-)recognition and retroactive ratification that will take some untangling. If we were to try to draw it, the result might look something like this:

ACO 1962   Skinheads 1968   ACO movie 1971   Skinheads

The copycat crimes that occurred in the wake of the film's release complicate things further still. As Peter Jachimiak puts it:

> The early 1970s saw skinheads transform into several mutant varieties – bootboy, smoothie, suedehead – all drawing, stylistically, from the recently released cinematic adaptation of Burgess's novel. [...] In particular, suedeheads went as far as wearing bowler hats and accessorising themselves with umbrellas that included 'sharpened metal points to aid and abet a few rounds of fisticuffs'. (156)

Post-film release skinheads, having (mis-)recognized themselves in the movie, remade themselves to conform with it and then adopted its particular brand of violence as a key element of style. Making things yet more interesting, there is the fact that the violent attack at HOME in the novel was based upon a 1944 attack on Burgess's first wife. While Burgess was away with the army, four deserters broke into his home and assaulted his pregnant wife, causing her to miscarry. Of course, the deserters, being army men, sported close-cropped haircuts – cuts which were even in the 1940s leading to soldiers being called 'skinheads' (OED). They were skinheads before there were skinheads, whose actions informed Burgess's invention of the skinhead as a youth culture, which then appeared on the streets only to be re-fictionalized in the film version of the novel, which in turn drove imitation in the streets – a form of imitation that begins to look an awful lot like traumatic repetition.

Attack 1944   ACO 1962   Skinheads 1968   ACO movie 1971   Skinheads   Copycats

The aesthetic ensemble that includes everything from the original attack in 1944 through the copycat crimes in the early 1970s that provoked Kubrick to withdraw the film from circulation in England presents as a multiphase cycle of violence, representation and (mis-)recognition. It's going to take us some work to sift through all this, and what it means for how we understand Burgess to be thinking *about* and *with* youth culture. Buckle up!

But before we get down to the specifics of Burgess's precognition of skinhead culture, some context is important. *A Clockwork Orange* was published in 1962, a year that is also significant for the trial and execution of Adolf Eichmann and for the first legislative efforts to walk back the British Nationality Act (BNA) of 1948. The Eichmann trial is important for this novel because it provides a way of thinking through the novel's complex morality. The Eichmann trial brought the monstrosity of the Holocaust back to earth – and therein lay its scandal. As Hannah Arendt so brilliantly recounted in *Eichmann in Jerusalem*, the scandal of the Eichmann trial was the banality of what it revealed: Eichmann was no monster, but just another schlub of the sort you see in the pub every day. If he could do what he was accused of having done, then how could we know who was and was not capable of such radical evil? Are we all? Is the power of authority such that any of us is potentially an Eichmann, as the infamous Stanford Prison Experiment – conducted in the same year as Kubrick's film was released – would eventually suggest? In terms of *A Clockwork Orange*, is the only difference between Alex and the average law-abiding citizen that Alex undertakes his violence himself, while others allocate the task to police, doctors, psychologists, guards and wardens? The effort to curtail the BNA is important because it marks the beginning of a legislative backlash against the flood of immigration that was rapidly reconfiguring how England looked, smelled, talked and thought. Though it would still be a long time before curry became the country's national dish,[2] it was already clear that things would never again be as they had been before the war, and the highly visible immigrant population became an easy target for frustrations over declining prestige on the world stage, a sluggish economy and decolonization abroad. As the decade played out, men like Enoch Powell traded on this set of allegiances and emotions to awaken many a Briton's inner fascist, scarcely twenty years after Hitler's defeat.

These crises of self-conception mirrored domestic changes and scandals that further eroded public confidence in traditional cultural institutions. The Profumo Affair of 1961, a political sex scandal with implications for national security, culminated in suicide, resignation, disgrace and a devastating blow to public confidence in government. Church attendance continued to decline, especially among the young, as television, rock 'n' roll music, films and youth clubs provided more than enough competition for young people's attention. And though national pride was somewhat restored with England's win in the 1966 World Cup, that rebound was undercut within a year by a 14% devaluation of the Pound Sterling. The abolition of capital punishment in 1965 and the legalization of abortion in 1967 likewise challenged long-standing cultural norms and cast doubt in some quarters upon the suitability of those in charge to sustain all that had not so long ago underwritten Britain's 'finest hour'. There is no better sign of this generally growing suspicion towards these traditional cultural institutions than the massively popular television show, *That Was the Week that Was*. Hosted by David Frost, the show featured a team of 'young Turks [...] [who] tore into the government and society with unbridled relish' (Pop Culture Correspondent n.p.). At a minimum, it is safe to say that the major cultural institutions of Church, government, school, police and prison were under suspicion if not in outright states of crisis – at least as far as the under-25 set were concerned.

Perhaps the most crucial of the cultural currents *A Clockwork Orange* tuned into was the ongoing crisis of masculinity that itself proved *the* driving factor behind the emergence of skinhead culture. We have already seen how this crisis was playing out in the 1950s in the work of Sillitoe and MacInnes. As it picked up steam in the 1960s, it found itself with even more to contend with. The year 1967 saw the legalization of abortion, giving women much greater control over their own reproductive health, an advance which positively paled in comparison with the introduction of the birth control pill in 1961 (for married women, extended to all in 1967). Also in 1967, the Sexual Offenses Act decriminalized homosexuality, presenting yet another clear and present threat to traditional hetero-normative masculinity. Exacerbating the problem still more was the increasing impetus to establish equal pay and working conditions for women – whose presence in factories itself was a not-always-welcome holdover from the war years. The Equal Pay Act of 1970 seemed to some young men in particular a perverse addendum to the introduction of the mini-skirt in the mid-1960s, at once a nod to women's increasing sexual freedom and a design intended to make it easier for them to 'run and jump' (Quant, qtd. in Watson n.p.). For some young men, who perhaps saw rights and freedoms as a zero-sum game in which gains for one group meant losses for another, such rapid advances for women translated directly into greater constraint upon men's rights (sadly, this view persists even today in so-called men's rights movements). More profoundly, if we understand masculinity as largely defined by its relationship to femininity, then we can understand (without necessarily condoning) how such sweeping changes in women's self-conception and expression presented as a direct threat to how men understood themselves. Put bluntly, women's gains intensified the perceived stakes of marking out a hard-core (of) masculinity. If the mods and rockers were still on deck, battling it out on the beaches and streets as Burgess penned *A Clockwork Orange*, the skinheads were already warming up in the on-deck circle.

Burgess presents youth culture as the flashpoint at which the key cultural institutions of Western civilization burst into flames. Responding to the notion that the youth of the day were '"barbarians in wonderland"' (Hoggart qtd. in Bentley 2010, 21), Burgess struggles to articulate a vision of youth culture as the true locus of anarchic utopianism. For Burgess, the droogs stand tall against all forms of (implicitly communist) collectivity except those that are necessary to defend the right to self-determination. Even the gangs with which Alex runs in the novel are temporary blocs, contingent configurations of free agents who are always bridling against any authority and seeking to assert themselves against the group. Alex's biggest mistake is to insist upon his leadership of his first gang: '"There has to be a leader. Discipline there has to be. Right?" None of them skazatted a word or nodded even. I got more razdraz inside, calmer out. "I", I said, "have been in charge long now. We are all droogs, but somebody has to be in charge. Right? Right?"' (30). His droogs' acquiescence leaves a great deal to be desired in terms of its enthusiasm, and Alex shortly discovers that discipline cuts more than one way. Burgess aligns the anarchic energy of youth with Western civilization itself. He sees youth culture's state of permanent revolution and instability as the epitome rather than the failure of the Enlightenment ethos. He aligns that anarchistic view with the Western canon of high art; to lose one's will is simultaneously to lose the capacity to enjoy Beethoven. What makes Western art great is precisely its individual nature, its origin in genius and its commitment to overturning conventions, be they social or aesthetic. Putting it in service of collective suppression of individual will and expression, as Dr. Branom does in the novel, is second only to threatening individuality itself. Discipline there must be, indeed, but the freedom to choose punishment over good behaviour must never be withdrawn.

Individual expression in *A Clockwork Orange* is defined primarily in terms of style, and especially of clothing style. Almost the first thing we learn about Alex and his droogs is what they are wearing. Insisting that they are dressed in 'the heighth of fashion', Alex details an outfit that is shockingly avant-garde for 1960:

> The four of us were dressed in the heighth of fashion, which in those days was a pair of black very tight tights with the old jelly mould, as we called it, fitting on the crutch underneath the tights, this being to protect and also a sort of a design you could viddy clear enough in a certain

light […] Then we wore waisty jackets without lapels but with these very big built-up shoulders ('pletchoes' we called them) which were a kind of mockery of having real shoulders like that. Then, my brothers, we had these off-white cravats which looked like whipped-up kartoffel or spud with a sort of a design made on it with a fork. We wore our hair not too long and we had flip horrorshow boots for kicking. (2)

The outfit is futuristic, as Burgess intended, but more importantly it is prescient. Picking up on elements of evolving mod style in the early 1960s, Burgess predicts here the emergence of both a hard mod style that will fuse a fashion-forward sensibility with readiness for violence with aspects of soft mod decadence such as cravats. More importantly still, Burgess envisions the fusion of hard mod style with elements of Jamaican-immigrant rude boy fashion to produce the skinhead aesthetic, years before it actually appears on London streets. The lapelless jackets with big shoulders anticipate the skinhead predilection for Harrington jackets, the tight pants (here actual tights, though) anticipate the skinhead demand for fitted but flexible dungarees or trousers, and of course the 'flip horrorshow boots' predict what is perhaps *the* key style element of skinhead fashion. As Richard Allen's prototypical skinhead put it nearly a decade later:

The boots were the most important item. Without his boots, he was part of the common-herd – like his dad, a working man devoid of identity. Joe was proud of *his* boots. Most of his mates wore new boots bought for a high price in a High Street shop. But not Joe's. His were genuine army-disposal boots; thick-soled, studded, heavy to wear and heavy to feel if slammed against a rib. (n.p.)

The boots are essential; they signify both working-class identity and para-military commitment.

And indeed, the boots persist against an otherwise wholesale shift in the clothing worn by Alex and his droogs by the novel's end:

We were dressed in the heighth of fashion, which in those days was these very wide trousers and a very loose black shiny leather like jerkin over an open-necked shirt with a like scarf tucked in. At this time too it was the heighth of fashion to use the old britva on the gulliver, so that most of the gulliver was like bald and there was hair only on the sides. But it was always the same on the old nogas – real horrorshow bolshy big boots for kicking litsos in. (Burgess 180–181)

The boots anchor this ensemble to the earlier one, bridging the two descriptions and fusing multiple elements of emerging skinhead style. This later description is perhaps even more striking than the first, in that it foresees the emergence of a particular hippie style of dress – the leather

FIGURE 2.1 *Hard Mod/Skinhead transition, UK, circa 1960s. (Photo by KEYSTONE-FRANCE/Gamma-Rapho via Getty Images.)*

jerkin over an open-necked shirt with the scarf tucked in – even as it goes beyond clothing to add one more aspect of skinhead style to the picture, in the shaved head. A 'britva' is a razor, and Alex and his droogs now style themselves by using it to shave all but a small bit of hair on the sides of their heads. Their ongoing commitment to 'real horrorshow bolshy big boots' completes the picture. Though they never combine the clothing style of the first description with the close-cropped hair style of the second to achieve a full-blown skinhead aesthetic, all the pieces are in place. Stylistically, they are prototypes of the skinhead who would shortly appear on the city streets.

Giving this stylistic evolution a potentially lethal edge, Burgess also predicts an amplification and expansion of violence among young male youth cultures. This amplification is part of the larger crisis of masculinity we have been tracing. Jachimiak notes that 'what youth culture understood as cool (their music, clothes, hairstyles, language, transport, etc.) was, by the late 1960s, undergoing a radical metamorphosis – as violence was, alarmingly, now being utilised as a measure of cool' (154). Jachimiak situates this evolution in the late 1960s, but as we will see, Burgess understands its inevitability much earlier. In their exploits in this line, Alex and his droogs outstrip even the violence of the Teds and the battles between the mods and rockers. This amplification takes shape in terms of both increased viciousness and the randomness of its targets.

First, the intensity of the droogs' violence surpasses that of the predecessor groups rather dramatically. Where the Teddy boys were vilified for a single murder in 1953, Alex alone commits two murders. There would be no skinhead murders until the second wave of skinhead culture flourished in England in the 1970s and into the 1980s, but the trend was already visible: Skinheads outwardly manifest a readiness to commit violence, and a steely commitment to see it through. The violence associated with skinhead culture in the 1960s upped the ante on youth-cultural menace even as the wider public grew somewhat inured to it, thanks in part to sensational newspaper reporting.

Second, Burgess's droogs focus their violent attention on random civilians, rather than engaging in pitched battles with other youth gangs, as the mods and rockers were doing even as he wrote the novel. Burgess seems to have seen beyond the limits of contemporary youth violence to its inevitable creep into the country's wider social life. In *A Clockwork Orange*, only one fight between youth gangs takes place, compared to multiple instances of theft, assault, rape and murder of members of the mainstream culture. For Burgess, the problem comes down to a fundamental boredom that drives the quest for ever more intense experiences. The repeated refrain, '"What's it going to be then, eh?"' signals a form of boredom in which each day threatens monotony, taken as a prompt to seek out new challenges. Alex sums up the deadly drift inherent in this slow boil when he says in disappointment, after one outing, '"But, myself, I couldn't help a bit of disappointment at things as they were those days. Nothing to fight against really. Everything as easy as kiss-my-sharries"' (Burgess 12). The life of privilege and ease for which the war generation had fought presents in this light as devoid of the challenges essential to establishing mature masculinity. It leaves young men in particular to their own devices as they seek to test themselves – and the only thing apparently hard enough to withstand such testing is society itself. The droogs are thrown back on their own devices, the law of the jungle, and an ersatz model of masculinity defined by violence and instinct in search of resistance against which to struggle – very much as the skinheads were in the late 1960s and into the early 1970s. In this development, Burgess appears to have foreseen not just the stylistic elements of skinhead self-presentation, but also the hardcore masculinity and fetishization of independence that undergird it.

We can now return to the complex temporalities by which Burgess's novel and skinhead culture are inter-implicated. It might be giving too much credit to the influence of this single novel on youth-cultural style to proclaim that Burgess's invention of skinhead style produced it on the streets, but the parallels are more than coincidental. Indeed, though there is no way to be sure that skinheads saw themselves in Alex before the release of the film in 1971, they most certainly did recognize themselves once the film came out:

> The skinheads' attraction to *A Clockwork Orange* was that, as well as paying homage to their aggressive style, it updated their look and provided it with some sort of futuristic whiteness, thus suggesting longevity for skin heads and associated violent masculinity. To skinheads, *A Clockwork Orange* promised both a pat on the back and recognition of their place in British subcultural history. Put more simply, by former skinhead Tony Parsons, '[s]omeone had been paying attention. And we were flattered beyond belief.' (Jachimiak 155–156)

Jachimiak's account of how skinheads received the film version of *A Clockwork Orange* introduces some trickiness with regard to the language of chronological ordering. When he writes that Kubrick's version of Alex and his droogs 'updated' the skinhead look in the film version of *A Clockwork Orange*, he introduces a larger problematic. As we saw earlier, Kubrick's version is itself an update on the prior stylings of the novel, in which skinhead style is invented in the first place. There are multiple overlapping temporalities in which the original is indiscernible. Burgess's novel may well have fed into the advent of skinheads, skinhead culture feeds into Kubrick's adaptation of Burgess's novel, and the skinheads recognize themselves in Kubrick's adaptation of Burgess's novel by way of skinhead culture. If you need to refer back to the graph earlier, please do. I'll wait. You back? OK. Making matters even more interesting is the likelihood that Burgess's own vision was influenced by the emerging elements of what would become skinhead culture, as they already appeared in the hard mod aesthetic of the early 1960s. The takeaway here is that the entire ensemble of prediction, influence and (mis-)recognition presents a compelling picture of how fiction and contemporary youth culture are related.

Perhaps more to the point, this tangle exposes the extent to which youth culture prefers ideology over sociology, accepting mystification over explanation and fetishization over ratiocination. The cycle of precognition, recognition and mis-recognition corresponds eerily to the logic of the dream. Often, in dreams, you transform from one thing into another only to find that you've been the new thing all along: 'So then suddenly I turned into a crocodile, but somehow I had been one all along, but nobody noticed, not even me.' Something similar is at work in the skinheads' self-mis-recognition in the film version of *A Clockwork Orange*. Having had their style of clothing, violence and behaviour predicted in the novel version of *A Clockwork Orange*, skinheads only discover after the film comes out that they are always already droogs. What's weird about this is that the clothing of the droogs in the movie bears little resemblance to actual skinhead style, apart from the boots. In the movie, the droogs wear all white, bowler hats and oversized jock-straps or codpieces. The film's style of violence apparently trumps such superficialities, though, and skinheads readily saw themselves in the celluloid psychopaths. This identification produces pleasure ('we were flattered beyond belief') and consolidates their sense that the onscreen droogs are versions of themselves, when the fact is that they are real-life versions of the novelistic droogs on whom their style is modelled in the first place. When they see themselves on-screen, they misrecognize the temporality at play, believing that the film comes after them, when in fact they come after the original upon which the film is based.

The novel stages precisely this cycle of mis-recognition, dream and reality in Alex's dream. After the first night's adventures, which conclude with Alex violently asserting his domination of the gang but foreshadowing his ouster as its leader, Alex dreams that Georgie is now in charge:

> In this sneety [dream] he'd got like very much older and very sharp and hard and was govoreeting about discipline and obedience and how all the malchicks under his control had to hump hard at it and throw up the old salute like being in the army, and there was me in line like the rest saying yes sir and no sir, and then I viddied clear that Georgie had these stars on his pletchoes and he was like a general. And then he brought in old Dim with a whip, and Dim was a lot more starry and grey and had a few zoobies missing as you could see when he let out a smeck, viddying me, and then my droog Georgie said, pointing like at me: 'That man has filth and cal all over his platties', and it was true. (36)

Dim pursues Alex in the dream while Alex tries to fend him off, until the ringing doorbell delivers Alex from his dream. Alex's dream is in one sense simple foreshadowing, predicting Georgie's actual attempt to take control of the gang later that same day. It also replays in reverse, as it were, the conflict of the previous night, where Alex tries to insist upon the necessity for discipline and leadership of the gang after striking Dim. Alex's awareness that he has overstepped and his bad conscience for having to appeal to precisely the sorts of authority he supposedly despises and kicks against – discipline, order – returns in the dream to punish him. So, the dream exposes how Alex's rebellion only re-inscribes military order, discipline and hierarchy as a reaction against their perceived absence. With 'nothing to fight against', the informal army of droogs turns inward and begins to tear itself apart in the name of precisely the same ideals it mocks in the parental generation. Georgie's identification as a general anchors this dream in the actual military, to which Alex directly compares his gang (15). It also predicts the ease with which the droogs will be absorbed into the government's disciplinary system (e.g. when Dim and Billyboy become police officers). This military bearing likewise calls to mind the skinhead tendency to close-cropped hair, an explicit rejection of the Teddy boys', mods and rockers' (not to mention the hippies') long hair – which was itself a rejection of the close-cropped style enforced by the army during the war years. Everything old is new again (again).

All this depends upon the manifest content of the dream, though, and ignores the key phrase: 'and it was true.' This phrase reactivates the dream logic, where Alex's clothes *becoming* filthy is simultaneous with the discovery that they *always have been* filthy. The dream encodes Alex's pre-existing investment in the logic of hierarchy and order. It indicates what I take to be perhaps the key element in the novel: The discovery that youthful anarchic energy has never been driven by individual will to self-determination, but is simply inherent to youth. The crucial element of Alex's dream is not that it reverses his role from leader to follower, or from punisher to punished. It's not even that he already abides by governmental logics long before he is sent to prison and subjected to the Ludovico technique. Instead, it's the indication that he has never had the free will he – and Burgess – supposes himself to have. Nor will he lose it, nor will he regain it, as I will demonstrate shortly. The consequence of this dream logic for understanding the dynamics of skinhead self-mis-recognition should be clear: That moment of identification in fact reveals that what passes for authenticity is without basis – its truth *is* betrayal.

As I've already hinted, masculinity is absolutely central to both Alex's and the skinheads' self-conceptions. Both depend upon a highly conventional understanding of masculinity in terms of strength, toughness, street smarts, sexual prowess, capacity for mind-altering substances (be they lager or milk laced with drugs) and of course the imminent threat of violence. As Beryl Schlossman has noted,

> Like the secret brotherhoods or societies of earlier centuries and the militaristic regimes of the modern period, this clockwork orange is a man's world, ruled by manipulative and unscrupulous men. With the exception of Alex's boo-hooey mother, a singer in a bar and a few victims, women exist on the fringes as objects of desire who are immediately available and quickly forgotten. (273)

Perhaps the most persistent reminder that we are in a book concerned with masculinity is the repeated refrain throughout: 'O my brothers.' The book is narrated by a man, and addressed in the language of fraternity only to other men.

The marginalization of women in the novel is a symptom of the epidemic tendency in post-war British novels of this sort to use youth culture as a means to think about masculinity. Thinking *with* his droogs, Burgess reinforces the popular conception that the violent youth-cultural groups in post-war Britain excluded young women. Of course, there were in fact skinhead girls just as there were Judies and female mods and rockers. But the ethos of the group seems to have been almost exclusively addressed to young men – its values are the most assertively masculine of any post-war youth culture, barring perhaps rude boys, from whose style and ethos the skinheads borrowed freely. As Alex makes unavoidably clear, this is a book that is first, last and always concerned with using youth culture to think about masculinity.

Crucially, this thinking is linked to a conception of traditional values that bypasses the cultural institutions that are supposed to sustain them. The skinheads and Alex both subscribe to a nostalgic ethos of traditional masculinity along the lines of the 'hard man', with a traditional, physically challenging presence anchored in a fantasy of manhood defined by hard work, self-sufficiency, group loyalty and independence. This fantasy gets around the existing cultural institutions such as school, church, government and so on by tapping into prior, less formalized, more potent and more affective sources. For the skinheads, it was the working man who stood for himself, his family and his clan independently of the bureaucratic weakness of modernity. For Alex, it is Western art music and a distinct predilection for the Elizabethan and biblical. His 'O my brothers' expresses both. The language here fits both the ersatz Elizabethan diction for which Burgess strove and, with its biblical 'O' rather than the more colloquial 'Oh', signifies that this story is also a prophesy, perhaps a lamentation. Its repetition anchors masculinity in the long lineage of patriarchal authority (we'll come back to this soon) via high cultural appeals to Shakespeare and Moses. Its egalitarian tone likewise ropes readers in, forcing them to identify with the narrator even before the relentless use of Nadsat penetrates our minds so that we begin to read without translating and even think in it when we are no longer reading. The repetition of 'O my brothers' mimics the homosocial community that dominates skinhead culture, just as Nadsat emulates the idiolects by which youth-cultural groups have always policed the boundaries of inside/outside. This much is relatively innocent, though, compared to the further articulations of masculinity in play here.

Developing the homosociality of the 'O my brothers' refrain, the edgier elements of masculinity in A Clockwork Orange are articulated along a continuum of violence and libidinal release that ultimately muddle the two so that all violence is sexualized and all sex is violent. Alex derives pleasure from doing violence, and it is an aesthetic pleasure, one that is tied irrevocably to literature, art and sexuality. The very first man the droogs assault, for example, is not just humiliated, robbed and beaten, but also stripped to his underwear. Stripping his clothes parallels the destruction of the pages of the books he is carrying, books which Alex and Dim pretend to find obscene, though they are in fact books about crystallography. Violation of the books becomes violation of the man's body, and the violence of beating him stands in for (homoerotic?) libidinal release. As Schlossman puts it, Alex 'enjoys his evil acts with a vivid and voluptuous enjoyment, characteristic of sociopathic criminals; *jouissance*, a word borrowed from French, gives a precise account of that enjoyment as use, misuse, or the act of taking possession' (274). Each successive encounter – with the drunken bum on the street, with the shopkeeper – plays out similarly, with Alex exploring his victims intimately and deriving pleasure from violating them. The evening culminates in the invasion of HOME, where Alex and his droogs beat F. Alexander and finally consummate their violent spree with the gang rape of F. Alexander's wife:

> So [Dim] did the strong-man on the devotchka, who was still creech creech creeching away in very horrorshow four-in-a-bar, locking her rookers from the back, while I ripped away at this and that and the other, the others going haw haw haw still, and real good horrorshow groodies they were that then exhibited their pink glazzies, O my brothers, while I untrussed and got ready for the plunge. Plunging I could slooshy cries of agony. (23)

Alex's ripping away of the woman's clothes replays his earlier stripping of the old man on his way home from the library, providing some continuity between the two episodes. Similarly, before the rape, Alex begins to read through the manuscript of *A Clockwork Orange* and then to 'tear up the sheets and scatter the bits over the floor' (22), further linking the episodes and heightening the connections between literature, art, violence and sex. The fusion of aesthetics with sexualized violence is finally achieved when Alex describes the woman's screams coming in 4/4 time ('four-in-a-bar') before he praises her breasts and, finally, almost anticlimactically, penetrates her. Her cries of agony provide the operatic crescendo to Alex's violation which, however, concludes uncertainly. Alex's violation of F. Alexander's wife is followed by three more *acts* in the same vein as each of the droogs takes his turn. The connection between violence and sex reaches its grotesque extreme in this rape, where it reveals the profoundly homosocial/homoerotic undercurrent that sustains its particular brand of masculinity. More troubling still, the homosociality with which the night began approaches the terrain of homoeroticism through the proxy contact of the four droogs, each sharing in a common female body.

Without all the right elements, though – that is, without the presence of Western art music – Alex seems unable to climax himself. As the violence winds down, and the droogs leave, he confesses to feeling 'that malenky bit shagged' (24), letting Georgie drive the car back to the city. My suggestion is that Alex remains libidinally frustrated by the night's experiences, and this is why he responds so powerfully to the woman singing in the bar:

> one of these devotchkas – very fair and with a big smiling red rot and in her late thirties I'd say – suddenly came with a burst of singing, only a bar and a half and as though she was like giving an example of something they'd all been govoreeting about, and it was like for a moment, O my brothers, some great bird had flown into the milkbar, and I felt all the little malenky hairs on my plott standing endwise and the shivers crawling up like slow malenky lizards and then down again. (27)

Alex's physical arousal is unmistakeable, as is his invocation of the homosocial validation so crucial to his masculinity ('O my brothers'). His aesthetic sense is awakened along with his libidinal sense, and the sequel is inevitably violence. When Dim irreverently interrupts her, Alex responds vehemently: 'I felt myself all of a fever and like drowning in redhot blood, slooshying and viddying Dim's vulgarity, and I said: "Bastard. Filthy drooling mannerless bastard." Then I leaned across Georgie, who was between me and horrible Dim, and fisted Dim skorry on the rot' (28). This violence threatens the fraternity among the droogs, as Dim declares he no longer wants to be Alex's '"brother"' (28), and leads directly to the crisis of authority and discipline that begins Alex's downfall. All the droogs fail to realize that Alex's violence is a display of sexualized aggression provoked by the gorgeous singing in the bar. They call a truce of sorts and head to their respective homes, where we alone are permitted to witness the real climax of Alex's night.

In his room, Alex re-invokes the feeling of hearing the woman sing by playing music that likewise calls to mind 'a bird of like rarest spun heavenmetal' as he envisions himself carrying out acts of violence:

> There were vecks and ptitsas, both young and starry, lying on the ground screaming for mercy, and I was smecking all over my rot and grinding my boot in their litsos. And there were devotchkas ripped and creeching against walls and I plunging like a shlaga into them, and indeed when the music, which was one movement only, rose to the top of its big highest tower, then, lying there on my bed with glazzies tight shut and rookers behind my gulliver, I broke and spattered and cried aaaaaaah with the bliss of it. (33)

It all comes together here (pun intended): violence, rape, sexualized assault, Western aesthetics and libidinal release. Alex's orgasm here is provoked entirely by what he sees in his mind's eye and hears playing on his stereo. The music is significantly, for him, 'gorgeousness and gorgeosity *made flesh*', not in a biblical sense, but in the profane sense of libidinal indulgence (33, my emphasis). The high cultural and specifically German purview of the music places it outside the moribund cultural institutions of Alex's world, and outside the English context to boot. It anticipates the war against the war generation that at least partly accounts for the skinheads' adoption of Nazi symbolism. Moreover, the music, crucially, is 'one movement only', in contrast to the four movements of the gang rape earlier, and it reaches its conclusion successfully as the previous encounter did not. As he drifts off to sleep listening to Bach's *Brandenburg Concerto*, Alex once again returns in his memory to HOME, considers what he had read in F. Alexander's manuscript pages and experiences a post-orgasmic urge to have been even more violent.

These connections – among masculinity, aesthetics, sexuality, authority and violence – achieve a new extremity the following day, when Alex has sex with two 10-year-old girls. In this case, Alex's masculinity takes on additional hues that are similarly permeated with libidinal urges and violent overtones. Despite being only 15 years old himself, Alex behaves like an adult in relation to the girls, clearly finding their way of talking alien and quaint (as Pete's wife will find Alex's language quaint in the novel's final chapter), taking them out to eat ('spaghetti and sausages and cream-puffs and banana-splits and hot choc-sauce' [44]) and then bringing them home to listen to their new records on his stereo. What's more, in addition to paying for their meals and treating them to a taxi ride to his house, Alex positions himself as an adult by calling himself ' "uncle" ' (44, 45) and arrogating for himself the role of teacher: 'No school this afterlunch, but education certain, Alex as teacher' (44). The dynamics of age, masculinity and authority are rounded out by Alex's claim that the girls 'would grow up real today' (44). The cultural institution of school is invoked only to be perverted, just as adulthood is invoked only to be parodied, and even the institution of the family is trodden under foot in Alex's figuration of himself as the girls' uncle.

The menace here is fleshed out by Alex's typical fusion of sex, violence and aesthetics, as Alex first injects 'growling jungle-cat secretion' into his arm to enhance his experience and then puts Beethoven's *Ninth Symphony* on the stereo as a soundtrack for his assault. Bored with 'nothing to fight against', Alex first has to use chemical stimulants to make the experience worthwhile. He then has to introduce the high-cultural short-cut by which he invokes the aesthetic and ideological ideal of masculinity in which he grounds himself, to make enjoyment possible. As the symphony enters the final movement, with the choral refrain 'about Joy being like a glorious spark like of heaven', Alex feels

> the old tigers leap in me and then I leapt on these two young ptitsas. This time they thought nothing fun and stopped creeching with high mirth, and had to submit to the strange and weird desires of Alexander the Large which, what with the Ninth and the hypo jab, were choodessny and zammechat and very demanding, O my brothers. (46)

The return of Alex's version of Nadsat here is striking, as he drops the charade of grown-up distance and indulges in his violent sexual urges. The musical accompaniment reinforces the experience for him, linking a feral animality ('jungle-cat secretions') to high cultural aesthetics via displaced patriarchal authority, all anchored in a violent sexuality that depends for its legitimacy on being shared among a group of like-minded men: 'O my brothers.' Alex's sexual violence expresses an uncanny parallel to the crisis of masculinity confronting early to mid-1960s youth cultures. Like the skinheads about to follow in his footsteps, Alex appeals to a masculinity anchored in a nostalgic value system that bypasses and derides contemporary cultural institutions. He asserts his masculinity through claims to authenticity, just as do skinheads: Alex through his superior aesthetic sensibility, Skins through their intense physicality. And, again like the skins, he enacts the whole through apparently random acts of violence whose real target is never the individual being assaulted so much as it is the entire social edifice he or she represents.

These connections find a real-world analogue and support in the persistent relevance of the War for post-war youth cultures and its pervasive presence in *A Clockwork Orange*. One of the consequences of sustaining the myth of the war as Britain's finest hour, and of keeping the joy of victory fresh in the minds of the populace, is that it gradually ceases to be associated with pain and suffering, and instead becomes associated with pleasure. The pluckiness of the survivors effaces what they had to survive, and their children – the baby boomers – are raised on a certain nostalgia for the sense of common cause, community and victory that attended the experience. We have seen this in operation already in the warm memories of desertion and solidarity among aunt Ada's family in *Saturday Night and Sunday Morning*, and in Vernon's sense of superiority over the Teenager in *Absolute Beginners*. In the memories of the baby boomers, recollections of post-war rationing and of having bomb sites as playgrounds stand as testimonies to character, ratifying a sense of entitlement to enjoy the fruits of victory.

As the source of a consoling myth of British global might, the war provides a ready model of masculinity that fits comfortably with traditional conceptions of men as hard, tough, strong, stoic, fraternal, implacable and imminently violent. These connections inform youth cultures from the Teddy boys through the staged battles between the mods and rockers, and include the skinheads perhaps most of all. Dressed in army boots or work boots, wearing a clear-cut uniform and with close-cropped or shaved heads, the skinhead aesthetic was anchored in an aesthetic of combat-readiness. That aesthetic was only reinforced by their sense of class- and neighbourhood-based fraternity, a sense that they stood in defence of a traditional England that was being eroded on all sides. Most notoriously, this retrenchment took the shape of increasing racism and right-wing nationalism. Though 1960s skinheads not only borrowed from rude boy culture, but listened to reggae music and fraternized with West Indian youth as well, many were from the start racist towards immigrants from Southeast Asia, especially Pakistan. The apparent contradiction here resolves itself if we understand skinheads in terms of their class and gender challenges, rather than the later fusion with football hooligans and bovver boys which have led to the caricature of all skinheads as neo-Nazis. Politically, then, skinheads are perhaps best understood as arising out of a growing sense that Britain is in rapid decline and must be defended – the government can't or won't do anything about it, so it is up to the citizenry to do it.

The paramilitary model of masculinity embraced by both Burgess's droogs and the skins infused their gangs. These gangs often styled themselves as small armies that mimicked the organizational and ideological underpinnings of victory in the war. One skinhead interviewed by Don Letts in 'The Story of Skinhead' explicitly characterizes skinhead violence in these terms. He notes that 'Well it used to be they'd sign 'em up and send off to fight wars, like. But like after the Second World War there wadn't any more wars to send the kids off, so they 'ad to release their' 'testosterone', Letts chimes in (17:40ff). In *A Clockwork Orange*, they are explicitly likened to small armies, and the violence between them characterized as war: 'Now in those days, my brothers, the teaming up was mostly by fours or fives, these being like auto-teams, four being a comfy number for an auto, and six being the outside limit for gang-size. Sometimes gangs would gang up so as to make like malenky armies for big night-war' (15). The organizational logic here is that of squads, platoons, companies and so on. The hierarchy even replicates the class distinctions in the British army, with the leader Alex alone capable of appreciating high culture, while Dim and the others are presented as uncultured ignoramuses. In the film version, this class component is highlighted still further in the accents of the actors playing Alex and his droogs, with Malcolm MacDowell's relatively posh tones clashing against Warren Clarke's broad working-class accent.

The violence that takes place between the gangs in *A Clockwork Orange* likewise explicitly recalls the violence of organized armies in war – and the chance to demonstrate authentic masculinity it presents. As compared to violence against helpless victims, a battle with other armed combatants comes with both higher stakes and greater opportunities. When Alex and his gang chance upon Billboy and his rival gang, Billyboy's crew are preparing to rape a young woman. When they spot each other, though, the prospect of rape is immediately dropped in favour of a real test: 'They viddied us just as we viddied them, and there was like a very quiet kind of watching each other now. This would be real, this would be proper, this would be the nozh, the oozy, the britva, not just fisties and boots' (15). Here, at last, would be something to 'fight against', an authentic test of masculinity. Armed conflict *mano a mano* is the gold standard for an authentic opportunity to perform and confirm one's masculinity. Lest there be any doubt about what is at stake, Alex commences the fight by taunting Billboy's masculinity. He calls him a 'eunuch' and threatens as the battle ends to have his 'yarbles off' soon enough (15, 17). Alex and his ilk quite literally play army by night, rehearsing a model of masculinity that is infused by the long shadow of the war.

The fundamental problem for Alex and the skinheads alike is that their effort to play war, and thus to achieve a mature masculinity as their fathers and grandfathers had done, involves them in a paradox. They fight, but have nothing to fight against. And, when they fabricate something to fight against, more often than not they end up pitted against contemporary society itself. This is in part a direct consequence of the generational conflict we have been tracing throughout, but it presents an interesting tension: To fight against the older generation by adopting that generation's greatest mechanism of authentication (trial by arms) risks a self-defeating irony. When Arthur Seaton, for example, imagines himself turning his machine gun on his officers, managers and factory owners, he crudely articulates this paradox. He wishes to destroy the very social reality that has allowed him to flourish in the first place. That he wishes to do it with the training he is receiving so that he can defend that social order is at least profoundly ironic, if not simply nihilistic.

For the skinheads, the paradox involved yet another temporal lag: They understood themselves to be fighting not for Britain as it was in the 1960s, but as it had been in the past, before it had been betrayed and undermined. Like the Teds, they anchored their identity in a Britain that belonged to the pre-war, the pre-First World War. This put them in the paradoxical situation of fighting for a nostalgic version of Britain against the current version of it. This paradox, fused with increasingly violent xenophobia, produced the odd phenomenon of young British men – the children, or perhaps grand-children, of the war generation – sporting swastikas and other Nazi regalia. Punks would do similarly in the mid-1970s, as we will see when we turn to *The Buddha of Suburbia*, precisely to amplify the shock effect latent in so oppositional a stance. In *A Clockwork Orange*, this effect manifests in Alex's alignment with nineteenth-century German music. It suggests that his nostalgia is not just for the past, but the enemy's past. His aesthetic ideology seems to place Alex doubly on the wrong side of history. In Kubrick's film version, the rival gang, led by Billyboy, is actually kitted out with Nazi gear, and the prison chaplain – complete with a toothbrush moustache – appears to raise the Nazi salute as he addresses the prisoners. Both Burgess's droogs and their real-life skinhead counterparts cast themselves as fighting against Britain, keeping the war going in the name of alternative traditions that seem to hold greater potential for authentic masculinity. Where Arthur Seaton wishes only to use the army's weapons to enact his violently antisocial fantasies, and the Teenager refuses to acknowledge the war's importance at all, Alex and the skinheads have begun the process of de-naturalizing it, turning it against the very society it was ostensibly fought to preserve. Their repurposing implies that the victory was at best Pyrrhic, leaving behind a nation whose institutions were only going to collapse anyway.

Burgess articulates this irony in the opening pages of *A Clockwork Orange*, when Alex and his droogs assault a drunk on the street. The drunk stands up to the gang, calling them out as little more than hooligans before he identifies himself as a former soldier by way of a snatch of song: 'O dear dear land, I fought for thee / And brought thee peace and victory' (14). The gang beat him viciously and proceed on their way, immediately coming upon Billyboy and his gang. The war is directly invoked here as a frame for the ensuing violence. The tension between the decrepit old man as the war's representative, versus the celebratory rhetoric of the song he sings plays out in Alex and Billyboy's pathetic imitation of war. These tensions illuminate a powerful anxiety of influence at work in how post-war youth cultures such as the skinheads used pseudo-military organization and violence to authenticate their masculinity. Richard Allen's iconic skinhead puts it most clearly of all, claiming that the 'conflict between the young and the State was, in fact, all-out war. A war threatening the authority that a country needed to keep it stable' (n.p.). Youth-cultural gang violence borrows the accoutrements of the war generation's self-congratulation. It mobilizes them against that generation in a paradox: At once coveting, resenting and rejecting its dependence upon that generation's model of masculinity. It presents generational tension as a war against the war generation.

Burgess understands these tensions as an inherent part of the paradox of Nazi atrocities. That paradox resides in the fact that men who had behaved as monsters were also sophisticated: Culture itself was no protection against evil. In *A Clockwork Orange*, Burgess traces this paradox by explicitly linking Nazi and Japanese atrocities with the Ludovico Technique. As Alex is reprogrammed through a combination of chemical treatment and aversion therapy, he is repeatedly shown video of firing squads, torture and concentration camps (112–118). In this, Burgess draws on the horror attending the revelation of these realities in the post-war years. Contemporary readers would have had a ready fund of shock and revulsion to draw upon at the mere mention of 'the prison-camps and the Jews and the grey like foreign streets full of tanks and uniforms and vecks going down in withering rifle-fire' (118). Alex refers to this as the 'public side' of the violence he is shown, while the 'private' side includes footage of just the sort of violence he inflicts: 'vecks with their gullivers smashed and torn krovvy-dripping ptitsas creeching for mercy' (118). Clearly, the intention of the technique is to parallel Alex's actions with those of the inhumane enemies defeated in the war. The larger effect, however, is to illustrate how Nazi and Japanese war atrocities parallel the Ludovico Treatment itself. Burgess uses the content of the Ludovico Technique to expose the similarities between behaviourist approaches to population management and outright torture. In both cases, the subject of the treatment is robbed of his or her humanity. For Western governments to pursue such methods is, for Burgess, to lose the war despite having won it. If the young really are at war with the state, it is nonetheless unconscionable for the state to adopt methods for winning the conflict that put it on equal moral footing with those it has just defeated.

Burgess brings this all together with the Enlightenment ethos just as he had done with Alex's aesthetics of violence earlier: through Western art music. Echoing Max Horkheimer and Theodor Adorno's argument in *Dialectic of Enlightenment*, Burgess links not just the war and the Holocaust, but the post-war society of control taking hold in Britain to 'the failure of the Enlightenment ethos' (Perloff 79). For Horkheimer and Adorno, the Enlightenment had been betrayed as critical reason had collapsed into instrumental reason. Thoughtful analysis was displaced by a mania for ever-greater efficiency. The result was both the fact of the Holocaust and the efficiency of its methods. The Enlightenment had become a myth in its own right, degraded into forms of rationalization that betrayed its original impetus. Burgess uses Beethoven as a metonym for the Enlightenment, confounding the equation of ethics with aesthetics. He insists that nothing at all – no philosophy, no aesthetic, no mechanism, no approach or method – will reliably produce positive results. Victory in the war guarantees nothing for post-war Britain, least of all the moral authority to attempt to resolve the problem of modern youth through dehumanizing re-education. Instead, Burgess warns, contemporary England must be on guard against becoming that which it has just defeated. It must welcome the volatility of true individualism as the price for remaining true to the promise and genius of Enlightenment art, literature, music and thought.

At least, that is what he'd *like* to do. Instead, he presents a vision of post-war Britain plagued by a massive crisis of faith in key institutions. Picking up on the critique advanced by Sillitoe and MacInnes, Burgess represents an ever-intensifying crisis of cultural institutions. The ease with which Western art music is repurposed as simply '"a useful emotional heightener"' (113), whether as a soundtrack to Alex's violence or reinforcement of Dr. Branom's conditioning therapy, indicates a fundamental crisis of Western civilization. Burgess gamely attempts to preserve Alex's human capacity for self-determination to the very end. But, ultimately, he presents instead a truly dystopian vision in which art and culture, newspapers, education, the penal system, the church and government are all revealed as bankrupt. We have come a long way from the unused church and school that Arthur and Fred pass on their drunken wander through Nottingham in *Saturday Night and Sunday Morning*, via the Teenager's disgust with the newspaper editorial about the riots in *Absolute Beginners*, to a sweeping view of near-total social collapse. It's precisely the kind of collapse that provokes young people to reaffirm traditional values, to hunker down into insular populations tightly defined by regional boundaries and to defend those values violently. In short, Burgess articulates exactly the cultural view already shaping an emergent skinhead ethos. Looking beyond the current cultural moment – the moment of mods and rockers – Burgess predicts the more extreme consequences of the post-war collapse of cultural institutions and bastions of normativity. The absence of 'anything to fight against, really' produces a scorched earth nihilism unlike anything we've seen so far.

Let's take each of these institutions in turn: family, mass media, the Church, Western aesthetics, education, the penal system, government and – perhaps most importantly of all – the family. Some of what follows may seem elementary to some readers, but as with Burgess's novel, my hope is that the accumulation of evidence will finally outweigh any tedium caused by enumerating it.

We begin with the family, which, in this case, is clearly in tatters. As I recounted in the Introduction to this book, the post-war economic boom which gave rise to the Teddy boys created what we might call wage-inversion: Young men just out of school could earn as much as or more than their fathers, who had years of experience and, moreover, may have just returned from the war. This challenge to the traditional order of bread-winners and dependents combined with the pervading sense of exhaustion among the parental/war generation. The combination made it relatively easy for young men in the post-war years to view their fathers as, at best, worn out and deserving of a rest or, at worst, weak and ineffectual. Arthur Seaton sees his own father in the first way, granting that he has earned the right to sit in front of the telly day in and day out. The Teenager in *Absolute Beginners*, though he is tender towards his father, also sees him as plainly ineffectual and stuck in the past. Alex's father is pretty much a dead loss. He lacks any authority in the family whatsoever, plaintively trying to coax Alex into treating his mother nicely and meekly accepting the ill-gotten money Alex gives him to shut up.

This state of affairs is the result of Alex having imported the threat of his street violence into the home, overthrowing both his parents' authority and establishing himself as a fully independent agent living on familial resources but owing nothing in the way of responsibility. The result is that his parents fear him and try to stay out of his way for the most part. His mother persists in trying to care for him, for example, by calling him to get up for school and leaving his breakfast to keep warm in the oven. Interestingly, Alex both accepts this mothering as his due and yet resists its potentially infantilizing effects. This aspect of the crisis in the family gains clarity when Alex returns from prison to find that he has been replaced by a proper lodger. The new man, Joe, not only pays his rent, he treats Alex's parents with deference, respect and protectiveness. Ironically, he uses the threat of violence to chase Alex out. He restores the boundary of the family unit, using violence to protect its integrity instead of to undermine it. That he inhabits Alex's room, from which all of Alex's belongings have been removed, further consolidates his place as a surrogate – and much improved – son. Of course, once the Ludovico Technique's effects are reversed, Joe is ejected and Alex moves back in with his mom and dad. Everything will go back to the way it was, with Alex in charge of his abject parents.

And yet, as Todd Davis and Kenneth Womack put it, 'Clearly, Alex subscribes to a patriarchal model and envisions a family system that consists principally of a wife who would bear his children' (35). I would go further, and say that Alex actively craves a normative family situation. This craving is already detectable in the little lies he tells his parents to cover up his real situation. When his mother calls him to get out of bed for school, Alex claims to have a headache, so he's going to stay home. If he were truly emancipated, Alex would more likely simply tell her to fuck off. Likewise, when his father starts to question him about what he does by nights, Alex presents a flimsy lie, backed up by a menacing stare, rather than simply telling him to … you guessed it … fuck off. This reticence indicates a deeply held longing for a traditional family. Consider Alex's sudden change of heart in the twenty-first chapter, where he sentimentalizes over a picture of an infant and dreams of a future in which he has a wife and a child. His encounter with his former droogie Pete, whose apparently normal relationship with his wife makes Alex aware of the foolishness of his continued delinquency, presents a vision of an alternative future he may not have known he wanted so badly until it walked right up and said hello.

In his commitment to a restrictively normative model of the family, though, Alex fails to present anything like a utopian alternative to the current social reality. His vision is clearly regressive in its sexism and hetero-normativity, and remains anchored in a view of both family and world history as irremediably stuck in cycles of hope and betrayal (I'll work this out in more detail later, when I turn to the book's final chapter). Joy McEntee has argued something along these lines with regard to Kubrick's adaptation of the novel, noting that 'Despite its excision of the problematic patriarchal institution of "Family", this is not a neutral adaptation that renders *A Clockwork Orange* amoral. On the contrary, it amplifies – or perhaps (re-)inscribes in provisional and problematic ways – the masculinism of its precursor text' (327). On this line of thinking, the crisis of the family Burgess registers may present a progressive opportunity, but it is equally clear that he has no intention of using it. Instead, Burgess, Alex and the hyper-masculine skinheads to follow will reject the perceived weakness of worn-out, ineffectual fathers and, once again, hearken back to older, more traditional models that guarantee a clearly demarcated and bounded masculinity.

Interestingly, the next cultural institution Burgess presents as being in crisis – the mass media – provides the only suggestion that parents may have some responsibility for the novel's plague of delinquency. As in *Absolute Beginners*, *A Clockwork Orange* presents the newspapers only to show how out of touch they are. After his first night's adventures, Alex reads the newspaper over his breakfast, linking in his mind the day's 'big article on Modern Youth' with previous editorials on the same topic. Alex 'smecks' at all the explanations on offer, from the sociological to the demonological:

> This learned veck said the usual veshches, about no parental discipline, as he called it, and the shortage of real horrorshow teachers. [...] Every day there was something about Modern Youth, but the best veshch they ever had in the old gazetta was by some starry pop in a doggy collar who said that in his considered opinion and he was govoreeting as a man of Bog IT WAS THE DEVIL THAT WAS ABROAD and was like ferretting his way into like young innocent flesh, and it was the adult world that could take the responsibility for this with their wars and bombs and nonsense. So that was all right. So he knew what he talked of, being a Godman. So we young innocent malchicks could take no blame. Right right right. (41)

Cynically, Alex both willingly accepts the papers' displacement of responsibility for their violence and rejects their efforts to understand it. The newspaper is so wide of the mark that Alex can readily accept its diagnosis and embrace the excuses it makes for him. Whether the official explanation tends towards the pop-sociological or the apocalyptic, the end result is the same: Young people are not responsible for their actions. As the voice of official parent culture, the newspaper utterly fails to comprehend the true nature of Alex's actions, further infantilizing him by denying him agency. The effectiveness of the newspaper's official line manifests in P. R. Deltoid's conversation with Alex on the same morning. There, Deltoid rehearses the newspaper's speculation, along with its sense of perplexity: '"What gets into you all? We study the problem and we've been studying it for damn well near a century, yes, but we get no farther with our studies. You've got a good home here, good loving parents, you've got not too bad of a brain. Is it some devil that crawls inside you?"' (39). As the voice of authentic insider knowledge, by contrast, Alex gives the lie to these adult explanations, and articulates an even uglier truth, one that had begun to haunt key lines of Western thought by the middle of the twentieth century.

In Walter Benjamin's terms, this truth lies in the notion that 'there is no document of civilization which is not at the same time a document of barbarism' (256). It's a dialectical view on offer as well in a wide range of psychoanalytical assessments making the rounds in the post-war decades. For Alex, the focus is not nearly so sweeping, though it resonates thoroughly with the novel's fusion of Western aesthetics, an Enlightenment conception of human agency and the recent history of industrial slaughter: 'I do what I do because I like to do' (40). Alex commits violence because it is pleasurable to him. It is aesthetically pleasing and provides a libidinal release, just like listening to Beethoven or reading the Bible. There is no elaborate sociological explanation, much less the devil abroad in the land, but instead what Burgess takes to be a dirty little secret – perhaps *the* dirty little secret – of Western civilization. The end result in terms of institutional faith, of course, is that both the official daily discourse of the newspaper and the legal apparatus which feeds off it are portrayed as utterly incapable of understanding what they try to explain. There is so little truth in the newspaper account, at least according to Alex, that it presents only a comforting fiction – one that provides cover for young men like Alex to continue their crimes.

On the spiritual side of things, A Clockwork Orange presents the Church as more or less totally bankrupt. The biblical explanation for youth violence presented in the newspaper finds its pale counterpart in the prison chaplain who tries to reform Alex. Alex continues in his cynical mode, accepting the chaplain's favours as a means of shortening his sentence and gaining access to both the music he so adores and the sex and violence depicted in the Bible. As he reads the Bible, Alex particularly lingers over Old Testament accounts of patriarchs sleeping with multiple women, including their own offspring, and massacring whole populations in bloody gore fests. In his reading of the New Testament, Alex delights in imagining himself as one of the Romans scourging and crucifying Christ, all with the 'useful emotional heightener' of sacred music. Again, Burgess shows that content is separable from form, so that holy texts and music can be turned to profane, even perverse, ends.

Alex's perversion of the Christian setting is not entirely his own doing, however. It is only possible because the institution itself is already corrupt. The chaplain himself does little to redeem the Church. He is habitually drunk and demonstrates breathtaking moral cowardice in refusing to oppose the Ludovico Treatment. Like Eichmann, he takes cover in just following orders and the presumed futility of his individual resistance. His preaching to the prisoners in Staja 84F is utterly ineffectual, as he relies upon armed guards to keep his flock in order. Rather than providing any moral or spiritual guidance, the Church appears here only as a tool of control (at best) and a time-wasting element of the prisoners' punishment (at worst). There is neither penitence nor redemption on offer here, and even when the chaplain finally does speak up – notably *after* the Treatment has been completed – he does so to no discernible effect and is quickly silenced. As far as crises of faith go, this one is at least doubly ramified: Neither spiritual nor social faith in the Church remains. As a parallel discourse to the newspaper, offering explanations for why the world works as it does, the Church is equally ineffectual, wrong and complicit with the very state of affairs about which it wrings its hands. The two together focus the crisis of faith in traditional cultural institutions that underwrites Burgess's vision of the droogs and feeds into the skinheads' reactive violence.

Just as Alex is capable of turning the Bible to his own perverse purposes, so Burgess shows that Western aesthetics can reinforce barbaric practices. Alex's use of Beethoven to enhance his enjoyment of violence is the most obvious reference point here, as is the Ludovico Technique's redeployment of the same music. Perhaps the most telling example of how Western aesthetics can be used to undermine the very tradition it had long been taken to uphold is F. Alexander's use of Beethoven to drive Alex to suicide. Having realized that Alex led the gang rape of his wife two years previously, and learned that the Ludovico Technique had made listening to Beethoven intolerable to him, F. Alexander imprisons Alex in an upper-storey room through whose walls he plays Beethoven loudly. The objective is to drive Alex mad, forcing him to leap out the window of the apartment to his death. The publicity of his death as a consequence of what the government has done to Alex will give F. Alexander's anti-government movement the momentum it needs to force the government out in the next elections.

It's the effort to drive Alex mad and then to kill himself that is most interesting here. First, this effort stands in direct contrast to the stated aims of the Ludovico Technique itself: '"You are being made sane, you are being made healthy"' (108). Turning the Ludovico Technique's achievements against itself, F. Alexander does not want to free Alex from his brainwashing, but to drive it to its logical conclusion. He thus starkly exposes the link between genius and madness, art and deviance, that underwrites the

Western cult of aesthetic genius. Driving Alex out of his mind with the very music that has been used first to heighten criminal enjoyment and then to heighten criminal discomfort, F. Alexander confirms that art and culture in themselves afford no security at all. The devastating revelations about Nazi guards listening to Beethoven before firing up the gas chambers that came in the immediate wake of the war point not to Nazi perversion of inherently good (morally as well as aesthetically) art, but to the inherently amoral nature of art itself. Any further confusion of moral with aesthetic goodness is impossible for Burgess, and all institutions and ideologies built upon that confusion stand revealed as utterly hollow.

The next major cultural institution upon which Burgess turns his jaundiced eye is education. The abandoned school in *Saturday Night and Sunday Morning* and the preference for education in the streets over anything approaching a school in *Absolute Beginners* manifests here in a reframing of education itself as a tool of domination rather than a path to enlightenment. In keeping with the emerging revolutionary sentiment of the 1960s, Alex only mentions school once, and then just to announce that he is not going to attend that day. Instead, we get a vision of how Western cultural practices have betrayed the Enlightenment principles behind public education – a nightmare vision that no doubt caused Matthew Arnold to roll over in his grave. No traditional curriculum appears in any guise in *A Clockwork Orange*, least of all the 'Lively Appreciation Of The Arts' recommended by the newspapers (42). The very notion that 'Great Music [...] and Great Poetry would like quieten Modern Youth down and make Modern Youth more Civilized' (42) is by now at best laughable, at worst cause for despair.

In place of such high-minded notions, we find Alex assuming the role of teacher, taking credit for Georgie's rebelliousness: '"I have taught you much, little droogie"' (53). Mindful that the student intends to surpass his teacher, Alex quickly reasserts his dominance as leader not by arguing the point, but by slicing up Georgie and Dim with his straight razor. As we have already discussed, Alex continues in his role as teacher when he sexually assaults the two 10-year-old girls he picks up in the record store. There, the logic of education as domination, as subordinating the student to the teacher's will manifests even more clearly. There is indeed no school that day for either the girls or Alex, but what he calls 'education' bears no resemblance to the Arnoldian ideals of the British system. Likewise, when Alex and his cellmates kill the new prisoner, they do it in the name of education – an education aimed at reasserting the right to exercise power: '"If we can't have sleep let's have some education. Our new friend here had better be taught a lesson"' (88). It's a new – and devastating – take on the old saying that education is power.

Even when education does take place in an institutional setting, it remains strictly a form of domination. First, Dr. Branom explains Alex's reaction to watching the violent film clips as a process of learning: '"Of course it was horrible," smiled Dr. Branom. "Violence is a very horrible thing. That's what you're learning now. Your body is learning it"' (108). Learning through bodily training is conditioning, not learning. It's what athletes and musicians do to create muscle memory. But, as with the notion of 'memory' in muscle memory, the 'learning' in Dr. Branom's explanation is metaphorical: it's a conditioned response. Shortly thereafter, Dr. Brodsky tries to finesse things by changing the explanation a bit: '"Right," said Dr. Brodsky. "It's association, the oldest educational method in the world"' (114). Though in some cases association may be a form of learning, that's not what they are doing to Alex. Instead, they are conditioning him just as Pavlov conditioned his dogs. Their version of education is little more than a form of stimulus–response manipulation that runs well below the threshold for the increase of human knowledge or intelligence. It is, in fact, an exercise of power that seeks to penetrate the mind and body of its subject, training it to respond in a given way to a given event, but nothing more.

Himself a product of the English school system, Burgess seems to have saved his most damning criticism for the Foucauldian nightmare of post-war regimes of discipline and punishment that pass for education. Small wonder that so many students chose to leave school at the earliest opportunity in the immediate post-war years, opting for gainful employment and relative freedom over the oppressive atmosphere of British education. Even smaller wonder, then, that the epitomes of undereducated working-class young masculinity – Teds, mods, rockers, but especially skinheads – used violence and tactics of domination to assert their authority in the streets. Perhaps they learned their lessons all too well, after all. (And if you hear the strains of Pink Floyd's *The Wall* beginning to sound, you're on the right track.)

Burgess follows what we now know of as the school to prison pipeline in his critique, moving from education to the penal system. Meant in principle to punish and reform the convicted, the penal system was in a certain sense low-hanging fruit in 1960 in large part because its methods so closely resembled those used by Axis forces in prisoner of war and concentration camps. As the governor himself says when he is visiting Staja 84F looking for candidates for the Ludovico Technique, the prisons do nothing whatsoever to reform prisoners. Instead, they only compound criminality through concentration, overcrowding and despair: '"Cram criminals together and see what happens. You get concentrated criminality, crime in the midst of punishment"' (92). He's not wrong. When Alex's already overcrowded cell gets yet another occupant, the result is not just violence but murder – the decisive murder that marks Alex out for the Ludovico Technique. Importantly, the extra prisoner is not just a violent personality, but queer as well. He tries to claim Alex's bunk for himself, and when that doesn't work, he simply crawls in alongside him while Alex is asleep and begins masturbating while talking dirty to him. In light of the novel's handling of masculinity, this is clearly a bridge too far. It illustrates the depravity to which prison exposes mere sociopaths like Alex and licenses Alex and his cellmates' brutal murder of the man.

The penal system isn't just corrupt, though; it is outright criminal. The Ludovico Technique is key here. As the penal system's most advanced technique, it is clearly portrayed as itself criminal, even if it is dressed up in the lab coats of scientific objectivity. Its direct lineage in Nazi human experiments and Japanese torture, as demonstrated in the film clips Alex is forced to watch, establish its place on the wrong side of Western civilization. As part of the thin blue line that supposedly safeguards civilization, the penal system is relentlessly cast in terms of total failure, collapse and betrayal of its principles in *A Clockwork Orange*. We should hardly be surprised to find that both Burgess's droogs and the skinheads they prefigure view violence as a viable solution to social ills.

The next major cultural institution Burgess exposes as having lost its moral authority is government. As the agency behind the penal and educational institutions, the government has already been implicated in Burgess's black view of post-war England. It is directly represented in the figure of the Minister of the Interior. The Minister is there when Alex is selected for the Ludovico Technique and presents the new approach as a socially responsible means of dealing with criminality. He warns Alex that the Ludovico Technique is '"not a reward. This is far from being a reward. Now, there is a form here to be signed. It says that you are willing to have the residue of your sentence commuted to submission to what is called here, ridiculous expression, Reclamation Treatment"' (94). The Minister appears to see the Technique clearly for what it is: A means of control, not reform. He situates it in the larger work of oppressive governmentality when he announces that though Alex will be the first to go through the new treatment, the government is fast-tracking its implementation because they anticipate an influx of 'political offenders' (92) within the year. When the Technique succeeds, the Minister is likewise present at the demonstration of the new and improved Alex. He approves of the outcome and cuts off debate over the morality of the process with the utilitarian pronouncement, '"The point is [...] that it works"' (129). It's brutal but effective, and there's just the breath of a chance still that we may read the Minister as acting out of a genuine impulse to social improvement, even if his methods are not very well thought out.

That chance vanishes in a puff of cynicism, however, when the Minister visits Alex in the hospital after his failed suicide attempt. Having sanctioned the Ludovico Treatment in the first place, celebrated its success and then been forced to have it reversed, the Minister visits Alex in the hospital to take credit for having 'cured' him (of what, exactly, is no longer clear) and to enlist him as a spokesperson for the government:

I and the Government of which I am a member want you to regard us as friends. Yes, friends. We have put you right, yes? You are getting the best of treatment. We never wished you harm, but there are some who did and do. […] There are certain men who wanted to use you, yes, use you for political ends. (177)

Charging F. Alexander with precisely what he himself has done to Alex – that is, use him for political ends – the Minister finishes off with a trifecta of cynical politicking: He tells Alex that he's safe from F. Alexander, who has been thrown into prison; he promises Alex '"a good job on a good salary"'; and he presents him with the gift of a stereo and plenty of recordings of Western art music (178). Someone yells '"Smile!"' and the Minister grabs Alex's arm for a photo opportunity that will no doubt feature in the very newspapers that will only reconfirm the official social narrative against which Alex has always fought. Cynical in the extreme, the government in *A Clockwork Orange* appears to be tendentially totalitarian and certainly more interested in securing political power than in governing justly. It's a grim vision of this last cultural institution with which to conclude the novel. Do I detect nihilism peeking around the corner?

Of course, this scene only concludes the novel in the truncated American edition. In the British edition, there is one more chapter. It is essential reading if we wish to understand exactly how Burgess undermines his own stated and carefully worked out faith in the utopian/anarchic potential of the youth revolution. I have already outlined how Burgess attempts to construct his novel as a defence of the most elemental form of Enlightenment ethos, with the self-determining volitional individual at its core. His account of the Ludovico Technique attempts to align liberal democratic governmental over-reach with the totalitarian regimes just defeated in the Second World War and ascendant in the Cold War Soviet Union. On this account, any encroachment upon individual liberty, even in the name of social order, is odious. As Jachimiak puts it, Burgess 'steadfastly uphold[s] the central tenets of liberalism – in particular, the triumph of the individual and persistence of free will' (149). Young people represent the utopian promise of radical freedom, of the capacity to choose how to act and what to believe, independently of any social norms or cultural pressures. Even if they choose evil, they must be celebrated as representing the kind of radical potential fundamental to truly utopian thought. If we are going to seek a new world, then we must be willing to countenance the destruction of all that presently exists, even if that destruction appears wanton – even evil – at first blush.

Burgess defends this reading of his novel in his famous essay 'A *Clockwork Orange* Resucked' (v-xi). The essay accompanied publication of the twenty-one-chapter edition of the novel in the United States, years after it originally appeared without the twenty-first chapter. In this essay, Burgess notes that the truncated American version leaves us with an Alex who has been 'conditioned, then de-conditioned' and who 'foresees with glee a resumption of the operation of free and violent will' (viii). He deems this ending unacceptable inasmuch as it fails on novelistic grounds, providing no moral growth for the protagonist: 'When a fictional work fails to show change, when it merely indicates that human character is set, stony, unregenerable, then you are out of the field of the novel and into that of the fable or the allegory' (viii). The problem is both aesthetic and moral. 'By definition', Burgess continues, 'a human being is endowed with free will. He can use this to choose between good and evil. If he can only perform good or only perform evil, then he is a clockwork orange – meaning that he has the appearance of an organism lovely with colour and juice but is in fact only a clockwork toy to be wound up by God or the Devil or (since this is increasingly replacing both) the Almighty State' (ix). Burgess recognizes that the last chapter does not aesthetically improve the novel. He notes that 'the book does also have a moral lesson, and it is the weary traditional one of the fundamental importance of moral choice. It is because this lesson sticks out like sore thumb that I tend to disparage *A Clockwork Orange* as a work too didactic to be artistic' (ix-x). He recognizes that it's not a very good novel, but stands by its morality, noting that the metaphor of a clockwork orange applies to Alex in that it stands 'for the application of a mechanistic morality to a living organism oozing with juice and sweetness' (x).

In terms of youth culture, Burgess articulates a profound optimism, one that sees young people as juicy, sweet organisms that make bad choices sometimes, yes, but ultimately do so as part of a moral education that will eventually see them mature: 'My young hoodlum comes to the revelation of the need to get something done in life – to marry, to beget children, to keep the orange of the world turning in the rookers of Bog, or hands of God, and perhaps even create something – music, say' (vii). It would seem that in Burgess we have found the spokesperson for the teenage revolution's true potential. Burgess puts this in basic utopian terms: Alex 'wants a different kind of future' from 'his devastating past' (viii). Such a reading depends, I submit, upon so complete a blindness to the realities of the text as to be plausible only to the author himself. It is only credible to those who already know they love the novel and believe what the author says about it, rather than the evidence of their own eyes. It sanctions even the increasing violence of skinhead gangs in the name of radical freedom, on the principle that such freedom is a necessary precursor to mature acceptance of human frailty in all its guises. It is horse-shit.

In the twenty-first chapter, Burgess upends the optimistic humanist reading of the novel with a single paragraph, one that uses the metaphor of clockwork to show that Alex never had free will about his prior actions, and that he has no control over his current transformation:

> Yes yes yes, there it was. Youth must go, ah yes. But youth is only being in a way like it might be an animal. No, it is not just like being an animal so much as being like one of these malenky toys you viddy being sold in the streets, like little chellovecks made out of tin and with a spring inside and then a winding handle on the outside and you wind

it up grrr grrr grrr and off it itties, like walking, O my brothers. But it itties in a straight line and bangs straight into things bang bang and it cannot help what it is doing. Being young is like being one of these malenky machines. (190)

To be young is to be a wind-up toy. To be young is to be a clockwork mechanism. To be young is to lack sufficient agency to change direction, let alone to make free decisions about how to live. Youth 'cannot help what it is doing'. It is a machine. *It is clockwork*. Alex has been a machine his whole life. He has had no moral agency. He has never partaken of the free individualism Burgess so passionately dreams about. His violence was inevitable, predetermined and mechanistic. Rubin Rabinovitz argues that 'Alex in his youth may be predestined to do evil; but with maturity comes freedom, when his determined phase is transformed into its polar opposite' (47). But this seems to me to miss the point and to lack evidence in the text. What matters is that with these few lines, Burgess ratifies the newspaper's absolution of young men like Alex for their violence. He and all 'young innocent malchicks could take no blame. Right right right' (41). Having earlier made fun of the newspapers for their total inability to comprehend the phenomenon of 'Modern Youth', Burgess turns around and parrots their misunderstanding as Alex's key moment of enlightenment.

But wait, there's more – it gets even worse. Alex contemplates his lack of responsibility for his 'devastating past' in terms of its inevitable repetition. His desire for 'a different kind of future' founders almost immediately on his conviction that the future will be exactly like the past:

My son, my son. When I had my son I would explain all that to him when he was starry enough to like understand. But then I knew he would not understand or would not want to understand at all and would do all the veshches I had done, yes perhaps even killing some poor starry forella surrounded with mewing kots and koshkas, and I would not be able to really stop him. And nor would he be able to stop his own son, brothers. And so it would itty on to like the end of the world. (191)

There's no utopian impulse here, no promise of improvement, however incremental. Youth-cultural rebellion will not improve a damn thing. Instead, the conclusion on offer here matches Arthur Seaton's grim meditation about life at the end of *Saturday Night and Sunday Morning*. What is to be done? Absolutely nothing. The future will be as the past, world without end, amen. 'And all it was was that I was young' (191).

Perhaps the lesson here is that there is no greater moment of delusion than that of conscious epiphany. I am not sure if the reversal is more astounding, or Burgess's own failure to see it, or decades of criticism's willing promotion of Burgess's own terrible reading. The very most we can say for this ending is that, with it, Burgess introduces a naturalism that displaces and gives the lie to the novel's supposed moral lesson. And yet, this is not even naturalism, but mechanism. It is a vision of humanity that is not even reducible to genetic competition or an indifferent universe, but one that readily sees it in terms of the nightmare of a generalized industrialism – industrialism as ontology. Instead of a moral lesson, it presents mechanistic predetermination as the truth of human existence. It might just be the most profoundly anti-existentialist ending in all of fiction, and certainly among the most profoundly anti-humanist. It normalizes the Nuremberg Defence and takes it to another level altogether: Alex was just following orders, not of human superiors, but of a wind-up universe. With this ending, Burgess gives the lie to both his novel and his defence of the novel. More: He makes fools of all those who have taken him at his word and empties youth culture of any and all utopian potential.

What this means for our understanding of youth culture generally and skinheads more specifically is profoundly depressing. Sillitoe and MacInnes at least tried to articulate some version of youthful energy that would stretch if not break the boundaries of tradition. Burgess, by contrast, presents a vision of young people as machinery to be allowed to run down over time. Mods and rockers battling on the shores of Brighton represent no larger social anxiety, no fear of nuclear annihilation, no anarchic energy unleashed upon a profoundly new world, but only an inevitable youthful impulse to violence and destruction. On this scheme, skinheads articulate no new-found class solidarity, fear of displacement by immigration or sense of betrayal over a post-war economy that has fizzled when it ought to have boomed, but just another form of aimless violence and wanton destruction. The specificity of their targets is accidental, and the viciousness of their attacks simply a result of a system with more fuel than it needs. It's an appallingly bleak vision, one conducive to nihilistic resignation.

This tension returns us to the skinheads' mis-recognition of themselves in Kubrick's film version of *A Clockwork Orange*. The film ends with the end of the twentieth chapter, with Alex announcing, 'I was cured all right' (179). This is the vision of Alex to which skinheads responded, and not the mechanistically matured Alex Burgess champions instead. On the one hand, this mis-recognition is itself an ideological operation, in which skinheads see themselves as Nietzschean *Übermenschen* taking their city and country back from an ineffective government and an invasion of foreigners bent upon uprooting and destroying English traditions. On the other hand, the fact that it is an ideological mis-recognition does not mean that it is without truth. Burgess anticipated the advent of the skinhead in part because he recognized the decline of the post-war establishment and the growing crisis of faith in its cultural institutions. Skinheads responded to his vision because it presented a world in which those institutions are in rapid decline, if not outright free-fall: The newspapers are full of lies and incomprehension, schools are defunct, the Church is corrupt, the government is cynically self-serving, the penal apparatus only enhances criminality and the police are every bit as thuggish as those they police. They responded with a stylistic assertion of independence from the preceding youth cultures, which were increasingly mainstream (e.g. the introduction of the mod TV show, *Ready, Steady, Go!* in 1963), and the parent culture's sanctimony about the War and lack of energy to remake the world in its wake. Hard, energetic, violent and menacing, the skinheads asserted themselves in terms just like those of Alex and his droogs. Both the novel and the film versions of *A Clockwork Orange* presented a world in which adults either cowered at home by night or else practiced inhuman experiments upon young people by day. As the 1960s screwed up their courage for the leap into the 1970s, the skinheads would continue to ride high in terms of youth-cultural influence, even as they were forced to make space for emerging countercultural groups such as hippies, glam rockers and eventually punks – no matter what Burgess thought of them.

3

Youth Culture Goes Metastatic: *The Rachel Papers* and *The Buddha of Suburbia*

With the 1970s, youth culture in England goes metastatic, remaining fixated on a common set of concerns even as it explodes in terms of the variety of youth cultures and the way young people understand them. First, the stakes of youth-cultural experimentation and rebellion are remarkably consistent even as we enter the heady 1970s – masculinity, identity, history, generational tensions – though they are predominated by a widespread concern with authenticity. As we will see, authenticity becomes a hotly contested element of various youth-cultural formations as the first glimmers of post-modernism begin to influence how writers such as Martin Amis and – quite a bit later – Hanif Kureishi represent the next generation. Second, these representations are likewise shaped by the explosive variety of youth cultures jostling for attention in the early to mid-1970s. Successive youth cultures begin to appear at closer intervals as the decade turns, creating a crowded scene: teds, mods, rockers and skinheads now shared the terrain with hippies, glam rockers, prog rockers and eventually punks. Finally, as a result of this proliferation, youth culture achieves a form of self-awareness unlike anything we've seen so far. It becomes something of which young people are increasingly aware, and on which they comment even as they participate in it. Young people begin to understand their specific cultures as having a history, and themselves as taking part in a cycle with precedents and likely followers. By the 1970s, a kind of template has formed for youth-cultural experimentation and behaviour, at the same time as self-reflexivity about that template begins to shape how youth cultures are represented in literature.

Two novels that exemplify this transition brilliantly are Martin Amis's *The Rachel Papers* (1973) and Hanif Kureishi's *The Buddha of Suburbia*

(1990). The astute among you will notice immediately that *The Buddha of Suburbia*'s publication date breaks with the precedent set in the previous chapters, where I have tried mightily to include only novels written in the decades they address. *The Rachel Papers* fits that bill, but I have had to turn to the later, and thus necessarily retrospective, *The Buddha of Suburbia* to flesh out our exploration of the 1970s. The key reason for this is that I have been unable to identify any novels written in the 1970s that directly engage with that decade's youth cultures. It really is as though the film version of *A Clockwork Orange* comes out and everyone stops writing about youth culture for rather a long time. Of course, the seventeen-year difference in publication dates of *The Rachel Papers* and *The Buddha of Suburbia* means that they have very different takes on the youth cultures of the 1970s, a fact I try to turn to good purpose as I work through them. Where they overlap, interestingly, there is a good deal of agreement, though of course Kureishi's views are shaped by nearly two decades of political and theoretical discourse dealing with race, ethnicity, sex and sexuality, history and identity.

Both novels continue the pattern of thinking *about* and *with* youth cultures. Presenting a wider panoply of youth cultures than any novel so far, these novels think *about* youth culture intensively. At the same time, they think *with* these youth cultures. They use hippie, glam and punk to address themselves to a turning point in the post-war crisis of masculinity and the advent of a self-reflexive youth culture. What marks this self-reflexivity out from that in, say, *Absolute Beginners*, is that now the parental generation is not just a collection of out-of-touch oldsters. Instead, adults are understood themselves to have belonged to prior youth cultures. Your dad is your dad, but he might also be an ageing Teddy boy, or at least have been a Ted in his youth. The young people coming of age in the 1970s are faced with the historically new phenomenon of having parents who themselves set the template for what a teenager was and did: They charted the initial formulations of post-war youth culture. This fact introduces a dizzying element to the generational tensions by which 1970s youth cultures still sought to define themselves and helps explain the dramatic move to challenge authenticity. If the prior youth cultures had grounded themselves in some form of faith in authenticity – that there is a core self, a stable identity, that could be expressed as the truth – the youth cultures shouldering their way onstage in the 1970s are no longer quite so sure. Putting paid to the hippie ethos of authenticity – 'Just *BE*, man!' – glam and punk called into question not only the possibility of such selfhood, but whether it was even desirable. This dramatic shift informs how *The Rachel Papers* and *The Buddha of Suburbia* use youth cultures to think with as they engage the perennial issues of generational tension, sex and sexuality, masculinity and history itself. Between them we see the transition to a new stage in the development of post-war youth cultures, a *crisis of authenticity* and the emergence of performance as a competing alternative. Taken together, they present a complicated form of self-consciousness (itself a chronic condition of youth culture) with a postmodern twist that expresses a rapidly shifting mood in which hippie sincerity gives way to glam or glitter extravagance, prog-rock's moody interiority and punk's snarling rage.

The 1960s had seen wild swings in youth-cultural affiliation from the battles of the mods and rockers in the early part of the decade to the hippie revolution of its latter half and the emergence of skinheads on the scene in the last couple of years. In large part, these movements emerged in reaction to the dawning realization that Britain's reduced role on the world stage was now the new normal. The Suez Crisis of 1956 and ongoing decolonization around the world meant that the British economy never experienced quite the same boom as the U.S. economy did. The rise of racism and racial tensions in England and the onset of the Troubles in Northern Ireland likewise fuelled the sense of decline that, though briefly alleviated by the World Cup victory over Germany in 1966, provoked youth-cultural reactions of both the traditionalist (e.g. skinhead) and non-conformist (e.g. hippie) varieties. Things only got worse, though, in the 1970s. Decolonization continued apace, and the economy continued to worsen. Inflation reached 25% in the first half of the decade and unemployment skyrocketed. As Nehring notes, 'Comparisons of the Great Depression with the late seventies were widespread' (283). Energy shortages took hold, an enforced three-day work-week was instituted, the Troubles in Northern Ireland led to bombing campaigns in London, racism and neo-fascism reached new highs with the National Front and Enoch Powell's famous 'Rivers of Blood' speech prophesying carnage in the streets if immigration were not reversed, and terrorism emerged on a global scale for the first time with multiple hijackings of airliners. The result was a growing sense among young people that if cultural institutions such as school, the church, the penal system and government were in crisis before, they were now utterly illegitimate. Margaret Thatcher's election at the decade's close only seemed to ratify this sense, summed up most succinctly in her declaration that 'There's no such thing as society' (qtd. in *Women's Own* magazine). Pity.

The Rachel Papers (1973) and *The Buddha of Suburbia* (1990) present the decade's change of temper on virtually every level. Between them, they take youth culture meta-static by forcing it to exceed itself in a self-consciousness that is dizzying in its potentially infinite regression. *The Rachel Papers* presents us with a narrator who is so obsessively self-fashioning as to be apparently unable to consider *anything* as genuine. His identity is a fluid performance, characterized by an ever-changing set of accents, lexicons, clothing styles, musical tastes, literary preferences, and opinions on all topics. He fancies himself a social chameleon capable of discerning anyone else's illusions about themselves and then mimicking them in whatever way seems most advantageous to him. *The Buddha of Suburbia* in turn thematizes this self-awareness in several ways, as the narrator Karim increasingly finds his métier in acting, his best friend Charlie morphs repeatedly through youth-cultural trends en route to rock 'n' roll stardom and the titular Buddha of suburbia – his father Haroon – becomes a career charlatan. For both novels, the question of what is original, authentic, enduring or true becomes less and less relevant as the characters learn more and more that they can fabricate the effects and appearance of authenticity – an *authenticity-effect* – out of whole cloth. The question of authenticity goes into abeyance, possibly for good, and is supplanted with the highly flexible potential of performance.

The Rachel Papers and *The Buddha of Suburbia*'s representations of the youth cultures predominating in the 1970s illustrate the crisis of authenticity in near-documentary terms. We'll begin with Amis's more general engagement with the problem of modern youth in *The Rachel Papers*. Amis frames his engagement in the general terms of youth, broadly understood, though his presentation of this large category is of course inflected by the youth cultures and preoccupations of his novel's moment. Then, we'll move on to discuss how the two novels represent specific youth cultures, notably hippie, glam/glitter, skinhead and punk. Throughout, we'll see common concerns with varying inflections and witness the emergence of a truly postmodernist understanding of youth culture.

The governing conceit of *The Rachel Papers* is that it takes place on the protagonist, Charles Highway's, last night as a teenager, meaning that he is explicitly concerned with youth and adulthood, and especially the transition between them: 'There were several teenage things still to be done: Get a job, preferably a menial, egalitarian one; have a first love, or at least sleep with an Older Woman; write few more callow, brittle poems, thus completing my "Adolescent Monologue" sequence; and, well, just marshal my childhood' (Amis 9–10). Charles's sense of weary knowingness, of being above it all even as he engages timidly with the mechanics of these various 'things still to be done' is paramount, and colours the entire narrative. For Charles, to be a teenager is to perform a certain list of tasks, not to achieve a form of identity or discover oneself. It is not a process of becoming who you will be for the rest of your life but of ticking off boxes on a form provided by the preceding twenty-five years of history. 'Teenager' has become a prescriptive rather than a descriptive category.

This templating effect licenses bad behaviour and self-indulgence – the sensationalistic sides of the teenage stereotype – and absolves young people of responsibility for their actions. By the time the novel winds down and Charles approaches the midnight at which he will cease to be a teenager, he has moved on from his teenage to-do list to an authoritative outline of the teenager as a rugged individual who 'is not designed for guilt but for canine lust; not for regret but for exultation; not for shame but for dismissive, ignorant cynicism [...] The true teenager is a marooned ego but his back is always turned to the new ships; he has a kind of gormless strength that can bear to live with itself' (201). Finally, as Charles's own generalizations here indicate, the templating process licenses the sort of universalizing impulse that lets MacInnes's Teenager blithely elide his own white, straight, metropolitan experience with that of all others in the same age group. Charles can, then, ultimately declare with a similar degree of self-absorption:

> So I am nineteen years old and don't usually know what I'm doing, snap my thoughts out of the printed page, get my looks from other eyes, do not overtake dotards and cripples in the street for fear I will depress them with my agility, love watching children and animals at play but wouldn't mind seeing a beggar kicked or a little girl run over because it's all experience, dislike myself and sneer at a world less nice and less intelligent than me. I take it this is fairly routine? (Amis 205)

This self-reflexivity, down to the claim that he even dislikes himself, announces Charles's coolness and expresses a basic anxiety about how to be in the world. The last line here, 'I take it this is fairly routine?' re-frames the preceding lines: Their conventionality takes precedence over their substance.

This meta-framing of teenage attitudes finds its keenest expression in the debate over youth in the middle of the novel. Here, at a dinner held by Rachel's parents, two of the guests begin to argue over youth-cultural mores. One of them takes the line that 'the ostentatious "unconventionality" of youth was, in point of fact, nothing other than a different sort of *conventionality*. After all, was not the non-conformity of yesterday the conformity of today? Were not these young people as orthodox, in their very different way, as the orthodoxy they purported to be subverting?' (128). Charles places a subtle spin on the conversation by taking up precisely this dismissive approach and apparently ratifying it:

> I couldn't agree more, Sir Herbert, though I confess I've never looked at it from quite that angle. It occurs to me that the analogy can be taken further – moral issues, for example. The so-called new philosophy, 'permissiveness' if you like, seen from the right perspective, is only a new puritanism, whereby you're accused of being repressed or unenlightened if you happen to object to infidelity, promiscuity, and so on. You're not *allowed* to mind anything any more, and so you end up denying your instincts again – moderate possessiveness, say, or moral scrupulousness – just as the puritans would have you deny the opposite instincts. Both codes are reductive, and therefore equally unrelated to how people feel. (128)

Charles cleverly satirizes Sir Herbert's view even as he appears to back it up. He quite openly declares that such vapourings have nothing to do with why teenagers do what they do. The very notion that there is any sort of orthodox ideology behind teenage behaviour is itself patently absurd. The infinite regress suggested here – that unconventionality is a form of conventionality so that being conventional is in a sense unconventional, which is in turn only conventional either avant-garde or après-tout – is precisely the point: '"What will that mind of yours get up to next?" I said, recognizing the self-congratulation behind this thought and the self-congratulation behind that recognition and the self-congratulation behind recognizing that recognition' (96). Self-reflexivity, congratulation, admonishment and anxiety are the order of the day, elevating style itself to the sovereign value. What one does has practically no importance when compared with how one does it: This is the essence of youth-cultural identity formation in *The Rachel Papers*. And style is, of course, appropriable, adaptable, tractable – performative.

I invoke Judith Butler's concept of performativity here precisely because it depends upon citation as its keystone element: To perform gender, for Butler, is to cite other examples of it, to act *like* a man or *like* a woman because you have been furnished with so many examples you can readily call to mind the templates by which your identity is shaped and to which your actions should correspond. In *The Rachel Papers*, Charles lives his entire life in these terms, even going so far as actually to cite his sources. As he walks 'soulfully down the Bayswater road', something he does repeatedly and even wonders at while he's doing it – 'Don't I ever do anything else but take soulful walks down the Bayswater Road, I thought, as I walked soulfully down the Bayswater Road' (73) – Charles acquiesces to his imaginary addressee's expectations by providing a description not just of the road, but of his mental state as well:

> Very well: demonically mechanical cars; potent solid living trees; unreal distant-seeming buildings; blotchy extra-terrestrial wayfarers; Intense Consciousness of Being; pathetic fallacy plus omnipresent *déjà vu*, cosmic angst, metaphysical fear, a feeling both claustrophobic and agoraphobic, the teenager's religion. The Rev. Northrop Frye fetchingly terms it 'queasy apocalyptic foreboding'. An Angus Wilson character terms it 'adolescent egotism', thereby driving me almost to suicide last Christmas. Is *that* all it fucking is, I thought. (73)

Openly committing the pathetic fallacy, Charles invokes multiple literary and philosophical precedents for his state of mind. He is a well-read young man who can easily convert his affective state into a series of clichés. He even attaches critics' names to the conventions he invokes, at once elevating them to existential significance and endowing them with an intellectual imprimatur. Tellingly, though, when he turns to the novelist, Angus Wilson, Charles discovers that the aesthetic is more devastatingly insightful than the academic and reacts with vehemence. Wilson's character's assertion that the grand feelings in which Charles shares come down ultimately to nothing more than 'adolescent egotism', nearly drives him to suicide – or so he would have us believe. The point here is that Wilson's insight in no way discredits the other terms Charles invokes, but rather adds a layer of self-awareness to them. 'Cosmic angst, metaphysical fear, [...] "queasy apocalyptic foreboding"' remain authentic affective experiences even if they are also characteristic of 'adolescent egotism'. The egotism only enters in when the person experiencing the affective states believes that he or she is unique, or uniquely sensitive, in having them. The turn here marks an incipient postmodernism that will become endemic to youth culture from here on out.

So much for Amis's attempt to think about youth culture more generally. Now, let's turn to some specifics. Here, Kureishi joins Amis as both novelists think sustainedly about the two youth-cultural movements arguably most obsessed with authenticity: skinheads and hippies. Though the film version of *A Clockwork Orange* had been released in 1971, leading many skinheads to celebrate their newfound understanding and mainstream representation, Burgess withdrew the film from circulation in the UK in 1973 for reasons of public safety due to copycat crimes modelled on Alex's depravity in the film. *The Rachel Papers* is published in the same year, and presents skinheads as already belonging to the past. In Raymond Williams's terms, skinheads were already a residual cultural element. They persisted, to be sure, as did Teddy boys, mods and rockers, but they had become part of the furniture in a sense. Their menace was understood, relatively confined and accountable – you could plan for it and avoid it if you wanted to.

The Rachel Papers' Charles understands them as simply another element of what makes the city both lively and dangerous, and he plans his travels accordingly. On his arrival in London at the outset of the novel, Charles opts to take a taxi to Jennifer and Norman's house rather than the tube because 'it was far, far too late to go on the tube without getting denounced by drunkards, or, alternatively, castrated by skinheads' (Amis 18). Denunciation by drunkards is on a par with violent assault by skinheads, both equally to be avoided if possible. Time of day is a key factor, then, in avoiding skinheads, who are understood to present, as is what one is wearing or whom one is with. No doubt in large part because he is white, Charles finds the skinheads to be a nuisance, but no more of a threat than most other tribal groups of the metropolis, noting that 'the fellows are quite tractable really' (50).

The Buddha of Suburbia seems to ratify this perspective, presenting a trio of skinheads jeering at Jamila and Changez as they move in to the housing co-op as being 'as respectable as Civil Servants' (217). And though they are clearly among the culprits who regularly vandalize and attack Anwar and Jeeta's store, their particular menace is conflated in this novel with the larger resurgence of National Front racist politics. For example, when Changez is attacked on his way home one night, he is beaten and has the initials of the National Front carved into his skin. The perpetrators are skinheads, but the real culprits are the National Front agitators who have given them political legitimacy. In this respect, Kureishi again benefits from hindsight. He knows from the perspective of 1990 how the skinheads will be mobilized by regressive political forces, transformed from being just the most offensive and violent of the inhabitants of the soccer ends into violent defenders of a particular version of traditional England. Consider Karim and Changez's attendance at a soccer match: The threat of violence is real, but restricted enough that simply having Changez wear a 'bobble-hat' (98) is sufficient to keep them safe: Karim's own dark skin presents a negligible risk of attack outside the context of National Front politics. Kureishi, unlike Amis, has seen not only the first wave of skinheads in the late 1960s and into the 1970s, but also the skinhead revival of the 1980s. This historical knowledge, along with the racial politics inherent in his representation of immigrant populations, leads him to present them as much more of a persistent social threat than Amis does. It permeates his representation of the skinheads and determines the climactic violence of *The Buddha of Suburbia* as a planned march by the National Front at which Jamila and her cohort plan a counter-protest rather than a spontaneous outbreak of violence as it was in *Absolute Beginners*.

In both novels, the particular language in which skinheads are represented carries remarkably dense associations. In *The Rachel Papers*, as Charles makes his way home from his last session with his English Literature tutor, he notes that 'It was light enough to risk the walk to Kilbourn [...] Maida Vale was reassuringly well-lit against the incipient dusk' (114). When he pops into a pub 'to consolidate' the gin he had drunk at his tutor's, however, Charles quickly retreats: 'I went into a ramshackle Victorian pub, and came out of it, quickly. Chock-a-block with teds, micks, skinnies, and other violent minority groups' (114). The problem isn't the Teds and skinheads per se, but the fact that Charles is still 'wearing a three-piece charcoal suit – from school, admittedly, yet quite flash all the same' (114). Charles's suit, though ostensibly excusable because it is a school uniform and therefore not conclusive evidence that he is worthy of attack, is nonetheless too 'flash' – too indicative of money and non-working-class status – to risk in the presence of 'teds, micks, skinnies'. The only three named of the various 'violent minority groups' in the pub, this trio of 'teds, micks, skinnies' is decisive for our understanding of how normalized skinheads had become, and how much they had lost any ratifiable claim to authenticity. First, the skinheads are here lumped in with Teddy boys, by now relics of a previous youth-cultural era (either they are ageing original Teds or young second- or even third-generation Teds). They overlap ideologically enough to occupy the same pub at the same time without too much disruption or violence, suggesting that in a very real sense the skinheads are simply a later incarnation of Teddy-boy machismo. The two youth groups have a very similar attitude towards class, and specifically their class affiliation, but expressed in near-diametrically opposed ways. Where Teds express their working-class pride by rejecting the historical clothing style of scarcity and need, skinheads embrace that history and dress it up. Where Teds continue to embrace what is by 1970 significantly outdated haute couture (from the early 1950s, now calcified as the Teddy boy uniform), skinheads clean up and sharpen up their working-class uniforms of dungarees, braces and boots. They bring the mod tendency to dress normally (for their class) but with a distinctive edge suggestive of menace to bear on working-class style. Both, however, share an affinity for black music – soul or R&B in the case of the Teds, reggae and ska in the case of the skinheads – even as they disavow its racial origins. Nonetheless, the Teds are clearly presented as relics of history, quite literally out of style. Their comfortable equivalence in the novel with skinheads marks the skinheads too as belonging to the past. Both groups have been overtaken by events, their edginess reduced to an element of style rather than social disruption, even if they continue to present a real threat of violence.

Crucially, the skinheads and Teds are lumped in here with 'micks': Irishmen. This alignment cuts two ways. First, it powerfully ratifies the reification of both skinhead and Teddy-boy identities, equating both groups with a national identity, an ethnicity. It shifts youth-cultural affiliation in the direction of national character, suggesting both that it is insuperable and ingrained. Class becomes genetics in this alchemy. Youth-cultural affiliation takes on a stability that makes it part of history in a much more enduring way than simple passing fads. But it also becomes part of history in the sense that it is not part of the future any longer; rather, it is an historical phenomenon whose legacy in the present must be dealt with, but which no longer represents any sort of futurity. Second, in a move we will see repeated in *The Buddha of Suburbia*, this alignment unsettles ethnic identity by suggesting that it is a matter of style more than anything else. To be a 'mick' is, it would seem, at least discursively equal to being a Ted or a skinhead. It involves a certain way of dressing, speaking, behaving, and thinking, but not necessarily more than that. It gives the lie to a mode of historical thinking that depends upon national character, upon the existence of an essential element that makes one people distinct from another. In this respect, it opens up the possibility of change, since identity thus becomes fluid and adaptable. And while this new vista is certainly being explored by 1973 in the emergence of glam rock in particular, it remains underdeveloped in *The Rachel Papers*. Suffice for the present to note that whichever way we read this grouping of 'teds, micks, [and] skinnies' skinheads are understood as established fixtures of contemporary London, as occupational hazards for city-dwellers, but hardly the revolutionary threat they had seemed only a short time before. Indeed, by the time we get to *The Buddha of Suburbia*, set only a few years after *The Rachel Papers*, we will see people of colour fight back against skinheads, Teds and other National Front racists in the name of a future that explicitly *excludes* them.

A parallel scene takes place in *The Buddha of Suburbia*, when Helen, Jamila and Karim walk into a bar to discuss how Jamila will respond to Anwar's use of a hunger strike to try to force Jamila to accept the arranged marriage to Changez.

In the pub, the Chatterton Arms, sat ageing Teddy Boys in drape coats, with solid sculpted quiffs like ships' prows. There were a few vicious Rockers too, in studded leather and chains, discussing gang-bangs, their favourite occupation. And there were a couple of skinheads with their girls, in brogues, Levi's, Crombies and braces. A lot of them I recognized from school: they were in the pub every night, with their dads, and would be there for ever, never going away. They were a little startled to see two hippies and a Paki walk in; there was some conversation on the subject and several glances in our direction, so I made sure we didn't eyeball them and give them reason to get upset. All the same, I was nervous they might jump on us when we left. (Kureishi 75)

The situation is strikingly similar to that in *The Rachel Papers*, with 'ageing Teddy boys' sharing the pub with skinheads, though there are rockers here too. This affiliation aligns all three groups with a racist politics and penchant for violence going back to the immediate post-war years: The Teds are from the 1950s, the rockers from the 1960s and the skinheads from the 1970s. It's a virtual museum of violent, imperilled whiteness articulated via (superannuated) youth cultures. The lot are presented as go-nowheres, maintaining a generational commitment to ignorance, violence, and alcoholism. There is no evidence here of the generational tensions that animated each youth group in its initial manifestation, but rather an agreed-upon regressiveness that morphs generational tension into class identity. This transition is critical, inasmuch as it signals a marked diminishment in the utopian potential that animated earlier self-conscious generational breaks. We are now well into the decade whose mantra will become, with punk 'no future', and these blokes know it all too well.

One of the most telling details on offer here is the rhetorical equivalence of 'two hippies and a Paki'. Multiple indeterminacies dog this line. First, though Helen is clearly one of the hippies, it is not clear whether Jamila or Karim is meant as the other one. Which is the 'Paki' here? In a sense, particularly in the eyes of the Teddy boys, rockers, and skinheads, it doesn't matter – they are all the same. Second, there is the fundamental mis-identification of the slur, 'Paki'. Neither Karim nor Jamila is from Pakistan; both were born in England. Moreover, none of their parents is from Pakistan; Anwar, Jeeta and Haroon are all from India, and Karim's mother is English. Of course, it is not the point of the slur to be ethnically accurate, but to denigrate and dehumanize – which is why in an earlier incident, Jamila responds to a 'greaser [who] rode past us on an old bicycle and said, as if asking the time, "Eat shit, Pakis"' by sprinting 'through the traffic before throwing the bastard off his bike and tugging out some of his hair, like someone weeding an overgrown garden' (53). Most tellingly of all, though is the rhetorical balance here: A hippie equals a Paki. Since 'hippie' is so clearly a stylistic adaptation – a matter of choice in clothing, music, substances, politics and so on – this parallel suggests that 'Paki' is similarly a stylistic ensemble rather than a determinate ontological category. Both categories are likely to irritate the pub's denizens, and to provoke similar kinds and degrees of violence. And even if the equation is ultimately philosophically untenable, it is pragmatically telling in terms of how it frames authenticity. Though the relationship is not precisely symmetrical, there is a clear transfer of discursive status from 'hippie' to 'Paki' such that the authenticity attached to racial categories is cancelled even as it is preserved in the mis-identifying slur. Our inability to know which of Jamila or Karim is identified as the 'Paki' returns to importance here: Only *one* of them is a 'Paki'. If the category were reliably anchored in some form of ethnic authenticity, both would have to be identified by the term, but they are not. One of them is exempted: His or her 'hippie' style trumps (mis-attributed) national descent. This rhetorical sleight subtly and powerfully illustrates the extent to which the 1970s crisis of authenticity empties out virtually all identity categories, even among subcultural groups that still rely upon them to determine their targets, to police the boundaries of belonging and exclusion.

The second, and much more prominently engaged, youth culture these novels situate in terms of a crisis of authenticity is hippies. In one guise or another, and with varying degrees of credibility, hippies appear throughout *The Rachel Papers*. Amis's novel furnishes a remarkable panoply of hippies, in fact, downplaying glam, which was just emerging on the scene, and punk, of which Amis had no inkling in 1973. By contrast, Kureishi attends to hippies in the context of glam and punk as well as progressive and experimental rock. Kureishi's hippies are, for the most part, older than the teenaged Karim and his friends, adhering to Maharishi-era Beatles decadent styles rather than the groovy pot-smoking vibe landmarked in the UK by the inaugural music festivals at the Isle of Wight and Glastonbury in 1969 and 1970, respectively. In both novels, hippies are represented as credulous fools who still believe in authentic experience and identity, and/ or as hopelessly out of style. In either case, they belong to the past, and their vague utopianism is simply mocked when it is not outright ignored.

In *The Rachel Papers*, whether they are credible hippies such as Charles's older brother Mark's girlfriend Elaine, arrivistes such as Geoffrey's younger brother Tom, ageing sell-outs such as Knowd the Oxford Don who interviews Charles, posers such as Sue and Anastasia the two girls Geoffrey brings over to Charles's room, or even simply inclined towards hippie styling like Rachel, all the hippies are either shown up as lacking authenticity or ridiculed for being so naive as to believe that authenticity remains possible. In fact, with the sole exception of Elaine, all the other hippies encountered by Charles are quickly compartmentalized and stereotyped. Each one is quickly characterized and filed away in Charles's system of character types, treated as though he or she is a hippie on the surface only. When he first tries to analyse Rachel's personality, Charles bemoans the fact that she is not more clearly categorized: 'Why couldn't Rachel be a little more specific about the type of person *she* was? Goodness knew; if she were a hippie I'd talk to her about her drug experiences, the zodiac, tarot cards. If she were left-wing I'd look miserable, hate Greece, and eat baked beans straight from the tin. If she were the sporty

type I'd play her at ... chess and backgammon and things' (45). Being
a hippie or a leftist is equivalent for Charles to being sporty. Bona fide
political commitment and/or pursuit of authentic insight are mere stylistic
fillips, always-already hackneyed and dismissible precisely because they
smack of effort. Even given the tendency of some young people to adopt
radical political causes without full insight into their complexity, or to
seek enlightenment through charlatanism or substance abuse (about
which much more when we turn to *Trainspotting*), Charles's reduction of
what are ultimately expressions of passion (at least some of the time) is
profoundly cynical. Any deeper sense of commitment, even where Charles
allows that it might exist, is relegated to yet another stylistic element
rather than an indicator of a genuine political consciousness; it becomes
something he can mimic and work to his advantage rather than engage
with and try to understand.

In fact, for Charles, virtually every hippie is either depressingly
predictable or else a walking contradiction. Sue and Anastasia, the girls
Geoffrey brings by Charles's room early in the novel present standard
specimens whom Charles easily reads, categorizes, and caters to: 'The girls
being hippies, I selected the most violent and tuneless of all my American
LPs, *Heroin* by the Velvet Underground. The immediate results? Anastasia
swayed in her chair and tapped a sandalled foot; Sue went glazed, craning
her neck in figure-eight patterns. There you go' (55). These hippies, and
by extension in Charles's world, all hippies, are utterly predictable and
quintessentially simple to manipulate. Geoffrey's younger brother Tom
bears out this reading by adding in the element of self-contradiction. For
him, 'hippie' is an aspiration he has yet to realize: 'Tom (apprentice hippie,
second class) fidgeted with the ludicrous bundle of scarves, bandanas and
lockets swathed around his boily neck to indicate the sympathetic nature
of his views on sex, drugs, Cuba, the fact that he *was* a hippie, despite
the contrary evidence of his as yet short hair and unfaded jeans, his
conventional though tolerably sweat-stained shirt' (169–170). Though he
is clearly not a bona fide hippie, Tom is trying – but of course *trying* is
itself the key signifier of failure. Effort is anathema to the sort of cool Tom
seeks, and indeed presents the contradiction at the heart of any fashion
that styles itself aggressively to show off its disinterest in the trappings of
commodity capitalism. This element of contradiction manifests perhaps
most clearly, though, in Rachel, whose 'hippie satchel' both announces
authenticity and yet rings a false note:

My use of the split-infinitive and the hippie colouring of my speech were
attributable, in part, to Rachel's hippie satchel – one of those tasseled,
ropey-looking nose-bags – which, or so she claimed, was made entirely
from natural fibres and dyes (i.e., snot, hair, ear-muck). I had remarked
on how nice it looked.
    'Yes. That's the trouble.' (96)

Charles modifies his speech to something conventionally incorrect (the split-infinitive) to conform with Rachel's bag in an attempt to come into line with the non-conformity the bag represents. He doubts Rachel's claim that the satchel is 'made entirely form natural fibres and dyes' and undercuts the value of the authenticity thus claimed by identifying those natural fibres and dyes as human bodily effluvia. He aligns the bag's authenticity-effect with the very hippie embrace of the natural body about which Rachel appears otherwise to be so squeamish. These latent contradictions find full expression in the Rachel's rejection of Charles's compliment: The bag looks nice, which is precisely the problem with it. Authenticity in this respect correlates with ugliness. The bag's nice appearance betrays its status as a commodity – that is, as inauthentic – even as its constitutive elements, or at least Rachel's claim about them, strain to produce an authenticity-effect.

As though this critique of hippie authenticity were not sufficient to illustrate the pastness of the style, Amis goes yet one step further by having the Oxford dons who interview Charles themselves be hippies. It is hard to imagine a more damning expression of Establishment acceptance than elevation to the status of Oxford don, particularly for a member of the counter-culture whose mantra is at least putatively 'turn on, tune in, drop out'. This commentary, coming as early as 1973, presents a powerfully cynical counterpoint to the hippie movement's total investment in authenticity, ultimately suggesting that hippie authenticity is in fact nothing more than a pose, a style anyone can adopt, and utterly bereft of political effectivity let alone youth-cultural credibility. This is not because Charles assumes that all other people are simply posing, but because he thinks of himself as existing above them, like a literary critic hovering over characters in a novel and interpreting them in the service of an argument. There is, no doubt, a lesson for critics here, perhaps a prophylactic attempt by Amis to ward off criticism that attends too closely to the specificities of his narrative. But characters in novels are not people, and leaving aside the paradox of holding Charles to a standard vis-à-vis characters in a novel while I excuse myself from it, I think the point stands. Charles reads others as texts that lack any substance.

In *The Buddha of Suburbia*, hippies are even more clearly outmoded. As Saglam notes, Kureishi portrays a moment in which 'the hippie movement has already lost its ideals and is practically middle aged by the time' the novel begins (557). For the most part, they form an older age group than they do in *The Rachel Papers* and ring an even more monotonous single note: India equals authenticity. As always in this novel, Charlie is the bellwether for youth-cultural fashion, and there can be no clearer sign that hippies are outré than the fact that he's already left its stylings behind by the time the narrative begins: It's literally prehistory. In that prehistory, Charlie was cutting-edge, though, establishing his hippie credibility by sneaking the Beatles' 'Come Together' onto the school record player in place of the Vaughan Williams piece the students were meant to learn to appreciate (9).

It's telling, then, that Karim begins the novel as a hippie – at least until he sees Charlie at Eva's house. There, Charlie bluntly informs him that his hippie clothes are no longer stylish:

> 'You've got to wear less.'
>   'Wear less, Charlie?'
>   'Dress less. Yes.'
>   He got up on to one elbow and concentrated on me. His mouth was close. I sunbathed under his face.
>   'Levi's, I suggest, with an open-necked shirt, maybe in pink or purple, and a thick brown belt. Forget the headband.'
>   'Forget the headband?'
>   'Forget it.'
>   I ripped my headband off and tossed it across the floor.
>   'For your mum.'
>   'You see, Karim, you tend to look a bit like a pearly queen.' (Kureishi 17)

Charlie has by this time already moved on to his prog-rock phase, replacing 'Come Together' with Pink Floyd's *Ummagumma*, which he recommends to Karim (14). Progressive or experimental rock music encouraged drug-induced detachment from the social or political spheres even as it articulated a powerful distrust of the parental culture's institutions (e.g. Pink Floyd's *The Wall*), and Charlie is again in the vanguard with his musical taste. Ever on the move, though, Charlie will only hold the prog-rock pattern for as long as it takes to change the disc before he's off to the Next Big Thing: Glam. We'll come back to that shortly, but there's one more significant constituency of hippies to account for: The adults.

All the real hippies in *The Buddha of Suburbia* are adults, who are thus by default either figures of fun or else nonentities. Eva, for example, may present as a hippie in some respects, though by and large she is simply a suburban bohemian. She is most characteristically hippie in her embrace of Haroon's ersatz Eastern mysticism. The guests at her séances are likewise borderline hippies, with the exception of Carl and Marianne, 'friends of Eva, who'd recently been trekking in India', and who stand out as grotesque caricatures of Maharishi-era Beatles hippiedom (30). Their apartment is filled with 'sandalwood Buddhas, brass ashtrays and striped plaster elephants' (30). They themselves stand 'barefoot at the door as [Karim and Haroon] entered, the palms of their hands together in prayer and their heads bowed as if they were temple servants and not partners in the local TV rental firm of Rumbold & Toedrip' (30). Karim usually lacks Charles's intensely critical sarcasm, but here he cannot hold back. Carl and Marianne's faux authenticity, guaranteed by the elevated spiritual state conferred upon them by their trip to India (where they have acquired no end of cheap tourist tchotchkes), simply rubs Karim the wrong way. When Carl declares '"There are two sorts of people in the world – those who have been to India and those who haven't"' he is 'forced to get up and move out of earshot' (30). In *The Buddha of Suburbia*, hippie style appropriates its authenticity from other cultures, bolstering it not by establishing its own bona fides, but by hosting an *actual Indian* to instruct others in the ways of wisdom and enlightenment. Here as in *The Rachel Papers*, hippies clearly fall under the rubric not only of false authenticity, but of a glaringly self-contradictory and yet unself-conscious false authenticity. Their moment is well and truly over in large part because the very moment of authenticity in youth culture is itself over.

Emerging from the psychedelic and art-rock movements associated with late-hippie stylings, glam fused space-age futuristic outfits with gender-bending costumes, fluid representations of sexuality and a resurgent dandyism that had not been seen since the 1890s. It is the first glimmer of post-humanism in the mainstream, breaking down boundaries around gender, sexuality, humanity and machines in the name of a future that would be nothing but performance. In such prominent figures as Marc Bolan, David Bowie, Mott the Hoople and Gary Glitter, glam fused powerfully queer aesthetics with aggressive masculinity and laddish behaviour: violence, promiscuity, substance abuse. It presented a no-holds-barred challenge to conventional masculine style even as it reinforced many of its characteristics. At the same time, it sanctioned sexual experimentation and especially male homosexual acts. It presented the possibility of dressing 'like a pearly queen', drinking and fighting in the streets, and giving one

FIGURE 3.1 *Stoned Hippie poses with elderly man, August 1971. (Photo by Jack Garofalo/Paris Match via Getty Images.)*

another blow-jobs, as part of a swirling ball of experimentation and anxiety. Further fuelled by the space-age ethic of other worlds, alien species, and the threat that technology would soon take over humanity, glam seemed to license pretty much anything, even as it anxiously clung to some strongly traditional notions of masculinity.

Charlie's first glam appearance borrows heavily from its early 1970s space-age iteration: He wears 'silver shoes and a shiny silver jacket. He looked like a spaceman' (35). Channelling Ziggy Stardust, Charlie evokes the futuristic vibe of glam, fusing his preternatural beauty to the space-age aesthetic in a fluid expression of gender identity that is, nonetheless, shored up by the presence of a young woman, as a sort of guarantee of his heterosexuality. Not long after this first appearance, Charlie turns up again in full glam drag, and this time he has become more fully androgynous, pushing the performative possibilities of glam: Charlie

> stood out from the rest of the mob with his silver hair and stacked shoes. He looked less winsome and poetic now; his face was harder, with short hair, the cheekbones more pronounced. It was Bowie's influence, I knew. Bowie, then called David Jones, had attended our school several years before, and there, in a group photograph in the dining hall, was his face. (68)

David Bowie, the consummate performance artist, famous for how rapidly and convincingly he adopted new identities (with each early album, at least), furnishes Charlie with his checklist for success: 'just be yourself' is not on it. On it instead is play, outrage, challenge, a defiant middle-finger offered up to conventional masculinity.

Punk, then. Punk manifests above all as an aggressive rejection of everything that came before it, giving youth culture its first genuinely nihilistic face. It reacts explosively to the growing sense of crisis in 1970s England, opening the sewers to public view. It doesn't detach like prog: Punk performances famously put the performers in direct contact with the audience, as against the arena shows of bands like Pink Floyd, in which the audience may hardly even be able to see the band. Nor does it escape through a utopian *ressentiment* like hippies. Instead, it spits in the face of the contemporary moment, unleashes dissonance as the only fitting soundtrack to a world in which discord has displaced anything like a melody. Harmony belongs to a naive past (which probably never existed anyway, or at least only ever existed on the backs of suffering others), and nihilism affords the only reasonable response to the day's realities. In effect, punk insisted that 1970s Britain was already a culture of nihilism and defeat, so it exposed it, revelled in it and identified with it. As The Sex Pistols paradoxically and menacingly put it, there is both 'no future for you' and 'we're the future, your future'. It's a negation of negation, but in no sense at all dialectical – this is simply nihilation.

FIGURE 3.2 *David Bowie performs live on stage at Earls Court Arena on 12 May 1973 during the Ziggy Stardust tour. (Photo by Gijsbert Hanekroot/Redferns.)*

Stylistically, punk owes a debt to the glam revolution of the early 1970s, to the New York music scene of the first half of the decade, and even to the hard-man traditions of the Teddy boys, rockers, mods and skinheads. But it pays that debt by violently rejecting its precedents, violating traditions – the more sacred the better – playing tunelessly, embracing disgust and filth, rejecting the trappings of stardom, and raging against anything that might even hint at optimism or positivity. It spews vitriol (and spit) at its audiences and vomits with rage at social hypocrisy. Though it was initially conceived by an impresario with a strong interest in the fashion world – Malcolm McLaren, along with Vivienne Westwood – punk made a style out of anti-fashion. Perhaps the first ever bit of English punk fashion is John Lydon's Pink Floyd t-shirt, on which he had scrawled with a marker, 'I hate', transforming the bit of fan ephemera into a snarling challenge. In this vein, punk settled for nihilism as authenticity, embracing negation, anger, disgust, the dark underbelly of Western civilization.

In another vein, though, punk played a key role in re-awakening the political consciousness that had animated some elements of hippie culture, anchoring youth culture in a sense of outrage and protest. As Nehring puts it, 'the punk subculture contained a much more explicit, widespread political consciousness' (316) that, though it looked very different from the tie-dyed psychedelia of the 1960s, nonetheless raged against the same Establishment. Bands such as The Clash exemplify this movement, leading the Rock Against Racism movement and paving the way for the 1980s explosion of political rock with groups such as U2, and the novel phenomenon of benefit concerts giving youth culture a seriously engaged image. 'Besides racism, punk also challenged to some extent the constructions of masculinity and femininity available in rock music' (Nehring 320; cf. 322). This version of punk thus heralded a re-awakening of authenticity in direct response to the mainstreaming of cynicism with the Thatcher government. If Sex-Pistols-style punk essentially articulated Thatcher-esque slogans, paving the way for Thatcher's most famous line of all, 'There is no such thing as society', Clash-style punk activated the music of the oppressed in its use of reggae rhythms to redeem youth culture as the voice of an authentic humanity. The emergence of two-tone bands (i.e. bands with both black and white members) in the 1980s marked this engagement with reggae out as distinctly different from skinhead appropriations, standing up for an authentic alternative to the politics of division and fear that held Westminster from 1979 to 1990.

Ultimately, though, punk's success became anathema to many of its key players, giving it little option but to burn out as quickly as it had flourished. The Sex Pistols even denied the authenticity of their own success, with Johnny Rotten famously asking the audience at the end of their very last set, 'Do you ever get the feeling you've been had?' Punk's origins in the activities of fashion-forward impresario McLaren (who in fact catered to a Teddy boy clientele until just a few months before he formed The Sex Pistols) dogged it with a sense of inauthenticity that was only compounded by the fundamental incompatibility between success-stardom and a truly punk rejection of the entire apparatus of commercial success and popular acceptance. For many true believers even today, punk had a brief intense period of authenticity, followed by a long tail of inauthentic rehashing, re-mixing and appropriation. This is the version of punk we find in *The Buddha of Suburbia*, and especially in the tension between the initial performance where Charlie and Karim see The Sex Pistols on stage and Charlie's long career as a punk frontman.

The initial performance takes place in a small pub in which the legacy of the 1960s persists in the form of 'the usual long-hairs and burned-out heads hanging at the back in velvet trousers or dirty jeans, patchwork boots and sheepskin coats, discussing bus fares to Fez, Barclay James Harvest and bread' (129). Outshining this 'usual clientele' is a small group up front: 'there were about thirty kids in ripped black clothes. And the clothes were full of safety-pins. Their hair was uniformly black, and cut short, seriously short, or if long it was spiky and rigid, sticking up and out and sideways, like a handful of needles, rather than hanging down. A hurricane would not have dislodged those styles. The girls were in rubber and leather and wore skin-tight skirts and holed black stockings, with white face-slap and bright-red lipstick. They snarled and bit people' (129). 'This alien race' presents a form of authenticity Karim and Charlie have not seen before. They are 'dressed with an abandonment and originality we'd never imagined possible' (129). They represent an authenticity that the grit of the city harbours, but which the suburbs cannot cultivate: 'I began to understand what London meant and what class of outrage we had to deal with' (129–130). Charlie and Karim decide that the whole scene is ' "too weird" ' and determine to leave, but before they can 'the band shamble[s] on':

> The fans suddenly started to bounce up and down. As they pumped into the air and threw themselves sideways they screamed and spat at the band until the singer, a skinny little kid with carroty hair, dripped with saliva. He seemed to expect this, and merely abused the audience back, spitting at them, skidding over on to his arse once, and drinking and slouching around the stage as if he were in his living room. His purpose was not to be charismatic; he would be himself in whatever mundane way it took. The little kid wanted to be an anti-star, and I couldn't take my eyes off him. [...] When the shambolic group finally started up, the music was thrashed out. It was more aggressive than anything I'd heard since early Who. This was no peace and love; there were no drum solos or effeminate synthesizers. Not a squeeze of anything 'progressive' or 'experimental' came from these pallid, vicious little council estate kids with hedgehog hair, howling about anarchy and hatred. No song lasted more than three minutes, and after each the carrot-haired kid cursed us to death. (130–131)

The 'carrot-haired kid' is undoubtedly Johnny Rotten. The band is The Sex Pistols. The effect is electrifying. The total rejection of style, of tradition, of social norms, even of bodily limits violently repudiates the inauthenticity of 'progressive' or 'experimental' rock of the sort topping the charts in the mid-decade. Rotten's total inversion of convention – wanting to be an 'anti-star', aiming 'not to be charismatic' – smacks the 'stoned-out' inauthenticity of lingering hippie commitment in the face. It hits Charlie and Karim in precisely these terms: 'Charlie was excited. "That's it, that's it", he said as we strolled. "That's fucking it." His voice was squeaky with rapture. "The sixties have been given notice tonight. Those kids we saw have assassinated all hope. They're the fucking future" ' (131). Charlie uses The Sex Pistols' own line about themselves – 'We're the future, your future' – and McLaren's own aspiration for them – he wanted them to be 'Sexy young assassins' (qtd. in Simpson) – to cement their authenticity. What could possibly be more authentic a response to the dire situation of 1970s England and the failure of hippie peace and love than pure nihilism?

Kureishi immediately introduces a tension, though, between the band's apparent authenticity and Karim and Charlie's situation:

> 'But we can't follow them', I said casually.
> 'Why not?'
> 'Obviously we can't wear rubber and safety-pins and all. What would we look like? Sure, Charlie.'
> 'Why not, Karim? Why not, man?'
> 'It's not us.'
> 'But we've got to change. What are you saying? We shouldn't keep up? That suburban boys like us always know where it's at?'
> 'It would be artificial', I said. 'We're not like them. We don't hate the way they do. We've got no reason to. We're not from the estates. We haven't been through what they have.' (131–132)

Two perspectives emerge. For Karim, authenticity is something you earn by going through hardship; the authenticity they've just seen on stage is *authentic*: It is not simply a style you can adopt. For Charlie, by contrast, the authenticity he witnessed is still just an effect, a stylistic achievement that can be mimicked, perhaps even improved upon. He recognizes the charisma

FIGURE 3.3 *The Sex Pistols in Concert, circa 1975. (Photo by © Hulton-Deutsch Collection/CORBIS/Corbis via Getty Images.)*

of the anti-star in a way that Karim does not, and understands that the impression of not caring on show is precisely the key to success. For Karim, punk authenticity is expressive; it is a function of *who the punks are*, not a performance. For Charlie, the expressive dimension never enters into things; it is all about performance. His repeated exclamation '"That's it, that's it"' marks not an authentic encounter with raw affect and rejection of the high-concept performativity of 'progressive' and 'experimental' music, but a discovery of the next big thing. Karim's insistence that the performance is beyond them forces a break between them – notably characterized by Charlie's sudden hatred of Karim (132) – that launches Charlie on the path to superstardom.

Punk's violently angry rejection of such platitudes of authenticity at last provides Charlie with the recipe for success. Achieving an authenticity-effect through its crackling nihilism, punk vehemently rejects any positive articulation of authenticity. Instead, it defines authenticity through hatred and loathing – of self fully as much as others. The result is intoxicating, tearing down the entire dichotomy of authenticity/inauthenticity itself, rather than embracing one over the other: 'Charlie was excited. "That's it, that's it," he said as we strolled. "That's fucking it." His voice was squeaky with rapture. "The sixties have been given notice tonight. Those kids we saw have assassinated all hope. They're the fucking future"' (131). Popular punk slogans such as 'we are all prostitutes' undermined any claims to the contrary by universalizing the experience of inauthenticity just as MacInnes's Teenager had universalized his experience of authenticity. Of course, such slogans also reserve a space of extra-authenticity for the sloganeer, a meta-stance that precisely captures the meta-static situation of 1970s youth culture. Such a position, both inside and outside the youth culture upon which it wishes to capitalize, is precisely what Charlie's been looking for. His bands have never been very good, musically, but with punk they don't need to be; instead, style can stand in for substance and Charlie's inherent coolness can provide the aesthetic distance necessary to shoot to stardom in a youth-cultural moment where irony is the paramount virtue.

'Charlie's big con trick', as Karim sees it, is to provoke authentic reactions in mainstream adult culture by performing outrage and disgust (154). As against the aura of authenticity conveyed by the band Charlie and Karim see at the bar – real anger, real hatred – Charlie contrives his appearance in a manner more reminiscent of Bowie-glam than guttersnipe filth:

One night, after a rehearsal and drinks with Terry, I came into the flat to find Charlie getting dressed in Eva and Dad's bedroom, prancing in front of a full-length mirror which leaned against the partition wall. At first I didn't recognize him. After all, I'd seen only photographs of his new personality. Hs hair was dyed black now, and it was spiky. He wore, inside out, a slashed T-shirt with a red swastika hand-painted on it. His black trousers were held together by safety-pins, paperclips and needles.

Over this he had a black mackintosh; there were five belts strapped around his waist and a sort of grey linen nappy attached to the back of his trousers. (151–152)

'Prancing' around in front of a mirror to ensure that he has achieved the right effect, Charlie has fully mastered the punk uniform as only someone with ready access to plenty of clothing options can. Again, the point of his dress is not to express an affective state or essential self, but to provoke, to create an authenticity-effect. He hits the mark with the swastika, which Eva begs him to take off: It is the one thing she cannot countenance about his outfit. This is gold for Charlie. Eva's authentic anguish over his appropriation of the symbol of Nazi atrocity is just the ticket, guaranteeing that he will keep it on. In other words, Charlie casts about, prancing in front of a mirror seeking just the right look to convey authenticity, but can ultimately only borrow Eva's genuine disgust at the swastika as evidence that he has found a winning combination. As Karim later puts it, 'Charlie was magnificent in his venom, his manufactured rage, his anger, his defiance. What power he had, what admiration he extorted, what looks there were in girls' eyes. He was brilliant: he'd assembled the right elements. It was a wonderful trick and disguise' (154).

As was largely true of punk itself, Charlie's adoption of the style is almost entirely a trick. It depends upon access to money, a strong aesthetic sense and a capacity for deception to produce the appearance of authenticity. For Karim the effect is nearly complete but for one tell-tale give-away: 'The one flaw, I giggled to myself, was his milky and healthy white teeth, which, to me, betrayed everything else' (154). Charlie's healthy teeth give away his class status and relative prosperity. For contrast, recall that John Lydon became Johnny Rotten at least partly 'because of his green teeth' (Saglam 566). As Karim notes, the punk style Charlie adopts, perfects and helps popularize depends upon having purchasing power in the first place: 'There were also many punks around now, dressed, like Charlie, in ripped black. This was the acme of fashion. as soon as you got your clothes home you had to slash them with razor-blades' (173). The irony is abyssal; in pursuit of an authenticity-effect that sanctions their 'manufactured rage', punks like Charlie actually participate in almost potlach-levels of conspicuous consumption, purchasing clothes precisely so that they can destroy them and wear the resulting rags.

Kureishi seems to be at pains to present Charlie as a pseudo-punk along the lines of Billy Idol. As Saglam notes, Billy Idol attended Kureishi's school just as David Bowie attended Charlie and Karim's (559), though both he and Winkgens oddly insist on identifying Charlie Hero with David Bowie instead (559 and 239, respectively). For my money, the parallel with Billy Idol is far more convincing. First, there is the simple fact that Charlie's punk stage name, 'Charlie Hero', is a thinly veiled repetition of 'Billy Idol. Second, Idol's substitution for Bowie suggests that he is similarly a master of performance, a chameleon who can put on and off personae at will. As Idol's own 'milky and healthy white teeth' illustrate with stark clarity, he is no council-estate ragamuffin, but a sharp performer, much more in the vein of David Bowie than of Johnny Rotten. Third, Idol stands in relation to the pre-eminent figure of punk authenticity, Johnny Rotten, as Charlie stands in relation to the 'carrot-haired kid' he sees on stage in his first encounter with punk in the novel (130). Just as The Sex Pistols explode on the scene in 1976 and are gone by the end of 1977, while Billy Idol's commodified version of punk continues to generate album sales and sold-out arena shows for years after, so the band Charlie and Karim see on stage at the Nashville has only a single appearance, while Charlie goes on to massive international success. By aligning Charlie with Idol, Kureishi slyly undercuts any hint that he discovers an authentic self when he turns to punk. Instead, he suggests that even if authenticity has brief, genuine, resurgence in the mid-1970s, it is almost immediately stifled by lightning-quick appropriation and commodification.

There's one more character to consider here: Karim's younger brother Allie. He is notable precisely for *not* adhering to any youth cultures at all, apparently charting a completely independent path. Interestingly, Allie represents an alternative mode of mature masculinity that is anchored in traditionally homosexual characteristics, but ultimately finds success in the grown-up world of the art, fashion, and design business. Initially presenting as stereotypically gay, Allie regularly reads 'fashion magazines like *Vogue*, *Harper's and Queen*, and anything European he could lay his hands on. In bed he wore a tiny pair of red silk pyjamas, a smoking jacket he got at a jumble sale, and his hair-net. "What's wrong with looking good?" he'd say' (19). Their mother works solely 'to finance Allie, who had decided to become a ballet dancer and had to go to an expensive private school' (19). Later, we hear that he has taken off to Milan with friends to peruse the latest styles (148), before finally appearing back at the family home looking 'pretty zooty' in clothes that are 'Italian and immaculate, daring and colourful without being vulgar, and all expensive and just right: the zips fitted, the seams were straight, and the socks were perfect – you can always tell a dresser by the socks' (267). Auntie Jean clearly suspects Allie is gay, noting that he plucks his eyebrows, dresses a bit too smartly for her taste and changes outfits several times a day (103). I'd be tempted to say that he is a late-blooming mod, were it not for the fact that his style choices seem to be motivated more by a sincere interest in the world of high fashion than in any youth-cultural rebellion.

Interestingly, it's Allie's independence of mind that allows him to achieve what none of the other young men in either novel do: A mature masculinity. Having been far more upset by Haroon's betrayal of their mother than Karim was, Allie ultimately rises to the challenge and charts his own path to independent, strong and successful masculinity. We see this, finally, at the end of the novel, when he takes Karim out to a club:

Allie took me to a new club in Covent Garden designed by a friend of his. How London had moved on in ten months. No hippies or punks: instead, everyone was smartly dressed, and the men had short hair, white shirts and baggy trousers held up by braces. It was like being in a room full of George Orwell lookalikes, except that Orwell would have eschewed earrings. Allie told me they were fashion designers, photographers, graphic artists, shop designers and so on, young and talented. (270)

The fashions here are influenced by the new romantic or new wave styles percolating in the early 1980s, but it's not likely more than influence. The men with earrings, the baggy pants, the suspenders – all are features of mainstream 1980s fashion, even if it is in some ways derived from the youth-cultural avant-garde of the day. Kureishi aligns Allie with sensible English masculinity by invoking Orwell, of all people, and rounds out Allie's heteronormative success by meeting the implicitly gay artsy crowd with his model girlfriend (270). Allie has arrived, and though he is not yet a father, he at least is well-launched in that direction.

So much for thinking *about* youth cultures. How do these novels think *with* them, as they engage with broader contexts? In what follows I'll try to link the youth cultures depicted with the larger issues framing them and informing their presentation. At the same time, of course, I'll also be trying to show how the youth cultures inform and shape how these novels approach those broader contexts. Especially with *The Buddha of Suburbia*, there are numerous other critics who have addressed some of the same issues, though they have not linked them to the specific evolution of youth culture. So, though some of what follows rehearses accepted understandings of the novels, it does so to realign those insights in ways that I hope will be illuminating in the end.

The crisis of authenticity manifest in these novels complicates previous novels' engagement with it, and introduces irony as the hallmark of youth culture. Where novels such as *Saturday Night and Sunday Morning*, *Absolute Beginners* and *A Clockwork Orange* made authenticity the coin of the realm, *The Rachel Papers* relentlessly calls it into question, as even Charles Highway's own ironic stance is itself ironized. *The Buddha of Suburbia* raises the stakes still further, presenting all identity – sexual, class, racial, gender – as fluid, and giving precedence to performativity over authenticity. The product, in both novels, is a paradox wherein ironic performance is itself identified with authenticity. Only by knowingly performing authenticity (thus undermining its status as authentic) can one implicitly lay claim to the sort of authentic ground necessary for irony to function in the first place. Authenticity thus becomes a negative function, something one can only imply by denying its effectiveness in the world.

With the benefit of nearly twenty years' more postmodernism, *The Buddha of Suburbia* presents the problem of authenticity and irony as exacerbated by the presence of race as a key element in the narrative. As Anthony Ilona remarks, 'Karim's generation see identity as a relational and mutable concept. Different identities are easily assimilable, easily performed' (Ilona

101). As numerous critics have noted, for Kureishi no identity category is sacred and performance is all (see, e.g. Stein, Finney, Sukhdev and Allen). Race no more holds the key to authentic identity than do sex, gender, or class. This is easily the most well-trodden critical interpretation of the novel, featuring in the majority of writing about it, though the odd critic still posits authenticity either as a key element of Karim's development (O'Reilly) or as the driving force behind Karim's performative choices (Winkgens 237). The novel begins with a wry statement of this problem, and of its relationship to English national identity:

> My name is Karim Amir, and I am an Englishman born and bred, almost. I am often considered to be a funny kind of Englishman, a new breed as it were, having emerged from two old histories. But I don't care – Englishman I am (though not proud of it), from the South London suburbs and going somewhere. Perhaps it is the odd mixture of continents and blood, of here and there, of belonging and not, that make me restless and easily bored. Or perhaps it was being brought up in the suburbs that did it. (Kureishi 3)

Karim's self-introduction ironizes his status as an Englishman, undercuts the value of being an Englishman, challenges pop-sociological explanations for his restlessness (signalling their implicit racism in the process), and deftly deflates the entire question of identity as simply a function of having grown up in the suburbs. It alerts us to the fact that this is not going to be a novel about a second-generation immigrant finding his roots and rediscovering the authenticity of his ancestors' traditions. But nor is it going to be a novel about how he finally achieves acceptance and belonging amongst the English in a colour-blind utopia. Instead, it introduces race (and thus Britain's imperialist past) only to undermine any claims to authenticity on racial grounds.

As Nathanael O'Reilly reminds us, the suburbs are where many, if not most, youth cultures have their origins, though most readings of race in *The Buddha of Suburbia* fail to connect the two. The problem of the suburbs is not just one of race, nor one of youth culture, but of their intertwining. The discontent and sense of displacement (or unplacement, perhaps) that drives Karim is simultaneously ethnic and generational. His adventures with ethnic authenticity and performativity are informed throughout by his adventures with different youth cultures, different ways of taking up and performing identities in the world. The dramatic shift away from hippie and skinhead authenticity towards the open theatricality of glam and punk helps give shape to Karim's gradual comprehension of race and national belonging as likewise arbitrary and conventional.

Karim's real education in authenticity and its discontents comes through his father's charlatanism. Initially invited 'to speak on one or two aspects of Oriental philosophy' (5) to a group of white suburbanites at Eva's house,

Haroon soon cobbles multiple traditions together into an ersatz form of Eastern mysticism that is only part Hindu (Haroon's own background) and otherwise cribbed from his 'books on Buddhism, Sufism, Confucianism and Zen' (5). Bluntly put, it is phony New Age vapouring. But, for his white audience, it is authenticated by the fact that Haroon is an Indian. His status as an immigrant, his skin colour, and his accent all provide the guarantee that what he teaches is true wisdom. The takeaway for Karim and Charlie, though, is not spiritual enlightenment, but the all-important lesson that actual authenticity does not matter if you can bring off its *effect*. As glam and punk illustrated in the streets, if you can dress, speak and behave authentically you can provoke an experience of authenticity – an *authenticity-effect* – in others. And that is every bit as powerful as actual authenticity would be. Eva announces:

> 'My good and deep friend Haroon here, he will show us the Way. The Path.'
> 'Jesus fucking Christ', I whispered to Charlie, remembering how Dad couldn't even find his way to Beckenham.
> 'Watch, watch closely', murmured Charlie, squatting down.
> [. . .]
> I hissed to Charlie, 'Let's get out of here before we're hypnotized like these idiots!'
> 'Isn't it just fascinating?' (12–13)

All Karim can see is fakery at first, but Charlie understands that what he's seeing is consummate showmanship. Karim recognizes that Haroon is 'going to wing it', while Charlie studies a natural performer, speaking intuitively in the language of his audience and showing them what they have already decided to see. Neither Karim nor Charlie, however, is on the guest-list.

Driving its point home, the novel aligns hippie dreams of authenticity with the parental generation. The young understand that authenticity is now – and may always have been – just an illusion, while Haroon and his clientele increasingly fall for its allure. As he witnesses his own success, Haroon comes more and more to believe that he is the genuine article. He becomes increasingly self-important, speaking with greater and greater authority on how a generalized 'we' in 'our culture' sacrifice happiness out of fear and so forth. It's 1960s pop-psychology mumbo-jumbo in many ways – a soup of the counter-cultural clichés that animated hippie youth culture in the 1960s – but he comes to believe in its authentic truth value. In the end, Haroon finally puts his money where his mouth is, as he's instructed and led others to do before, by quitting his job so that he can 'teach and think and listen' full time (266): '"I want to help others contemplate the deeper wisdom of themselves which is often concealed in the rush of everyday life. I want to live intensely my own life! Good, eh?" "Karim," Haroon announces with finality, "this is the meaning of my life"' (266). Such certainty eludes Karim, as it does an increasing number of young people. He remains just as 'restless and easily bored' as he was on the novel's opening page. When Karim's uncle Ted asks him, '"D'you live an untrue life"', Karim immediately replies, '"Yes"' (265). For him there is no option; to believe that you are living a true life is simply to misrecognize the authenticity-effect for authenticity itself. It is to forget you are acting when all the world's a stage. And for the youth cultures coming into their own in the early 1970s, such a lapse is unforgivable. It means taking yourself seriously, mistaking performance for essence, citation for originality.

Perhaps more to the point, for Karim it would mean being locked into an identity he finds alienating, and which invites aggravation on a daily basis. It would, in brief, mean inauthenticity, a false comportment in the world. For Kureishi, writing nearly twenty years after his novel is set, this insight carries with it the benefit of watching as hippie and skinhead appeals to authenticity gave way to glam's over-the-top performativity, prog-rock's psychedelic divagations and punk's snarling rejection. He works much of this dynamic between authenticity and performativity out in Karim's acting career, where it is focalized through the problematics of race and belonging. These topics bear distinct affinities with the particular direction youth-cultural evolution was taking in the 1970s. Our understanding of both them and the relevant youth cultures will benefit from some mutual enframing. What we'll see emerge is a new element of youth culture: Irony as the only possibility of authenticity.

As we have seen, Karim presents a difficult ground for figuring out what authenticity would even look like, let alone where he could find it. He

1. has a half-Indian background,
2. compounded by Haroon's sudden self-presentation as a yogi,
3. combined with the fact that he is born and bred in the London suburbs,
4. to a mother who herself grew up in Orpington,
5. living in a city where his skin colour itself causes white people to mis-identify him as being of Pakistani descent,
6. and/or to question whether he even speaks English (258) even though
7. he is unable to speak Urdu (81),
8. and is routinely called racial slurs, threatened, and actually assaulted.

If he is indeed a 'funny kind of Englishman', as he says, then he's also in many ways an allegorical figure for the shifting nature of what it means to be *English* at all, as many critics have already pointed out. His very existence poses a challenge to the idea that national or even racial identity is in any way essential rather than relational. Instead, his status varies with the situation, requiring of him different performances in different circumstances.

It's perhaps unsurprising, then, that Karim admits to acting aspirations from the novel's outset. When Haroon marches into the house on the decisive first day of the narrative, strips down to his underwear, assumes a headstand and commands Karim to read to him out of a book on yoga, Karim obliges in a manner that at once recognizes the theatricality of Haroon's new undertaking, thereby ironizes it, and situates himself as someone who is always already on stage, performing: 'I imagined myself to be on the stage of the Old Vic as I declaimed grandly' (5). Irony, authenticity and performativity are all folded into the very fabric of the narrative from its outset.

These tensions are played out most clearly with relation to race, as Karim is first cast to play Mowgli, then humiliated by being forced to wear body paint to darken his skin and adopt a caricatured Indian accent to heighten his performance's authenticity. Having been cast for authenticity, purely based on his skin colour, Karim must still perform an identity to be convincing as Mowgli. Both accent and skin colour have to be affected so they appear to be more authentic, though Karim was cast precisely because he is not an actor but an authentic specimen of the type of person Shadwell imagines Mowgli to have been. These demands come from his white English director, whose racism takes the shape both of imposing such stereotypes and belittling Karim for not speaking either Urdu or Hindi, and for never having visited India (141). Shadwell rubs salt in the wound by suggesting that Karim has failed even the British imperialist project. He claims that Karim would be a disappointment to the 'pioneers from the East India Company' (141) precisely because he does not live up to a preconceived model of Indianness. He does this all on the basis of an essentialist logic of identity formation that can only be described as residual by 1973, and certainly out of step with the exploding youth-cultural challenge to authenticity itself in the 1970s. Shadwell's ignorance brilliantly exposes how the parental culture, here elided with white mainstream British culture, remains committed to an ideology of authenticity that it mis-recognizes as fundamental, enduring, true. It is of a piece with Carl and Marianne's insistence that India is *the* locus of authenticity, as their Maharishi-era Beatles commitment demands of them. The contortions required to produce the authenticity-effect so essential to his play's success themselves speak to the decreasing legitimacy borne by authenticity itself.

Our real interest in this episode derives not so much from how it challenges racialist logic, however, but from its insight into the quandary faced by youth cultures in the 1970s. This insight issues from a shift in perspective. The problem with Karim's performance is not that it presents an inauthentic fantasy of Indianness, as opposed to an authentic version. Rather, it is that there is no authentic original to begin with. The novel is written at the height of post-structuralist critiques of identity and origins, and is clearly influenced by them. The crisis of authenticity it encodes is profound: Taken to its logical extreme, it means the simultaneous collapse of both authentic and inauthentic as two halves of a binary that structures an ideological relationship by *producing* the very effect it claims to express. If there's no authenticity, then there's also no inauthenticity, and the whole paradigm vanishes in a puff of logic. Karim could not have performed his role authentically enough for anyone, since the very role he was assigned is itself inauthentic. It can only strive to produce an authenticity-effect for a particular audience by conforming to that audience's preconceptions. It can, by contrast, shatter the authenticity-effect by refusing to play along.

With the benefit of 1980s theoretical insights behind his representation, Kureishi is able thus to detect youth culture's incredibly savvy solution to this problem. He shows that the only way Karim can lend an aura of authenticity to his performance is by playing it ironically. As he settles into the role, Karim immediately begins ironizing it: 'I started to relax on stage, and to enjoy acting. I sent up the accent and made the audience laugh by suddenly relapsing into cockney at odd times' (158). Later, when he is acting in Pyke's play, Karim will adopt a similar strategy, hamming up his version of Changez on stage to such an extent that one of the other actors objects that he is ruining the play (220). In both cases, though, Karim is a hit. He achieves the height of success by camping up his roles, by playing them for more than they are worth. That is, he achieves success by adopting precisely the same strategy as glam rock and later punk will use: by ironically performing authenticity. For both Karim in particular and youth cultures more broadly in the 1970s, the crisis of authenticity means that the only possibility left for something resembling authenticity is irony. Performance is the name of the game. Authentic authenticity is no longer possible, persisting on the margins of youth culture only as a spectral after-image, an *authenticity-effect* that can be activated from time to time in specific contexts, but makes no commitment to essential identity formations.

For Amis and Kureishi, this challenge to authenticity surfaces powerfully as another stage in the ongoing crisis of masculinity we've already seen elaborated in the work of Burgess, MacInnes and Sillitoe. Critics have approached this problem in Amis's work primarily by noting his consistent misogyny – something we will also do. With Kureishi, though, the focus has relentlessly been on ethnicity and postcoloniality. As Winkgens has noted, only a tiny number of critics have taken note of Kureishi's engagement with the crisis of masculinity (231, 235, 244). Sticking to our guns, we will continue the line of inquiry we've already established with preceding novels. As we will see, the crisis of masculinity in *The Rachel Papers* and *The Buddha of Suburbia* is most fully worked out in terms of the relationships between fathers and sons first, and sex and sexuality second. Generational tensions govern both of these aspects of the crisis of masculinity, as the youthful effort to break with the parental generation is echoed in a deep (but repressed) anxiety over procreation. In their approaches to these problems, Amis and Kureishi register the shifting attitudes among 1970s youth culture, as registered in the promiscuous-but-heteronormative excesses of hippies, promiscuous-and-ambiguous hyper-excesses of glam and the nihilistic-anti-sex ethos of punk (Nehring informs us that Johnny Rotten 'was especially sour on romance and sex' [296]).

The Rachel Papers and *The Buddha of Suburbia*'s take on the crisis of masculinity begins with a normalized challenge to the traditional family structure. Both novels feature fathers who leave their wives for other women, disrupting the stable core of conventional English identity formation: Charles's father keeps an apartment in London in which he pursues his affairs during the week, and Karim's father leaves his wife to move in with Eva, again in a move further into the city. In keeping with their divergent temporalities, *The Rachel Papers* trades on a model of generational conflict still valid in 1973 – that of hippies and skinheads – that sees the conflict in relatively clear terms as a matter of hypocrisy versus honesty. *The Buddha of Suburbia*, from a later historical perspective, presents instead an array of father figures that complicate any such simple understanding of generational tension in these terms. Instead, it fleshes out the ambivalence Charles Highway records in his attitudes towards his father by outlining the impossibility of either understanding fathers as figures of authenticity *or* their rebellious sons as presenting authentic alternatives to their oldster hypocrisy. Together, these novels present the problem of how to progress to mature masculinity precisely in terms of the vanishing binary, authentic/inauthentic. For Amis, the solution is flight and deferral of mature masculinity; for Kureishi, it's displacement, irony and tentative alternatives to the traditional model. In both cases, mature masculinity is understood as a performance without an original, a matter of infinitely regressing citations, and thus a plurality of potential performances.

In *The Rachel Papers*, Charles manifests his anxiety about masculinity in his deep ambivalence about his father's infidelity. Though his parents have apparently arrived at some sort of understanding about Gordon's activities, Charles cannot quite reconcile himself to them. He longs either to break decisively with his father – who is, after all, modelling a promiscuous mature masculinity to which Charles would like to aspire – or to shame him, establishing in either case his moral – or at least aesthetic – superiority. Part of the problem is that Charles's father is performing a model of masculinity that properly belongs to unmarried, experimenting youth: promiscuity. He thus colonizes some of the space of masculinity Charles would like to claim as his own, especially as it is modelled in hippie and glam challenges to conventional morality.

This sense of having been usurped by his father – of having had their roles reversed in some key way – eludes Charles's outright consciousness, though it fuels his vacuous performance of Oedipal rage. The emptiness of his performance is obvious to his schoolmates from the start. They laugh at him for '"actually hating" [his father], who wasn't villainous or despotic, after all, merely dismissible' (11). Unable to articulate a rationale for his hatred, Charles responds to his friends' teasing with an overly intellectual reply that gives the lie to his proclaimed affect:

> You miss the point. Hatred is the only emotionally educated reaction to a sterile family environment. It's a destructive and ... painful emotion, perhaps, but I think I must not deny it if I am to keep my family alive in my imagination and my viscera, if not in my heart.
> Cor, I thought, and so did they. (11)

Charles recognizes that there is a template for how young men should relate to their fathers, and struggles mightily to conform to it. But, he can only justify it in terms of an aesthetic project: Keeping his 'family alive in [his] imagination and [his] viscera'. The ellipses in the phrase 'destructive and ... painful emotion' is a further contrivance of Charles for communicating thoughtful uncertainty whereas the speech is in fact well-rehearsed. Charles feels nothing of what he says he feels. He justifies it only in terms of 'the only emotionally educated reaction' possible. That is, he views it as formally necessary, even if the content it tries to convey is absent. His self-congratulation at the end thoroughly marks this outburst as a performance. It's a staged justification for an affective posture that is otherwise motivated only by generic expectations: A teenaged male is just expected to hate his father.

Charles never manages to bring his perspective to a full and open articulation, and accidentally exposes his stance as one of repressed self-critique. It's a mode of self-critique that extends to the youth-cultural shift taking place in the early 1970s, introducing irony as a permanent mode of being in the world. He views himself as possessed of the truth: The total absence of substance, and the supremacy of performance as the only intelligent way to navigate the path to maturity. As such, Charles scorns his father's simpler mode of mature masculinity. In the very midst of his own morally questionable activities, Charles snipes at his father who, in fact, has a very clear sense of his own values and their effects on his family. In this respect, Charles utterly fails to break decisively with his father, and his criticisms only become legible if we understand them as a displaced form of self-critique. That is, Charles is equally as guilty, if not more so, of the very things he charges his father with. The self-reflexivity of early 1970s youth culture presents here as a time-warped mode of critique. The much-ballyhooed letter to his father that Charles works on throughout the narrative (but whose content he conceals) is really a letter to himself. It configures conventional generational tension in an ironic mode wherein the author of the letter is its most immediate, obvious, and vulnerable target. It affords a view of youth consciousness in 1973 as at once idealistic, disappointed in itself, and ironically aware of its own failure to live up to its ideals:

> This may be bluffing, but I think that one of the dowdiest things about being young is the vague pressure you feel to be constantly subversive, to sneer at oldster evasions, to shun compromise, to seek the hard way out, etc., when really you know that idealism is worse than useless without example, and that you're no better. The teenager can normally detach his own behavior from his views on the behavior of others; but I had no moral energy left. (216)

Charles at last lacks the moral energy to detach himself from the ironic truth of his own – and a widely shared – conception of what youth culture should look like and how it should relate to the parent culture. The dual consciousness so essential to remaining an uncompromising teenager, to believing in authenticity for oneself not only at the expense of but as a function of 'oldster' inauthenticity, collapses into an ironic attitude. It's not so much a case of the old eating the young as the young eating their youth, in a sense. Maintaining a sense of authenticity and promise has become work, work that is no longer sustainable for Charles. His lack of sufficient 'moral energy' to continue that work ultimately confounds his sense of decisive difference from his father, and presents a symptom of youth culture on the brink of collapse.

If Charles's relationship with his father is troubled by a self-contradictory fantasy, Rachel takes things one step further, by replacing her absent father – we never do learn what has become of him – with a fantasy of a hostile, philandering parent any self-respecting teenager can really get behind. She tells Charles initially that her father had been ' "such a bastard" ' to her mother, that he lives in Paris with his mistress, and that he still calls her ' "when he's drunk and shouts at" ' her (71). Not only does Rachel outstrip Charles by furnishing exactly the kind of parent the teenage stereotype circa 1973 requires, she also outdoes him in sass, telling him that her father ' "rang last week, actually. Wanted to know whether I was on the pill or not, can you believe. I said, 'Look, mate, if I get pregnant I won't come running to you!' That shut him up" ' (71). Rachel beats Charles at his own game here, fabricating a scenario that illustrates a decisive generational gap between the father and the child, introduces the cutting-edge youth-cultural phenomenon of the birth-control pill, and sets the stage for thinking about youth in terms of its eventual adult state. The use of 'mate' in her dialogue puts her on equal footing with her imaginary father, as does her claim to have shut him up with her unanswerable put-down.

Of course, Rachel has made it all up. In one of their very last conversations, she admits to Charles, ' "You know all the things I've told you about my father. All lies. I've never seen him or spoken to him or heard from him in my life" ' (202). The next lines crucially reveal precisely the shifting ground of authenticity and identity in youth culture I've been tracing throughout *The Rachel Papers* and *The Buddha of Suburbia*. Charles suggests that perhaps Rachel has fabricated this fantasy because it makes her feel

'"What? More ... substantial? More ... *definite* about yourself?"' (203). That is, he immediately concludes that she has concocted the fantasy in order to produce an authenticity-effect, to consolidate her identity. He's wrong, though: '"Suppose so,"' Rachel answers, then, '"No. It's not that. It just makes me feel less pathetic"' (203). Rachel's rationale is not that of the traditional generational divide, but that of the young person without precedent, the child without a father. So strong is the cultural mythos of the teenager rebelling against his or her father that Rachel feels unmoored without it, a figure of pathos in need of bolstering. Tellingly, the fantasy she weaves is not that of the idealized father figure who has gone away to lead a life of daring philanthropy or achievement, as is often the case among children who lose a parent. Instead, it is a fantasy of generational discord that desperately tries to reinstate the conventional tension that had so comfortably served in the previous decades, but is increasingly losing its purchase. As the graduates of previous youth cultures get older – but don't necessarily grow up – they unsettle the template for youth-cultural rebellion they themselves helped create. The result is some impressive improvisation. Just as Charles discovers a deep ambivalence in his attitude towards his father, so Rachel likewise produces an ambivalent situation in which the generically conventional conflict can only be produced through fantasy.

If things just ended there, we would already have sufficient cause to read *The Rachel Papers* as engaging a new stage in the post-war crisis of masculinity, but we would miss a fundamental piece of the puzzle: *The babies.* Yes, babies, in the plural. Jenny's and Rachel's. Jenny, of course, has a confirmed pregnancy. It is the source of much of the tension in her relationship with Norm. In that case, after asserting his masculine privilege, the allegorically named Norm gives way and grudgingly accepts his new family situation because, as he so eloquently puts it after detailing all the ways having a child will make Jenny's body less sexually desirable, '"I don't fuck her that much now"' anyway (207). It's not exactly a utopian vision of mature masculinity at ease with itself, and it portends a future of infidelity that itself promises to repeat damaging conventions of masculinity. But, at the very least, Norm accepts responsibility – he admits it is his child – and seems determined (resigned?) to supporting it. I won't get too optimistic and suggest that he'll become a model father, but he will at least temporarily accept the role, right?

In Rachel's case, the baby is unconfirmed, but still likely. The last time Charles has sex with Rachel, the condom breaks. Rather than tell her, Charles keeps this alarming fact to himself, in part to cover up for his cheating with Gloria. Even he realizes that he must tell Rachel the truth, though, and prepares to do so at their last meeting. And here's where things go sideways. Call it a return of the repressed – or, better still, a repression of the return. At the last minute, Charles decides *not* to tell Rachel about the broken condom, after she confesses that she has made up the story of her abusive father. The sequence is important, since Rachel's confession ironically gives

Charles the sense that he, too, can lie – and specifically about paternity. It marks a moment when the crisis of masculinity comes to a head, when the young man supposedly making his steady way into adulthood can veer away, back into irresponsible adolescence. The example of Norm fails to have any effect, Norm otherwise having been degraded in Charles's eyes by his class status and boorish behaviour, not to mention his violence towards Jenny. The example of his father is little better, presenting only the illusion of a responsible family man, when the reality is adulterous irresponsibility. Balking at the prospect of having to walk the talk, as it were, Charles instead lamely confesses to Rachel that he's decided not to go to Oxford after all. As confessions go, this one is a real yawner that leaves a huge issue unbroached. Making matters worse, Charles's next communication with Rachel is his break-up letter. When she comes to see him he *still* holds his peace on the subject of her possibly being pregnant, apparently even having forgotten himself. In doing so, Charles may have created for Rachel's child exactly the situation in which she grew up: with an absent father. The logic of generational conflict we've seen worked out so far thus takes a new twist. Tensions between fathers and sons become all the more complex, as sons in many cases become fathers themselves either before they have established the conventional conflict and distance from their own fathers or in lieu of doing so at all. By and large, they remove themselves from the concrete, living, evidence of their successful performance of masculinity, taking its crisis into a new stage of development.

The Buddha of Suburbia tries to navigate these tricky waters by furnishing a number of different fathers, struggling at times, even with the benefit of an additional decade and a half of hindsight. In the cases of Charlie's absent father, Jamila's relationship with Anwar and Karim's relationship with Haroon, Kureishi plays around the margins of various models of generational conflict and how they can shape youth-cultural responses. Taken together, they illustrate a complicated engagement with the crisis of authentic masculinity typical of 1970s youth culture.

Charlie's father appears to have been absent Charlie's whole life, and never appears in the novel. He's only even mentioned twice, first on the night of Haroon's first session at Eva's house, when we learn that he is having a nervous breakdown '"in a kind of therapy centre where they allow it all to happen"' (11), and again when Karim is trying to antagonize Charlie by asking him how is father is doing in front of a crowd of their peers (69). In this generational narrative, the father is broken and absent. He doesn't even provide the excuse for a fantasy of conflict, as Charles's father does for him. Instead, he leaves the field of mature masculinity relatively undefined, leading Charlie to look to popular culture for his models. Winkgens argues that Charlie's father's mental collapse has to do with Eva's overpowering personality and the challenges it poses to his masculinity. If this is so, then the situation is all the more dire, since the model Charlie has before him is of a mature masculinity that finds strong women insanity-inducing.

Eva the Amazon (she even has only one breast) functions in this role as a castrating menace whose suffocating love for her son likewise threatens to keep him from becoming a man – whatever that might mean. As with Charles in *The Rachel Papers*, the result is a confused generational and sexual dynamic. Where Charles found that his father behaved more like the young rake than Charles himself could, Charlie finds himself locked into the quasi-erotic love object of his own mother: 'from the start Eva had insisted he was talent itself, that he was beautiful and God had blown into his cock. He was Orson Welles – at least. Naturally, long knowledge of this divinity now pervaded his personality. He was proud, dismissive, elusive and selectively generous' (118). Charlie plays out no Oedipal drama because there is no father to kill; he already occupies pride of place with his mother. He is accorded the authority and freedom of mature masculinity without ever having earned it, and without having aligned himself with any particular model. It's not an accident that he's consistently depicted as feminine – fragile, delicate and beautiful – rather than rugged, strong and handsome. He represents something new in our experience so far: A masculinity completely unmoored from traditional expectations and free to find itself in successive performances.

In this, Charlie represents a near-total triumph of style over substance, presenting an ideal of cool to which Karim can only aspire: 'an attitude or personality type that [... combines] three core personality traits, namely narcissism, ironic detachment and hedonism' (Pountain and Robins 26). He is defined by his ambition, seeking success as the ultimate reward and recognizing that creating an authenticity-effect is key to achieving it. Unlike Haroon, who charts a path to authenticity and adheres to it from beginning to end, Charlie quickly morphs through various styles as they come into and out of fashion, adopting identities the way Charles Highway adopts accents. The generational disparity here, between the authenticity-prone Haroon and the performance-junkie Charlie, speaks volumes about the shift taking place in 1970s youth culture. This shift is down not only to the traditional opposition between youth culture and the parent generation, but between a self-aware youth culture bucking a parent generation that itself still subscribes to the shibboleths of its prior youth-cultural heyday.

In stark contrast to Charlie, we have Jamila, whose father Anwar represents a throwback to absolute patriarchal authority. He both speaks to traditional English family structures and ironizes them by situating their truth in the figure of the immigrant. It's a neat bit of displacement, allowing Kureishi to play out the generational tension between the parental culture and emerging youth culture in something of a time-warp, reactivating 1950s (or earlier) paternal authority in the figure of Anwar even as he puts him into conflict with his very 1970s women's liberation social justice activist daughter Jamila. Jamila is by turns a hippie, social activist and spiritual punk, accepting no pre-existing model of gender relationships, let alone of masculinity, femininity, or sexuality. If combat rock has a female standard-bearer, Jamila is she. The resulting time-lapse between Anwar's outré masculinity and Jamila's avant-garde rejection of it presents a stark contrast to every other child–father relationship we have seen.

When Anwar forces an arranged marriage upon Jamila, Kureishi names the lucky fiancé Changez, giving him a withered arm, and making him effectively useless as a son-in-law. His name clearly indicates that he is a force of change, his arm indicates the misshapen dimension of Anwar's traditional beliefs, and his uselessness – along with Jamila's total rejection of him as a husband – illustrates that the line of traditional patriarchal authority, not to mention the family name, is conclusively over. Adding insult to injury, Changez has no intention of assuming the proper role of the son-in-law, preferring instead to indulge in fantasies of masculinity by reading endless hard-boiled detective novels, with occasional breaks for the sexual adventures depicted in works by the likes of Harold Robbins. Though Changez has no youth-cultural affiliation to speak of, he participates in the widespread crisis of masculinity and authenticity being articulated by the succession of hippie, glam, prog and punk cultures. He actively repudiates the model of masculinity set for him by Anwar and, though he would prefer to have sex with Jamila, is completely unprepared and unwilling even to try to play the authoritarian domestic-rapist husband to her. His masculinity will find other outlets, and in the end furnish the only genuine alternative we will see in all the works under consideration here.

Even though Jamila ultimately concedes victory to Anwar by agreeing to marry Changez, the narrative nonetheless awards the final point to Jamila by way of irony. Anwar wins, and in winning he loses: He gets a useless son-in-law, he loses his daughter's affection and he alienates his wife. There *will* be a grandchild, it is true, but not the way he would have preferred (more about this soon). That Anwar represents an outmoded and frankly grotesque model of masculinity is illustrated most clearly in the manner of his death. Denied sex by Jamila, Changez has taken on a regular prostitute as his sexual outlet, and they are returning from the sex shop when Anwar, outraged by everything Changez represents, attacks. Changez extracts a large pink dildo from his bag and wallops Anwar over the head with it. The blow itself does not kill Anwar, but he subsequently dies of a heart attack. A large. Pink. Dildo. The size articulates both a cartoon masculinity and typical masculine anxiety about penis size. The colour marks it out as racially white. The fact that it's a dildo aligns it with performativity and fakeness.

Lastly, we have Karim's relationship with Haroon, which turns on a shifting ground of performance and authenticity. It reveals the extent to which *The Buddha of Suburbia* sees claims to authenticity as the real problem for masculinity: Masculinity can only be in crisis where a notion of authenticity undergirds it. Karim loves his father, admires him and simultaneously considers him a thoughtless charlatan. This belief provides the key to their harmonious relationship: Haroon provides a template for masculinity and authenticity that itself is pure performance. Karim's sense of irony is so finely wrought that it is actually impossible for him to imagine Haroon as a guide to authentic experience. He sees his father's self-reinvention as a parallel to Charlie's rapid style changes, both of them articulating shifting and ephemeral models of masculinity. Perhaps because he is so temperamentally given to performance from the beginning, Karim sees Haroon's separation from his mother as revitalizing, and uses the newfound liberty to chart his own path. His break-up of the family home makes possible Karim's own exploration of an acting career, sexual experimentation and freedom to move around the city. In this respect, Karim has little to resent, and nothing against which to rebel.

The irony in this relatively – and atypically – harmonious relationship emerges as Haroon gradually comes to believe in his own authenticity. Where Karim sees only performance, opportunity (and opportunism) and fluid identity, Haroon increasingly sees a quest for inner truth, essential identity and lasting wisdom. It's a Mobius strip of masculinity in which the father's path is turned inside out by the son, ironized through over-adherence into its opposite. There is no direct break, no final confrontation, but rather an eversion in which Karim finally gently allows Haroon his illusion while he himself faces a much bleaker reality:

'I want to live intensely my own life! Good, eh?'
'It's the best thing I've heard you say', I said gently.

There is compassion here, but not the compassion of a guru for his devotee so much as the compassion of the nihilist for the true believer for whom the truth would be, as Conrad once had it, 'too dark altogether' (162). Centred by a rediscovered sense of his authentic manhood, Haroon will continue to live 'authentically'. Karim, on the other hand, will spend considerable time with Charlie, witnessing both the fragility of various performances and the increasingly desperate quest by which Charlie seeks stability in limit experiences.

One crucial difference between *The Buddha of Suburbia* and all the other novels we are discussing here is that this one features a baby who lives – and presents a provocative alternative mode of masculinity in the process. It does not reassert a traditional or stable mode of masculinity in the process, but presents a novel take on the performative aspects of masculinity instead. The child in question, Leila Kollontai, is Jamila's child by her boyfriend Simon. Simon does not stick around to be a father to the child, though, preferring the route of abandonment Charles Highway possibly chooses in *The Rachel Papers*, and Brenton Brown will certainly choose in *Brixton Rock*. But Kureishi is not concerned with Simon so much as with Changez. Having already compartmentalized the traditional facets of masculinity by segregating his marital love for Jamila from his sexual life with Shinko, Changez finds an outlet for his paternal affection in Leila. He eschews any delineation of masculine and feminine roles, and simply functions as her primary caregiver. In this, he goes one better than the gender-bending extravagance of glitter, without adopting the nihilism of punk. He presents a new model of masculinity which is performative in the extreme, shifting its manifestations according to circumstance and anchoring itself in selfless devotion to another. That Leila is not Changez's biological child is key here, since his devotion obviates any charge of genetic selfishness or patrilineality. He neither asserts, nor performs, nor ironizes masculinity, but places it out of consideration altogether. By the same token, he explodes the tension between authenticity and performance per se: If there is no question any longer of performance, then there is likewise no question of authenticity. There is only affiliation and a deep ethic of care. In Changez, then, Kureishi proffers a utopian alternative to the crisis of masculinity struggling its way through the post-war decades. Unfortunately, it remains in the realm of utopian possibility, presenting something like abjection as the only way out of the quandary facing so many young hippies, glitter rockers and punks. Not everyone is as liberated as Changez, and the problem of masculinity remains capable of producing some truly regressive instances of the quest for authenticity.

And now for the part you've all been waiting for: Sex! Always central to the youth-cultural experience, sex and sexuality come in for radically direct handling in these two novels. The open attitude towards sex fronted by the hippies assumes new dimensions of fluidity in glam and punk as the 1970s progress. The novels capture this fluidity at the same time as they chart how it is held in tension with the dynamics of power, authenticity, and performance that undergird the crisis in masculinity. As we might expect, though, the seventeen years between *The Rachel Papers'* 1973 publication and *The Buddha of Suburbia*'s 1990 publication yields a profound difference of perspective. Where *The Rachel Papers* presents a decidedly laddish understanding of sex and sexuality, *The Buddha of Suburbia* benefits from a decade and a half of theoretical work in the area to articulate a more fluid and nuanced understanding. Where *The Rachel Papers* pays lip-service to queerness and women's sexuality, thanks in large part to the recent advent of the Pill, *The Buddha of Suburbia*'s main character Karim is confirmedly bisexual and moves with relative ease through a world of sexual freedom. Both novels mobilize the 1960s legacy of free love and clearly take the revolution in reproductive health brought about by the Pill as preconditions for their treatments, though they also continue the legacy of casual misogyny and sexualized violence that often underwrote the sexual revolution. One result is a real uncertainty about whether sexual exploration really can bring us closer to authenticity. Another is the even darker possibility that sexual violence quite simply *is* the real locus of authenticity – a conclusion that upends the entire discourse of 1970s youth culture by changing the question at hand. At issue is no longer simply whether authenticity is possible, but whether it is ultimately desirable at all.

The Rachel Papers offers up an ostensibly free view of sex and sexuality that is in fact deeply heteronormative and laddish. Any sexual freedom in the novel is restricted to heterosexual promiscuity and a casual attitude towards hygiene. Charles has sex with a number of young women in the course of the narrative, though it is all rather banal and highly conventional. The adventurous part comes in with regard to things like the actual physical dirt of the bodies in question, as when Charles recounts looking down

> at the undulating area between my stomach and the stomach of a girl I just so happened to be poking at the time (in a sweaty, hungover state, I might add). What I saw there were worms of dirt – as when a working man, his day done, strides home rubbing his toil-hardened hands together, causing the excess grit to wriggle up into tiny black strings, which he soon brushes impatiently from his palms. Only these were on our stomachs and therefore much bigger: like baby eels. (17)

Even the effort to align this filth with authentic honest hard work fails, and Charles becomes squeamish enough at the sight that he is 'back in Oxford for lunch that same day' (17). Alternatively, Charles's sexual experimentation extends to the grotesque bedroom farce of ushering one girl out the door just in time to admit a different one to his room, and as a consequence having to re-use a condom (200). The result is not so much a vision of sex as the locus of authenticity for Charles as a vision of sex as a compulsion, a competitive event in which he excels even when the going is tough – marked by his apparent ease in delivering multiple orgasms to his various lovers – and his laddish commitment to pulling as many women as possible, even in the midst of his supposed love affair with Rachel. Even his sex with Rachel is perfunctory, mechanical, choreographed, and though it results in orgasms all around, finally unsatisfying. It certainly does not bring Charles anywhere near epiphany. Amis's over-coding of sex and sexuality with inauthenticity perhaps peaks in Charles's openly fraudulent claim that he 'was queer, too, once upon a time' (29). The prospect of a non-heteronormative sexuality appears only briefly here, though, only to be exposed as a typical instance of Charles comprehending everything through stereotypes. Having read, 'in a doped half-state, [...] a Chunky Paperback on Sigmund Freud' and considered such evidence as a single homoerotic encounter in school, the fact that he sang soprano, remained a virgin and masturbated less than his friends said they did, Charles concludes that he is a homosexual. He reads through 'the collected works of Oscar Wilde, Gerard Manley Hopkins, A. E. Housman, and (for what little it was worth) E. M. Forster' in preparation for a highly conventional undergraduate career of homosexuality (30). As soon as he turns away from the clichéd and stereotypical, though, and actually tests his sexuality by leafing through a muscle magazine 'waiting equably for an erection', Charles discovers that he is not in fact queer at all: 'Never felt less sexy in my life' (31). No, if authenticity resides in sexuality in *The*

Rachel Papers, it resides someplace other than Charles's banal explorations. It resides, in fact, in his misogyny and the fantasies it produces – and it is not pretty.

A partial catalogue of Charles's misogynist views should be sufficient to establish that his perspective is one of profound disgust for all but the most nubile, young bodies. Of his own sister, Charles notes that 'In particular, her hair was long, shiny, and quite thick for a Highway; and, remarkably, even though she was mousy-blonde, big-boned, full-breasted, wide-hipped and generally slightly sallow, there was no reason to believe that with her clothes off she would smell of boiled eggs and dead babies' (19). This last comment is even more ghoulish in retrospect, given how close Jennifer comes to having an abortion at her husband Norman's insistence. Of middle-aged women in general, Charles invites his readers' corroboration that they are unfuckable: 'Take a look at the scaly witches round your local shopping centre, many of them with children. Grim enough with their clothes on. Imagine them naked! Snatches that yo-yo between their knees, breasts so flaccid you could tie them in a knot. One would have to be literally galvanized on Spanish Fly even to consider it. Yet it gets done somehow. Look at the kids' (22). The woman who does the intake for the tutor's where Charles will prepare for his Oxford entrance exam earns his vicious insults for no apparent reason other than her looks: '"Yes" (you stupid bitch, you dull clit) [...] She was most unpleasant to look at. I won't go into it, but she was about thirty-five, had eye-brows as big as teddy-boy quiffs, and her teeth bucked out from her gums at right-angles' (26). Part of this revulsion comes down to a generational cluelessness, according to which only youth equates to sexual promise and desirability, a perspective that literalizes the notion that sexiness is only skin deep and thus inherently ephemeral and inauthentic. But it clearly goes beyond simple generational tension to a much deeper sense of masculinity – a particular form of masculinity – as authentic. Even girls of his own age come in for insults. Any girl left unattached at the end of Rachel's party he presumes must be 'pretty seriously deformed' (37) if she's been left on the shelf, and even one of his memories of sex involves a girl whom he considered 'quite hideous, [who] had smelled of unclothed open wounds and graveyards, etc.' (45). The 'etc.' concluding the sentence is telling: For Charles, the continuing list of unpleasant associations with women's bodies is so conventional and predictable as not to need completion – the reader knows anyway, and can fill it in for himself (yes, *him*self). At stake here is a presumptive model of masculinity that is fraternal – Charles assumes that his presumably male audience will 'get it' – and profoundly anxious. The tensions around achieving a viable mature masculinity that is neither a performance nor emasculating that we have seen over and over since the end of the war are clearly animating Charles's own conflicted, aggressive, formulations.

Notably, Charles's only models of mature masculinity at this point include his father, who is having an affair with a much younger woman, apparently having arrived at the same conclusions about his mother's sexual desirability as Charles himself has:

> What a heap. The skin had shrunken over her skull, to accentuate her jaw and to provide commodious cellarage for the gloomy pools that were her eyes; her breasts had long forsaken their native home and now flanked her navel; and her buttocks, when she wore stretch-slacks, would dance behind her knees like punch-balls. The gnomic literature she was reading empowered her to give up on her appearance. Off came her hair, on came the butch jeans and fisherman's jerseys. In her gardening clothes she resembled a slightly effeminate, though perfectly lusty, farm labourer. (13)

The other option is Norman, whose depth of character is revealed most tellingly in the fact that he wants Jennifer to abort her pregnancy not out of any concern for her well-being, but because having a traditional vaginal birth will ruin her sexual functioning (for him):

> 'Their cunts', he flicked off the heater, 'turn to mush. Tits' – we pulled away – '*smell of bad milk. And they hang. Pancake tits.*'
>   '*Really?*'
>   '*Yur. Jungle tits.*' (207)

Clearly not a man of great sensitivity and complexity, Norman presents not only here but throughout the novel as a deeply frustrated and angry person. He beats Jenny, drives recklessly and drinks to great excess. He is, in a telling word, a *lad*: An arrested adolescent who has managed to divorce the process of getting older from that of growing up. In the absence of a viable model of mature masculinity, Norman has opted simply to avoid becoming a man in any responsible sense, preserving instead his youthfulness through a pattern of self-indulgence and violence. Amis's insight on this is critical, as it points to how important the post-war crisis of masculinity is for understanding youth-cultures. If authenticity is on the ropes in the 1970s, and the very category of 'man' to which all young male Britons are inevitably moving is further in crisis, then only two options seem to present themselves. Either the category must be reimagined as purely performative (as glam, and especially David Bowie, illustrated) in terms that break decisively with both long tradition and any sense of gender essentialism, or it must be reaffirmed in unambiguous terms through violent domination of the other: Women.

I argue that if authenticity exists anywhere in *The Rachel Papers*, it does so, depressingly, in two key moments where Charles lets his persona slip and exposes both his own, Amis's and a significantly wider youth-cultural anxiety about masculinity. The first of these moments occurs at Charles's family's country house. Charles and Rachel are meant to spend the weekend with his family, but on the first night Charles's rival for Rachel's affections, DeForest Whittaker (an American, significantly), melodramatically arrives in a lather, crying and begging Rachel to return to London with him. She goes, leaving Charles on his own. The next morning, as he idly watches television, Charles quite suddenly divulges a disturbing fantasy:

> I was about to turn over when a pea-headed American gravely announced that what we were about to see was the women's semi-finals.
>
> Now I greatly revered women tennis players. When they came on the court, smiling in trim uniforms, they seemed plain, remote persons: yet, after an hour of sweat and malice ... A couple of years back, there had been a particularly simian little number: squat torso, arms like legs, and a face as contorted and spiteful as you could possibly wish. She had obsessed me all through the Wimbledon fortnight. Not an afternoon passed without me thinking how much I'd like to corner her after an eighty-game, four-hour final (which she had lost), wrench off – or aside – her porky pants, bear down on her in the steamed-up dressing-room, or, better, much better, in some nicotine-mantled puddle, and grind myself empty to her screams. (134)

The American announcer corresponds to the American DeForest, leaving us with little option but to consider the tennis player as a version of Rachel. The fantasy is disturbing for its violence, yes, but also for its insistence upon degradation. The tennis player is 'simian' and must be fucked after she has 'lost' a long match. Charles plans to 'corner' her and attack her, presenting a near-psychotic indifference 'to her screams' as he not only rapes her but also possibly impregnates her. Of critical importance here is how the fantasy gets away from Charles. For someone who has his every thought pre-scripted, and who indulges in self-reflection at the slightest provocation, Charles seems not to be in control of his own stream of consciousness here. This lack of control manifests in his on-the-fly revision – 'or, better, much better' – wherein he adjusts the details of a fantasy he has supposedly had many times before in the process of relating it to us. My sense is that this slip betrays the revelatory nature of the passage. Like a dream narrative, it both displaces and overtly articulates an unconscious truth – an authentic truth – that is otherwise inadmissible to consciousness. That truth is that every aspect of Charles's relationship with Rachel is inauthentic, masking and keeping at bay the barely contained violence she provokes in her direct challenge to his anxious masculinity.

Conclusive evidence for this reading appears in the next of Charles's violent sexual fantasies. At the tail-end of what appears on the surface to have been a deliriously enjoyable two weeks' cohabitation, marked by regular, easy and gratifying sex – that is, a perfect youthful fantasy of adulthood – Charles suddenly articulates a profoundly unsettling plan for the rest of the evening:

I'm fucked (I thought) if I'm going to tool into that bedroom tonight, bung on one of those feelthy heedeous condoms, and complete the hushed, devout routine. I was being at least fifty-per-cent sincere when, prior to The Pull, I said that enthusiasm and affection were enough, that French tricks were unimportant. But then again, then again ... No. Tonight, my lad, *you* are going to get laid. Selfishly. You're going to get gobbled for a kick-off. You gonna bugger her good. You gonna rip out her hair in fistfuls, fuck her like a javelin hurled across the ice, zoom through the air, screaming. Then, whether she wants to or not, and especially if she does not want to, she is going to ... let me see. (184)

Where to begin? The passage starts off with Charles's characteristic self-awareness, providing the parenthetical information that 'I'm fucked' is merely something he 'thought', but it quickly degenerates into a linguistically strange and violent fantasy that, I suggest, has important parallels with the tennis player fantasy and likewise inadvertently reveals more than it intends to. The reference to the 'feelthy heedeous condoms' invokes a distinctively non-English dialect (perhaps a caricature of a French, Hispanic or Russian accent), linking back to the racist characterization of the tennis player as 'a particularly simian little number'. The increasing break-down of the grammar and pronunciation here likewise signals an alignment of this aggressive masculinity in a series of racist stereotypes where machismo seems to correlate with the use of unspecified idiolects: 'you gonna ... you gonna.' At the same time, the passage is clearly inflected with Charles's consciousness in its elaborate similes – 'like a javelin hurled across the ice' – and its occasional return to fully articulated phrasing: 'and especially if she does not want to' versus a possible 'expeshully if she don't wanna'. The passage reveals, I argue, a masculinity in crisis, one that conflates sexual gratification with violent domination, forced oral sex with ripping out 'hair in fistfuls', sexual intercourse with aerial attack. Again, the tip-off that this is not a prepared speech or a carefully cultivated thought is that it lapses into indeterminacy. Just as the tennis player fantasy gave way to revision in its final phrase, so this fantasy peters out into uncertainty: 'she is going to ... let me see' All we can be sure of here is that whatever Charles comes up with next will take cruelty as its key feature – she'll do it *especially* if she doesn't want to.

Such moments provide exceedingly rare glimpses into the only locus of authenticity in *The Rachel Papers*. They chart a profound crisis of masculinity in terms that are so extreme that they break the mimetic contract. Even Norman's beating of Jenny, which is shocking in its own right, fails to achieve the level of shock captured in these two fantasies, fitting much more comfortably into Charles's wryly humorous presentation: 'Perhaps- yawn- she just meant that he was "murdering" her love for him. The sound of what could have been a forearm slam came from above, then a muffled crash, as of a body making speedy contact with the floor. I blew my nose on some lavatory paper and thought hard about Rachel' (57). The contrast between this actual incident of domestic violence, to which Charles remains almost completely indifferent and the intensity of the fantasies he constructs invites us to consider them as indicating a deeper perspective on what is perhaps the paramount struggle of post-war youth culture: How to achieve mature masculinity in the absence of so many previously viable contexts, guidelines and norms. It indicates a deep sense of frustration with the failure of previous youth cultures – teds, mods, rockers, hippies, skinheads – to present useful alternatives. In response, it articulates a proto-nihilistic vision of youth culture as an endless series of performances, only occasionally punctuated by eruptions of angry sexualized violence. It's at best an ugly authenticity that survives.

The Buddha of Suburbia presents a significantly more catholic view of sex and sexuality than The Rachel Papers, though it remains allied to a fundamental crisis of masculinity, and an overwhelming sense that authenticity is simply not in the cards. This translates into a view of youth-cultural identity exploration and formation in a truly postmodern key, where performance and performativity are given pride of place. As John Clement Ball puts it, 'In this collapsed "world" in downtown London – a world of parody, pastiche, simultaneity, and simulacrum – they are no more authentically Indian in their roles than Charlie is authentically punk or Eva authentically artsy. But when the image takes over from the actual, when notions of authenticity and inauthenticity fall by the wayside (Jameson 62), the artificiality may not matter' (23; see also Finney). In Foucauldian terms, bodies and pleasures take priority over identities. Nonetheless, sexual violence still persists, primarily as a form of masculine assertion (importantly configured along generational lines) and sexual exploration still holds down a spot as a possible avenue to authentic self-discovery.

The sex in The Buddha of Suburbia is famously fluid and experimental. When they visit Matthew and Marlene Pyke at their home for some casual multi-player sex, Eleanor tells Karim ' "whatever happens, we mustn't deny each other experience" ' (198), making sexual liberty an ethical imperative that seems to be embraced almost universally in the book. The couplings on offer here include the homosexual (Karim and Charlie, Karim and Matthew, Jamila and Joanna), commercial (Changez and Shinko, Charlie and Frankie) and heterosexual (Haroon and Eva, Marlene and Karim, Karim and Eleanor, Karim and Helen, Karim and Jamila). There's committed relationship sex, friends-with-benefits sex, paid sex with prostitutes, casual one-off sex, and, yes, violent sex as well. People pay for sex, use it to control one another, use it to relieve stress and use it to compensate for a multitude of other forms of anxiety. In terms of a burgeoning youth identity, Karim and Charlie have by far the most varied experiences, though ultimately they do not arrive at stable form of sexual identity that can serve as the basis for a strong adult sexuality. Instead, they perform a variety of acts with a variety of partners, embracing the fluidity of their sexual desire in a manner that advances well beyond the pseudo-liberatory sexual politics of the hippies by embracing glam play and rejecting the long-standing notion (going back at least to Freud) that sexual identity is the core for all other forms of identity – the anchor for an authentic understanding of oneself. *The Buddha of Suburbia* is, in brief, a novel saturated with sexual experimentation not in the name of self-discovery but simply in the name of performance and pleasure. In a strong sense, this returns us to the affiliation of pleasure with bad behaviour first mooted by Alex in his declaration in *A Clockwork Orange* that 'I do what I do because I like to do'. Two key episodes shadow this apparently non-judgemental approach to sex, and the youthful utopianism it promises, with a certain degree first of menace, and then of a kind of *mise-en-abyme* of authenticity: Matthew's unwelcome sexual use of Karim and Charlie's exploration of 'the ultimate experience' with the dominatrix Frankie.

The episode in which Karim and Eleanor visit Pyke and Marlene's house for a *ménage-á-quatre* stands out for its depiction of a generationally inflected battle over masculinity. From the outset, Pyke is in control. He has told Karim that there would be a dinner party, but in fact only Karim and Eleanor have been invited. Karim is upset by Eleanor's earlier demand that they not 'deny each other experience', and by the fact that 'Pyke had lied' about the party (199). Nonetheless, things go more or less smoothly, with Eleanor pairing off with Pyke and Karim pairing off with Marlene to begin with. They have all been smoking dope, and Karim is profoundly disoriented. He is not in control of what is happening, or even of his own body: 'The dope made me drowsy and held back sensation and reaction' (201). Pyke, on the other hand, is not only in control, he directs the action, either by peremptorily telling others what to do or – much more importantly – by simply taking pleasure from them without their consent:

> 'That looks like fun', his voice said.
> 'Yes, it – '
> But before I could complete the sentence, England's most interesting and radical theatre director was inserting his cock between my speaking lips. I could appreciate the privilege, but I didn't like it much: it seemed an imposition. He could have asked politely. (202–203)

Ever the director, Pyke ensures that the other actors in this little drama play their roles as he wants, deriving as much pleasure from his control over them as from the bodily sensations they produce for him. It's a key moment of masculine dominance, delineated along generational lines. As we discover somewhat later, this is only the beginning. After this initial assault, Pyke 'had fucked [Karim] up the arse while Marlene cheered us on as if we were all-in wrestlers – and while Eleanor fixed herself a drink – [and] had virtually ruptured' him (219). Now, Karim continues, 'I began to be certain, the fucker was fucking me in other ways' (219). Pyke asserts his dominance over Karim by degrading him, making him an instrument of pleasure. Even when Karim responds to the unwelcome privilege by giving 'his dick a South London swipe' Matthew only responds by 'murmuring his approval' (203). The fact that Karim's sexuality is fluid – he tells us that he 'liked to sleep with boys as well as girls' (55) – is irrelevant here, since what is at stake is not pleasure but power. However we configure this scene, Karim is subordinated by Pyke through the extension of a series of privileges that come with a hidden cost. Pyke has driven Karim around in his fancy car, told Eleanor to get together with him, fed him supper and given him the gift of sex with his wife. The cost is status and agency: Karim pays for these privileges not by being shown a model of mature masculinity to follow, but by being held in a subordinate subject position.

Ironically, Pyke only gets away with his assaults because Karim understands identity, sexuality, and authenticity in performative terms rather than stable categories. As he says, 'I liked strong bodies and the backs of boys' necks. I liked being handled by men, their fists pulling me; and I liked objects – the ends of brushes, pens, fingers – up my arse. But I liked cunts and breasts, all of women's softness, long smooth legs and the way women dressed' (55). He experiences sex and sexuality in terms of bodies and pleasures: He expressly does not say of himself, 'I am gay' or 'I am bisexual' or even 'I am pansexual'. At issue is not identity so much as performance, activity, desire and pleasure as they occur not as they constitute his authentic self. The irony in Pyke's dominance thus manifests most clearly when he announces to Karim that acting is a 'strange business [...] you are trying to convince people that you're someone else, that this is not-me. The way to do it is this, he said: when in character, playing not-me, you have to be yourself. To make your not-self real you have to steal from your authentic self' (219). It seems that Pyke has not gotten the memo. The very concept of an 'authentic self' is in near-total collapse, having been acquired in a hostile takeover by performativity. Karim intuitively recognizes this fact, while Pyke still adheres to a belief system anchored in an outmoded youth-cultural view of authenticity. His statement that 'The closer you play to yourself the better' captures this parallax distortion nicely: For him, the emphasis is on 'yourself', while for Karim the emphasis is on 'play'.

The novel apparently comes full circle in terms of how it understands sex and sexuality in relation to authenticity and identity in its closing treatment of Charlie, the ultimate figure of youth-cultural performance and hipness. This view emerges in Kureishi's depiction of him pursuing an authentic sense of self through sexualized pain, though ultimately even this gesture remains at best highly ambiguous. Charlie hires a professional dominatrix named Frankie to come to his apartment so he can explore '"the ultimate experience"' through BDSM (bondage, domination, sadism, masochism) sexual activity. Importantly, this pursuit of the authentic can only take place once Charlie is bound to his bed, his head covered with a leather hood. As Karim puts it, 'And now it wasn't Charlie: it was a body with a sack over its head, half of its humanity gone, ready for execution' (254). Only reduction to bare life, to a mere suffering body, promises an experience of the authentic for Charlie. Only by being rendered abject, he believes, can he attain something like subjectivity. As Frankie pours hot wax on Charlie's body and attaches painful clamps to his nipples, Charlie apparently confronts a core self, one which overlaps with authenticity only in limit experience. And yet ... the novel suggests likewise that maybe this pursuit of authentic experience is only possible via inauthenticity. It is surely ironic that Charlie's BDSM experience re-actualizes the abstraction of punks wearing bondage trousers and trashy see-through clothes in the streets. What had been adopted in the first place to signify social abjection by alluding to underground practices of domination and sado-masochism – as well as to shock – is re-situated in its original context by Charlie. Or nearly, so: Charlie does not visit a dominatrix's dungeon, an underground sex club or some other edgy venue outside the mainstream. Instead, he hires a dominatrix to come to his expensive Manhattan apartment and to dominate him in his own bedroom. Moreover, Frankie is not someone who cares deeply about Charlie and his emotional growth, but with a sex worker who is by definition paid to produce specific affective and physical states in her client. These facts by themselves do not necessarily reduce the authenticity of Charlie's experience. But when we consider them alongside Charlie's need for an audience for his experience it points in that direction. Charlie wants Karim to watch him have sex with Frankie, to witness his humiliation and to ratify the authenticity of his experience. Or perhaps we should say 'the authenticity of his *performance*'. I honestly don't know, but the novel's dedication to irony as *the* key element of 1970s youth culture makes it impossible simply to accept that Charlie at last discovers an authentic core.

The 1970s were tumultuous and complicated. In terms of youth culture, they were more crowded than any decade thus far, seeing more transitions than any other decade in the post-war era. I've argued here that this messiness is in part the result of the fact that the leading-edge baby boomers had begun to reach adulthood and that a certain meta-stasis of youth culture ensued. Youth culture began to recognize itself as youth culture, and to adopt a distanced perspective on itself. As a consequence, irony manifested as perhaps *the* key characteristic of youth-cultural cool in the 1970s, and a profound crisis of authenticity reached critical proportions. *The Rachel Papers* concludes with a relatively clear avowal of this state of affairs, circa 1973. Charles, having been challenged by the Oxford don Knowd to drop the charade and simply inquire into his own authentic response to literature, chooses instead to avoid self-exploration by turning down the offer of admission. He breaks up with Rachel, thus dodging the possibility of having to deal with her potential pregnancy and the responsibility that would entail. And, he decides not to deliver his letter/speech to his father, lapsing instead back into comfortable self-delusion in a manner not unlike the concluding delusions of the Teenager in *Absolute Beginners*. Benefitting from a decade and a half more postmodernism, *The Buddha of Suburbia* concludes with the triumph of the simulacrum. Karim has discovered independence, but only by accepting a role on a television soap opera – where he will 'play the rebellious student son of an Indian shopkeeper' (259), that is, a male Jamila. The novel's final sections increasingly formalize this triumph of the simulacrum as they become more and more episodic. Karim visits each group of characters in turn to wrap up the various storylines in which they have been implicated, and the novel concludes with a cinematic scene in which he hosts a lively dinner party for all the main characters. The novel has become a simulacrum of a television series (into which it was eventually made by the BBC in 1993 complete with a song called 'Buddha of Suburbia' by David Bowie, completing the simulacral circle). Together, these novels constitute something of a requiem for the first stage of youth culture, a stage during which authenticity functioned as both an ideal and an unmarked background, an assumption upon which you could proceed as you experimented with styles of being in the world. As we turn to the 1980s next, our focus thus necessarily changes as well. Alex Wheatle's *Brixton Rock* explores racial consciousness in youth-cultural fiction of the post-war, putting a slightly different spin on the questions of authenticity, style, generational tension, race and sexuality.

4

Sojourn in Babylon: *Brixton Rock* and *East of Acre Lane*

If 1970s youth culture moved with dizzying speed from organic hippie sincerity through glam artificiality and prog-rock detachment to punk outrage – and then part way back again – in a scant ten years, the 1980s upped the ante even more. At least as eclectic and diverse as its predecessor decade, the 1980s sought to outdo the 1970s by charting new ground in how youth-cultural energies were dispersed, re-energized, adapted and countermanded. The syncretic quality of youth culture proceeded apace, as all the youth cultures we've seen so far persisted, and were supplemented by yet more innovations. The field is flat-out crowded by this point, as Teds, punks, hippies, mods, skins and glam rockers increasingly rub shoulders with rockers, jazz enthusiasts, prog rockers and new romantics – not to mention movements we have not had the chance to discuss at all, such as goth, heavy metal and northern soul. At the same time, pop gets bigger than ever with groups such as Duran Duran launching a new era of mega-concerts. By and large, these youth cultures continue the concerns we have been tracking since the Teddy boys, addressing themselves to the perennial problems of masculinity, sex and sexuality, gender, class, economics, ethnicity, history and above all generational tensions. For the most part, they remain closely focused on the foreground of adolescent angst. The new romantics fuse a toned-down glam aesthetic with synthesizers to join pop in purveying standard radio fare. Northern soul renews its commitment to the mid-1960s Motown sound, while heavy metal gleefully tweaks noses by inviting moral panic. But something else happens too. Something that has long been an accompaniment to post-war youth culture's musical stylings, though it has rarely – except perhaps with the hippies – risen to the status of leading melody. That something is a political consciousness.

That political consciousness appears in distinct forms in white and black youth cultures, though the two streams are anything but distinct. Generally speaking, white youth cultures found themselves galvanized around the political anthem-rock of U2 and grandiose benefit concerts. U2's first major hit album, *War* (1983), established the band as a political force for peace and cooperation against the heightened antagonisms of both the Troubles in Ireland and the Cold War. Even at their height, though, U2 was as nothing compared with the massive impact of mega-band Band Aid, with its hit single 'Do They Know it's Christmas?' (1984) and its massive trans-Atlantic concert, Live Aid. Band Aid kicked off a decade-long mania for collaborative benefit projects with overtly political goals – most notably for our purposes the 1985 Artists United Against Apartheid hit, 'Sun City'. Importantly, these projects were driven by white musicians and producers, though they directly took up issues of racial discrimination and economic inequality. Black youth culture found a more inclusive approach in the less grandiose, but arguably more sincere, attempts to articulate a politics of inter-racial harmony of the continuing Rock Against Racism shows and new, mixed-race, bands: 2Tone groups like The Specials, Madness and UB40. Perhaps most importantly of all, at least for our purposes, reggae went mainstream as it had never done before. In large part, this was due to its appropriation by white groups such as The Clash and The Police. These appropriations signal the growing influence of reggae – and its politics – for youth cultures across the board. For black youth-cultural audiences, reggae played a vital role, fusing a personal, immediate sense of oppression to a longer historical narrative and – crucially – furnishing a potential utopian resolution. Whether you were white or black, political activism was hip again, and music could chart a new future.

Alex Wheatle's first two novels illustrate the extent to which reggae – along with soul, funk and disco – was integral to the black youth cultures of 1980s England: rude boy, sweet boy, Rastafarian. *Brixton Rock* and *East of Acre Lane* concentrate on a small group of black Londoners living in *Brixton* during the early 1980s. Characters who appear in *Brixton Rock* reappear in *East of Acre Lane*, and the timeline is more or less linear, moving from *Brixton Rock* through to *East of Acre Lane*'s climax in the 1981 riots. Structurally, then, and in terms of how they are positioned vis-à-vis historical events, Wheatle's novels have clear parallels with *Absolute Beginners*. Indeed, in many respects, Wheatle's novels may almost be read as a form of writing back to MacInnes's utopian fantasies. But, the differences are important. First, MacInnes's protagonist is a hip young white man from a solidly middle-class family. He elects to live in an impoverished neighbourhood, though he remains welcome to move back to the 'ancestral home' whenever he likes. Wheatle's characters, by contrast, have more in common with MacInnes's Mr. Cool: They are young black men who have no choice in where they live, lack fathers (they sometimes lack family altogether) and know Borstals as home more than anything like a suburban bungalow. MacInnes's Teenager is a highly particular sort masquerading as generic and universalized. He is mobile, can make money easily, enjoys sexual freedom and gratification, finds opportunity dropped into his lap, benefits from extraordinary good luck even in the midst of a riot, has a loving father, finds love with Suze and is utterly at home in the world, going so far as to take it upon himself to welcome new arrivals to London in the novel's final paragraphs. He speaks for the mainstream out of a narcissistic ignorance of his own highly privileged specificity. Wheatle's characters, by contrast, are highly particular. Brenton's anonymity is not a result of privilege, but of misfortune, as he begins *Brixton Rock* with no family at all, and his individuality is often the source of unspoken comment by his friends – Floyd frequently wonders at the fact that he is *not* like all the others. Biscuit, in *East of Acre Lane*, has no money, pursues criminal activity out of necessity (as opposed to indulging in morally suspect activity out of choice as MacInnes's Teenager does), is sexually frustrated, lacks opportunity, experiences tremendous bad luck and comes from a broken non-traditional family (his mother has three children by three different men and now raises them by herself). He is dislocated in the world, perpetually menaced by Brixtonian 'bad men' and the Metropolitan police: harassed, oppressed and intensely frustrated with his lot. Brenton is in equal straits, the climax of his narrative outstripping Biscuit's in a violence that far exceeds anything that happens in MacInnes's cartoonish rendering of the 1958 riots. One can only imagine what either Brenton or Biscuit would have to say to the planeload of African new arrivals so enthusiastically embraced by the Teenager at the end of *Absolute Beginners*.

There are two relevant historical contexts here, both of which must be introduced if we are to understand fully how Wheatle both thinks *about* the black British youth cultures of the 1980s and uses them to think *with*. The first pertains to the setting of the novels: 1979–1981. The second pertains to the time of their publication: 1999–2001. This disparity means, as it did with *The Buddha of Suburbia*, that we sacrifice some of the fuzzy immediacy of novels written *in* the moments they are *about* – novels such as *Saturday Night and Sunday Morning*, *Absolute Beginners*, *A Clockwork Orange* and *The Rachel Papers* – but gain something in clarity. The longer perspective lends an enhanced clarity to Wheatle's depictions, allowing him to identify which elements have turned out to be the most salient in hindsight, even if they did not always appear so clearly so at the time. That hindsight is not neutral, though, and herein lies another of the gains attendant upon the time lapse between the times of setting and writing: historical inflection. Put simply, Wheatle the writer at the end of the 1990s knows what is coming for his characters stuck in 1980 or 1981. That knowledge necessarily inflects his depiction of what happens to them, orienting the action of *Brixton Rock* and *East of Acre Lane* towards the political and youth-cultural changes to come. Thus, though Wheatle depicts only the 1981 Brixton riots at the end of *East of Acre Lane*, he does so knowing full well that they will repeat in 1985. Likewise, the significant Rastafarian undercurrent to the novels, along with the characters' dawning awareness of their African roots, cannot but be informed by Wheatle's later knowledge of the successful struggle against *apartheid* in South Africa, and of Nelson Mandela's release in 1990. So, I am going to treat the whole of the 1980s as relevant context for these novels, even as I give extra weight the pivotal years covered by the novels: 1979– 1981. The result, I hope, will both illuminate some of the conditions under which youth culture evolved in the decade and set the stage for the final novel in this study – *Trainspotting*.

On to the 1980s, then, the 'me decade', the age of Thatcher and entrepreneurship, individualism, free enterprise, imminent nuclear threat, a devastating recession, heightened racial tensions, the 'final' victory of capitalism over communism and an emerging global communications network that could transmit news and events around the globe 'live'. For our purposes, the decade begins with Margaret Thatcher becoming prime minister on 4 May 1979. Just two weeks earlier, New Zealand-born Blair Peach had been killed by riot police as he protested against the racist National Front. His death and Thatcher's ascension set the template for much of what would follow as the decade swung wildly among extremes. The year 1981 saw the wedding of Prince Charles and Lady Diana Spencer in the grandest display of pomp and circumstance since Queen Elizabeth's coronation in 1953. In the 1982 Falklands Crisis, Margaret Thatcher dispatched the mighty British navy to reclaim a tiny group of rocky islands just off the coast of Argentina after the Argentinean government declared sovereignty over them. In that incident, the navy steamed half way across the world to prosecute a 'war' whose only purpose could have been to restore the empire's crumbling prestige. It was a hugely expensive, and shockingly successful, public relations campaign. At the other extreme, the Troubles in Northern Ireland continued into their second decade, with the Irish Republican Army stepping up their attacks on British soil, earning support from Libyan strongman Muammar Gaddafi, and provoking Thatcher to respond with increasingly violent repression in Ireland. Top it all off with the first signs of a massive drug abuse problem, the onset of the AIDS/HIV epidemic, ongoing struggles over Scottish independence and of course the famous 'summer of love' rave-fest on the island of Ibiza, and you have a decade perhaps best summed up by one-hit wonders Love and Rockets as a 'ball of confusion'.

Thatcher's determination to remake Britain coincided with a deep and lasting recession as the economic crises of the 1970s extended into the 1980s. Not since the 1930s had Britain seen such numbers of unemployed (something on the order of 22% of the working-age population), accompanied by such gutting of the social safety net, and reversal of the mid-century's commitment to the welfare state. The situation was both exacerbated and felt most acutely by the immigrant populations in Britain, most of whom were now second or even third generation. For this group, unemployment was a majority experience: As much as 55 per cent of young black men in England were unemployed. And, as is all too often the case, this economic and social disadvantage was shadowed – harassed, really – by disproportionate policing, thanks in no small part to the new suspect law (the 'suss law' of popular parlance), which empowered police to stop, search and detain individuals for behaving suspiciously even if no crime had been witnessed or reported, and for which no evidence was present. The Cass report on the police murder of Blair Peach in 1979, not released until 2010 (!), noted that the officers likely responsible operated outside their mandate and that at least one of them had 'a collection of Nazi regalia' in his possession (*Guardian* 'Blair Peach' n.p.) (https://www.theguardian.com/uk/2010/apr/27/blair-peach-killed-police-met-report).

Interestingly, as Wheatle's novels document, though racial tensions existed, economic hardship crossed racial lines, leading underclass blacks and whites to make common cause against Thatcherite policies and their enforcement by the police. The riots in Brixton in 1981 and 1985, as well as those in Liverpool, Manchester, Leeds and Birmingham, were disproportionately motivated by economic disparities rather than by racial injustice. And though the two are ultimately inseparable, the riots took energy from a sense that police persecution has as much or more to do with economics than with race. We will see this complex, often ambiguous, dynamic worked out in detail in Alex Wheatle's treatment of youth cultures in *Brixton Rock* and *East of Acre Lane*. The novels chart a range of youth-cultural responses to the decade's challenges, surprisingly framing economics as the root of the problem. Race furnishes the terrain on which battles over authenticity, masculinity, generational tension and style are fought, but in the end economics trumps race as the most significant challenge to be confronted.

Wheatle's engagement with this complex set of concerns manifests in a multi-faceted opposition: reggae versus soul. This opposition, and the youth cultures it delineates, structures both *Brixton Rock* and *East of Acre Lane*. In them, Wheatle stages the tensions between soul and reggae, though he spends the bulk of his time on reggae and its religious side, Rastafarianism. The link to Ethiopia resides in this connection. Reggae was aligned with the Rastafarian belief that Haile Selassie, emperor of Ethiopia in the 1930s, was the messiah. Ethiopia thus came to stand for all of Africa in reggae/Rasta's devotion to roots music that would reverse the slave migration. Where white imperial history had transferred Africans to America and England, Rastafarianism would re-awaken black pride and reconstitute black history to move from exile in Babylon/England back to Zion/Africa. As the narrator of *Brixton Rock* puts it,

> The songs reflected the struggle for black freedom and the persecution of the black race throughout world history. The lyrics also had a rebellious slant against the Western world's way of doing things – or, as Floyd and many other blacks called it, Babylon. As [Brenton] meditated on the words he enjoyed the cussing of the people who represented power. He listened more fervently, and especially liked one song that was about the

Rastafarian religion and the connections this faith had with the Good Book. (23)

Rasta's red, gold, green colours correspond to the colours of the Ethiopian flag, and the heavily biblical lexicon and diction of much reggae music participates in Rastafarianism's reorientation of the Bible as a living account of black oppression. In this respect, as Wheatle shows, Rastafarianism provides the intellectual armature of reggae's populist aesthetic. The counter-history it promotes recovers and redeems black achievement and pride across the spectrum of intellectual and cultural enterprise. It re-articulates the suspicion of master narratives and long-standing British cultural institutions with which we began in *Saturday Night and Sunday Morning*, and *Absolute Beginners*. *Brixton Rock* and *East of Acre Lane* are direct descendants of the post-war anger and frustration that gave rise to rebellious – but tendentially utopian – youth cultures in the first place. These parallels, and their common focus in the early 1980s on Ethiopia, will inform my reading of Wheatle.

Central to that reading is the surprising revelation that for Wheatle class affiliation outweighs race or ethnicity as the determining factor in youth-cultural affiliations. Wheatle is a product of the Windrush Generation, the first wave of immigrants who came to England following the 1948 British Nationality Act. That generation provided an infusion of new blood and talent to such black British writers of the pre-war as C. L. R. James, Jomo Kenyatta and George Padmore. Writers such as James Berry, George Lamming, Sam Selvon, V. S. Naipaul and Wilson Harris constituted a powerful new stream of literary talent in England after the war. Responding to the confusing and contradictory way their generation were received in England, such writers directly engaged with the legacies of imperialism and challenged the increasingly open racism of English society. They forced a reconsideration of Englishness itself that infuses many of the novels we have already discussed, especially *Absolute Beginners* and *The Buddha of Suburbia*. Wheatle's novels directly invoke Windrush in their reference to a parental generation that is first-generation immigrant, and in their use of youth cultures such as rude boys, sweet boys, and Rastafarians to engage with larger problems of class, economic hardship, masculinity, generational tension and sex. And yet, Wheatle differs from many of his predecessors in a somewhat shocking way: For him, the chief problem facing young black men in England in the 1980s is not racism so much as economic hardship. It's an interesting move that registers a shift away from race as the key identity category (as it was in *Absolute Beginners* and even *The Buddha of Suburbia*, for example) back towards a traditional English Marxist understanding of social realities in which to be young is to be working-class, unemployed, downtrodden. Though it may once have been true that 'the positions "youth" and "Negro" are often aligned in the dominant mythology' (Hebdige 1979, 44), the situation would appear to have changed in a subtle but dramatic way by the 1980s. For my money, this shift is itself part of a generational conflict in which second- and third-generation immigrant writers simultaneously declare and disavow their ancestors. This is why Wheatle comes at the larger issues he tackles through youth cultures: why he uses them to think *with*. Doing so embeds generational conflict in the very form of his novels, making them part of the historical predicament they describe. In a very real sense, then, his novels think about generation, empire, history and so on as an inherent part of their thinking about youth cultures.

They do this thinking primarily by following the fortunes of two young Brixtonians, Brenton and 'Biscuit'. Brenton and Biscuit struggle throughout Wheatle's narratives against racism and enormous economic odds to support themselves and/or their families, and to achieve mature standing as men. The only regular work available to them is that of hustling – selling drugs and thieving – and they live in a constant state of imminent conflict with the police. The 'suss' law, allowing police to stop and search people on the basis of suspicious behavior, and dating all the way back to the 1824 Vagrancy Act, had become the focus of charges of police abuse of power in the late 1970s. It pervades the novels' settings, lending them a paranoid aura in which simply being black and on the street is cause for search and detainment. And if you're detained, you may well also be beaten. Crucially, though, the police force is clearly understood to be oppressive and profoundly racist in both novels, the larger horizon of communal identity for Brenton and Biscuit is that of a colour-blind underclass. White characters such as Frank, Biscuit's next door neighbour, find common cause with their black peers, suffer many of the same pressures and share the rage and frustration that finally explodes in the riots of 1981. White reggae adherents dancing to music in the *Brixton* high street draw no scorn or resentment, and there is little anger about white appropriations of black cultural influences on display.

This equanimity is somewhat surprising, given the long-established tradition of white youth cultures borrowing from black influences, erasing their origins, and repackaging them as the latest cool thing. This practice extends at least as far back as the Teddy boy predilection for gospel and blues influences, re-recorded and fused with country and western by white artists, and extends to the mods' love of cool jazz, the skinheads' preference for ska, northern soul's adoption of Motown, and punk's absorption of reggae (see Hebdige 64–67). For the first time, we are dealing with a novel that takes up those influences in their native contexts, if you will: Reggae and soul appear in Wheatle's novels not as influences on white youth culture, but as the key poles of black youth culture's musical world. Providing a counterpoint to Kureishi's view of second-generation immigrants as having abandoned authenticity in the name of performativity, Wheatle instead portrays the power of reggae in particular to provide a powerful sense of rootedness and authenticity to young people who feel profoundly excluded from mainstream culture. In Hebdige's words, 'reggae is transmogrified American "soul" music, with an overlay of salvaged African rhythms, and an undercurrent of pure Jamaican rebellion. Reggae is transplanted Pentecostal. Reggae is the Rasta hymnal, the heart cry of the Kingston Rude Boy, as well as the nativised national anthem of the new Jamaican government' (140). It provides a powerful counterpoint to the more digestible soul music associated with the Motown sound. Wheatle thinks *about* and *with* these overlapping youth cultures, focusing in particular upon the two poles of soul and reggae (itself subdivided into Rastamen and rude bwais). In his thinking *about* these poles, Wheatle demarcates a binary system. In this system, soul is aligned with sex, the personal, various forms of emasculation, and a perverse or abortive futurity. By contrast, reggae is associated with politics, the public, masculine assertion and the past. At the same time, he uses these youth cultures to think *with*. He traces a complex youth-cultural engagement with problems of history, empire, masculinity and authenticity.

This portrayal necessarily involves an engagement with History and its others – official History versus its occluded conditions of possibility or marginalized facets – in a way we have not seen quite so clearly since the works of the 1940s and 1950s. In drawing out for us how black youth culture is shaped in 1980s England, Wheatle's works take up the question of how black people came to be in England in such numbers in the first place, what sorts of lasting impacts that history has had on their lives, and what kind of futurity it implies for them. By and large, Wheatle takes this topic up through family romances, using the personal situations of Brenton and Biscuit to invoke the larger conditions of paternity, heritage, belonging and identity. He supplements this allegorical approach with bouts of Rasta wisdom provided by his novels' resident wise man, the one-eyed visionary Jah Nelson. Particularly at the end of *East of Acre Lane*, Jah Nelson looms large as the voice of rootedness, recovering the black history that has been elided by white imperialism and the history of slavery. What emerges is a crisis of faith in master narratives (literally, the narratives of the masters) that is attended by a still-unresolved crisis of masculinity and deep suspicion of cultural institutions: School is a non-issue for Wheatle's characters, church is a locus of what Nietzsche called slave morality, the government is at best useless and at worst actively working against its underclass citizens and the penal system's institutional violence is captured perhaps best in Sceptic and Biscuit's wry despair over the name of the Minister responsible: ' "de 'Ome Secretary. Wassisname? William Whitelaw, innit?' 'Da'ts kinda spooky, man', commented Biscuit. 'White law' " ' (85). For Wheatle's characters, the whole adds up not to a *system* but to a *shitstem*. It's a system that has both created the conditions in which the characters live and which punishes them for trying to survive in it, that equates their economically motivated criminal activity with racial essence, and that exercises extrajudicial violence upon them while bringing the full force of the law to bear on anyone who dares to resist.

One of the few areas in which the characters have some degree of autonomy is style. Typically for members of a youth culture, Brenton, Biscuit and their 'brethren' place a high value upon dressing stylishly, gaining and maintaining credibility through their performances of masculinity and savvy, and their commitment to authenticity. This last element is schematized in part as a tension between official History (which is inauthentic) and the shadow history told by Jah Nelson (which is authentic). The tension between the two manifests in the musical contradiction between soul and reggae, and between the sweet bwai devotees of the former and the bad bwai (or rude boy) adherents to the latter. As Wheatle describes them, sweet bwais style themselves lovers rather than fighters: 'Sweet-bwais were dressed in loose-fitting shirts that were often unbuttoned to reveal gold rope chains. The latest hairstyle was semi-afro which was shampooed and "blown out", giving an appearance of carved black candyfloss. No one calling themselves a sweet-bwai would go to a party without their Farah slacks and reptile skin shoes' (*East* 9). Brenton's friend Floyd in *Brixton Rock* is a would-be sweet bwai, dressing as sharply as his meagre means will allow, and even wearing holes in his feet as he walks to an all-night party so he can show up in his cheap fake crocodile shoes. He is completely consumed by the need for female company and the very best fashion his money can buy.

By contrast to both sweet bwais and full-blooded Rastafarian reggae fans, rude boys conform to a sleeker, more mod style – which, in fact they influenced extensively. Where the Rasta man sports dread locks and often wears traditional clothes (e.g. Jah Nelson's 'African-type robes' [*Brixton Rock* 190]) or military/guerrilla-style clothing, the rudie presents a cool, clear, crisp look. He wears sharp suits that have sleek lines, with well pressed shirts and trousers, narrow ties and pork-pie hats. The style originates in the mean streets of Kingston, Jamaica, but travels extremely well, infiltrating not only black British youth culture, but the world of soul and R&B as well – as witness the classic rude boy style of The Blues Brothers. As Dick Hebdige puts it:

> The rude boy lived for the luminous moment, playing dominoes as though his life depended on the outcome – a big-city hustler with nothing to do, and, all the time rocksteady, ska and reggae gave him the means with which to move effortlessly – without even thinking. Cool, that distant and indefinable quality, became almost abstract, almost metaphysical, intimating a stylish kind of stoicism – survival and something more. (145)

In England, the rude boy is commonly associated with criminal activity and the masculine economy of menace and cool that sustains it. It remains staunchly anchored in reggae through the rudies' loyalty to one or another of the sound systems that play all-night raves and engage in musical battles for youth-cultural supremacy at massive dances. In contrast to the sweet bwai, who is clearly identified as a lover, the rude boy is identified as a fighter, a warrior of cool who, nevertheless, would not hesitate to cut or shoot an enemy – or even a friend who makes the wrong move. Brenton and Biscuit move in this orbit, though they lack sufficient funds and gangland affiliations to really qualify for the name. Brenton, in particular fits the mould as he transitions from a damaged young man in *Brixton Rock* to a full-fledged 'bad man' in *East of Acre Lane*. Though we do not get much information about his clothing choices apart from his near-morbid fascination with the state of his trainers, it is clear that Brenton stands as the counterpoint to Floyd's sweet bwai persona: He is dangerous, angry, potentially violent and clearly involved in the world of crime. The tension Floyd and Brenton present is another iteration of the old opposition between lovers and fighters that is characteristic of troubled masculinity, but here given the added baggage of political commitment and the binary of assimilation (soul) versus resistance (reggae).

Crucially, for the first time since we began our study, we find ourselves now facing members of a youth culture for whom the style of the moment is only an aspiration: Though Biscuit, Brenton, Floyd, Sceptic and the rest all urgently want to dress as either sweet bwais or rude boys, they lack the money to do it. If youth culture originates in the early 1950s with the Teddy boys' hijacking of Savile Row's haute couture lines thanks to their abundant cash, it runs into a barrier in the 1980s. Punk had met a similar obstacle by making a virtue out of necessity, and creating a style out of filthy, ill-fitting, torn clothes. Rastamen do likewise, dressing down to emphasize their renunciation of Western consumerist values. Sweet bwais and rudies, however, face an increasing gap opening up between the values of the youth

FIGURE 4.1 *Sandy Raggamuffin DJ of Saxon Sound system, London 1987. (Photo by: PYMCA/UIG via Getty Images.)*

culture they identify with and the means of performing it through their clothes. And with the British economy as bad as it has ever been – certainly at its worst since the war, especially for young black men – the only avenue of access to sufficiently stylistic gear is to sink deeper into crime, and to embrace an ever more dangerous lifestyle with even fewer possibilities for escape.

If Brenton, Floyd, Coffin Head, Biscuit and the rest are only aspirational in their adaptation of rude boy styles, they are fully engaged when it comes to the typical rude boy pastime of attending DJ battles to back one or another 'sound system' in competition – at times violent – against others. Just such a scene unfolds in the middle of *Brixton Rock*, when Floyd and Brenton attend the battle to be named the '"Champion Sound of London"' (139). They enter to a crowd savouring 'the almost ritualistic atmosphere, feeling a sense of belonging as they marvelled at the red, gold and green colours. Rastafarians wore their long locks proudly and black females, adorned in their African-type dresses, added a spice of culture to the event' (138). Pictures of Haile Selassie hang on the walls and 'the aroma of West Indian cuisine' drifts through the air (138). It's a scene so powerfully redolent of Jamaica that when it ends and the crowd pours out into the street the narrator tells us that 'the scene at the bus stops could have been the warm streets of downtown Kingston' (140). That is to say, we are fully immersed in the immigrant youth culture of reggae, Rasta and especially rude boys. The tracks played are exclusively imports from Jamaica, as was typical for rude boy raves from the 1960s on in the UK. Four sound systems compete for the title: 'Soferno B, Jah Shaka, Sir Coxone and Moa Anbessa' (139). As each takes the floor, their followers jump, shout, dance and cheer in support. There is also a strain of danger in the scene, as Brenton in particular keeps a weather eye out for Terry Flynn and his group who, notably, support a rival sound system to the one Brenton and Floyd support. 'At around eleven o'clock, the competition came to a climax, and the judges declared Jah Shaka the winner. Jah Shaka's followers hollered and whooped their approval, along with the illegal bookmakers. Floyd and his posse, backed up by others, barked their disappointment as they threaded their way out of the building' (140). The evening ends with the racist police rolling up, calling Brenton and Floyd 'niggers' and 'wogs' (141) and then chasing them into a housing estate. Brenton and Floyd escape, buy some marijuana from a dealer and close out the evening by connecting with Sharon and Carol – though both men long for a 'war in the streets between us and the beast' (145). Everything here bespeaks the rude boy youth culture, from the battle between sound systems to the air of violence permeating the night; from the West Indian food smells to the Rastafarian colours, clothes and music; and from the encounter with the police to the consumption of marijuana and persistent sense of injustice. Brenton, Floyd and the rest make up for their inability to buy proper rude boy clothes by more than sufficiently playing the part. It's a part that sets them at odds not just with the police and mainstream white

British culture, but with the more orthodox Rastafarians like Jah Nelson and especially with the world of soul, which is almost exclusively associated with the women in their lives.

In Wheatle's novels, soul is invariably characterized as superficial dance music. It has no political thrust and instead codifies many of the dominant culture's attitudes: It is a force for assimilation rather than revolution. In *East of Acre Lane* it is aligned with Denise and Biscuit's cousin Ruth. Ruth is a church-going girl who has had little to no exposure to reggae, Rastafarianism or drugs. She is one or two levels above Denise and Biscuit socially, and her family has translated that difference into an assimilationist perspective that is at once quietist and submissive, preferring the promise of a reward in the afterlife to the advancement of blacks in contemporary England. At one point, Ruth invites Denise to come out with her to 'different places' than the reggae dances she frequents, so she can meet men who do not make their money by selling drugs or through other criminal means. Denise instantly recognizes what kinds of 'different places' Ruth means and dismisses soul clubs for precisely these reasons: '"Whatya mean different places?" replied Denise. "Don't expect me to go do dem soul clubs where dem white bwai try to act black an' dem black bwai skin up dem teet' checking dem white girl an' try to act white"' (*East* 96). Soul clubs represent a profound inauthenticity for Denise. They are where white kids try to act black and black kids try to act white. The repeated phrase, 'try to act' illuminates her view of things: In soul clubs there is only performance, and it is performance in direct conflict with what she takes to be authentic identity. White kids ought not to act black and black kids ought not to act white. The mention of 'dem black bwai […] checking dem white girl' gives her dismissal an explicit element of fear of miscegenation: '"Dem idiot soul 'ead black bwai ju' wanna dilute, man"' (*East* 96). In a rare comedic moment, Ruth marvels at her cousin Denise's political frame of reference: 'Ruth fell silent, wondering if her mother's charge that reggae music was corrupting the ghetto youths was true. Why else would Denise mention a rabble-rousing black power-monger like Marcus Garvey? Ruth wondered whether her cousin smoked herb as well' (*East* 96). Tellingly, Ruth links Garvey to reggae in the context of corruption. For her, reggae means a mix of Rasta and rudie, but with a decided emphasis upon the rudie side of things: black nationalism, criminality, drug-taking, violence and the politics of direct action. She much prefers soul music, a smoothed-out black identity that threatens no one. Musically, it is harmonious and sleek, well-timed on the beat and focused on the personal aspects of romance and desire. In a broader sense, it articulates an Enlightenment individualism that places self-fulfilment and the pursuit of romantic satisfaction ahead of communal consciousness and social justice.

In *Brixton Rock*, soul is even more clearly aligned with inauthenticity, perversion, and the problematic elevation of personal gratification over community. In that novel, it is primarily associated with Brenton's half-sister

Juliet. Juliet's name is the first clue that all is not going to go well here: It is a clear and direct reference to Shakespeare's Juliet, complete with her tale of 'star-crossed lovers' ending in misery, if not death for the mis-guided couple. Brenton and Juliet's incestuous romance provides the plot line in Wheatle's novel, turning upon their choice of personal gratification over social cohesion, cultural norms, or even the weight of their own consciences – up to a point. When Juliet finally breaks things off with Brenton, a single chapter pivots the narrative abruptly, delivering the break-up, the loss of Brenton's job, Brenton's near-suicide in the Tube, news of Juliet's pregnancy, Brenton's battle with Terry Flynn and their mother's discovery of the affair. The promise of a happy ending is abruptly shut down, just as it is in Shakespeare's play: comedy punctually turns to tragedy. The miscegenation hinted at by Denise in *East of Acre Lane* finds both a concrete historical referent in Brenton and Juliet's mother's past – Brenton is the product of an extramarital interracial affair she has while studying to become a nurse in the 1950s – and a sublimated contemporary referent in the incest between Brenton and Juliet.

Soul provides the sound-track for this drama, beginning with Juliet's tapes of 'lover's rock', which she and Brenton play on their stereos as they fall in love and then into bed. The romance finds its legs when Juliet convinces Brenton to come out to The Lyceum with her, instead of going out raving at an all-night reggae party: '"The Lyceum, that's a soul place, innit?" Thoughts of black guys with parted hairstyles and wearing baggy trousers, granddad shirts and winkle-pickers made him smirk' (*Brixton* 90). Brenton understands soul clubs in similar terms to Denise in *East of Acre Lane*, where 'black guys' dress like 'sweet bwais' – lovers rather than fighters – and devote themselves to the pursuit of romance. The vibe at the Lyceum is notably different from the rude boy vibe at reggae events, too, lacking the threat of imminent violence that characterizes his preferred scene: 'He'd been used to the sometimes menacing atmosphere of reggae raves, especially blues dances, where one false step could lead to a stitched cheek' (*Brixton* 93). The missing sense of menace comes with a decidedly less political and serious vibe: The DJ runs a wet t-shirt contest in the club and previews precisely the apolitical rave mindset that will sweep through white youth culture as the 1980s give way to the 1990s: 'Onstage the DJ seemed intent on playing non-stop dance music until everybody before him collapsed from exhaustion' (*Brixton* 92). Though Brenton does not put his distaste for the soul setting in clearly political terms, he remains resistant to its charms, feeling that they lack something vital, if dangerous. When Juliet apologizes for leaving him on his own so she could dance, Brenton replies, '"That's all right, I ain't the type to freak out anyway. I supposed the club is all right if you are a soul-head, and it's all friendly and t'ing, but I must admit I prefer my reggae"' (*Brixton* 93). Brenton's isolation in the midst of a crowd in the soul club manifests in his vague sense that though everything there is friendly, still the communal vibe of a reggae rave is preferable even with – perhaps because of – its air of rude boy menace.

The evening concludes with a rare cab ride for Brenton, and the first sign that his sister fancies him: 'Before Brenton could ask his sister what she meant, Juliet kissed the tips of her digits and gently touched her brother's forehead. Dazed, Brenton watched Juliet turn her key into the front door as the taxi did a U-turn. His brain was so spin-dried; he had to pause before being able to direct the taxi driver to his hostel' (93). The cab ride is important here, since it signals very clearly the gap in socio-economic standing between Brenton and his sister, just as the church-going Ruth stands a rung or two above her cousin Denise in *East of Acre Lane*. In Wheatle's world, soul clearly resonates with upwardly-mobile black youth, forming a musical accompaniment to varying degrees of integration into the mainstream. In class terms, then, soul appeals to the *working* working class, while reggae appears more palatable to the *non-working* working class: the underclass. As with *East of Acre Lane*, *Brixton Rock*'s view on this standing is clear as well, as soul is linked directly to dizzying romance, the libidinal whirligig of incestuous desire that takes place in isolation from social pressure – or sanction. Tellingly, and in a manner completely consistent with Juliet's greater integration into mainstream English culture and its stricter morality, Brenton is entirely unbothered by the fact of their incest, while Juliet is tormented by it. Intuitively, he has already moved beyond the hypocrisies of 'Babylon', and into an idiosyncratic rudie morality where what feels good is by definition right. As Burgess's Alex notes in *A Clockwork Orange*, when laughing at mainstream culture's hand-wringing over morality and the good, '"what I do I do because I like to do"' (40). Though Juliet tries gamely to rationalize her actions, ultimately her guilt drives her to break off the relationship. Soul's affiliation with mainstream integration, Christian morality, romance, individualism and sex is thus clearly established. Throughout the remainder of the novel, when Brenton and Juliet meet to make love, the musical accompaniment is inevitably soul music, with the angry, offbeat, aggressively masculine tones of reggae held at arm's length.

The reggae nexus in Wheatle's novels articulates a dramatically different perspective, anchoring their engagement where rude boy and Rastaman meet: masculinity, history, politics and authenticity. As with Juliet, Brenton's name deserves some comment in this regard. Just as 'Juliet' anchors *Brixton Rock* in perhaps *the* iconic story of ill-fated young love in the English tradition, so Brenton Brown's name calls to mind Pinky Brown, the teenage protagonist of Graham Greene's 1938 novel *Brighton Rock*. The titles clearly resonate as well, though Wheatle rather disingenuously tries to mask the reference in his Afterword to the novel, claiming that 'Some have asked me where does the "*Rock*" come from in the title. Well, it's quite a simple explanation: *Brixton* was *rocking* at the time with reggae music' (251–252). The mention of reggae here is important, and we will return to it shortly, but first there is the matter of Wheatle's more or less explicit lie here. I won't pretend to guess why he disavows Greene's influence in the Afterword, but the evidence more than countermands any inclination to take him at his word. The title is a clear echo of Greene's title, Brenton and Pinky share the same last name, the action of Greene's novel takes place in Brighton while Brenton's youth care home is located 'on the way to Brighton' (32), and both novels are pervaded by a sense of menace culminating in climactic violence. Whatever else Wheatle means his title to invoke, it invokes Greene's precedent first. The resonance it creates is important in that it aligns Pinky and Brenton, a white man and a black man, on class terms rather than racial terms. Both lead lives of criminality partly out of necessity and partly out of choice, though Pinky heads up a vicious gang where Brenton is the victim of such a gang leader in Terry Flynn.

Adding to this mix of allusions is the title of *East of Acre Lane*, which clearly evokes John Steinbeck's East of Eden – itself a narrative about economic hardship driving men to violence and desperation – and, more importantly, the biblical source for the phrase. In the Bible, Cain's punishment for killing his brother Abel is exile into 'the land of Nod, on the East of Eden' (Gen. 4:16). The 'East' invoked in Wheatle's title is a biblical as well as a literary allusion to expulsion from a promised land, into a future of exile and torment. It also calls to mind the tradition of commentary that sees Cain as the first black man, reading the biblical curse or mark of Cain as referring to dark skin, and identifying people of colour as the descendants of the original biblical fugitive or wanderer. The mark of Cain makes him readily identifiable to strangers as cursed, and at least part of his punishment is exclusion from the family unit and a lifetime of nomadism (notably, *Brixton Rock* begins with a 'Prologue' entitled 'Solitary', with Brenton in a jail cell by himself, cut off from his community – though it's not solitary confinement per se). Much of this applies more or less directly to both Brenton and Biscuit, giving their contemporary plights a historical weight that they might otherwise lack. Perhaps more importantly still, these references provide a direct connection to reggae and its link to Rastafarianism. The promise of a return from the East (of Acre Lane, of Eden) is a promise of redemption for everyone of African descent and the conclusion of a history typified by oppression, enslavement and imprisonment.

As I mentioned earlier, reggae is perhaps the primary means by which the Rastafarian gospel was circulated and promoted among young black Britons in the 1980s. Briefly, Rastafarianism maintains three key positions:

1) that Africans are one of the lost tribes of Israel;
2) that Haile Selassie the Emperor of Ethiopia in the 1930s is the Messiah returned to earth;
3) that an eventual return to Africa for all diasporic blacks will manifest as the concluding establishment of Zion in the promised land.

It is an Old Testament theology that borrows heavily from Islam and Judaism, but also Christianity in its chiliastic orientation towards an imminent redemption of history. It emphasizes roots, history, authenticity and blackness as characteristics for which people of colour have long been oppressed, but which will in the end become markers of privilege and salvation. One of its most powerful attractions lies precisely in the promise of a renewed esteem of black people for blackness itself, a restoration of self-regard that has been eroded on both the micro- and macrocosmic levels for centuries. Rastafarianism's historical awareness keeps the transition from Africa to the Caribbean, and thence to England present to mind, and urges a reverse journey that will restore African descendants to their African homelands. In this key respect, Rastafarianism encodes an understanding of history (or, rather, History) as an imperialist project, one that has seen multiple dislocations wherein black fathers and mothers were violently separated from their children. The generational discontinuities that result continue to produce dysfunction and rupture on the intimate familial level and on a day-to-day basis. Problems of generation, history and historicity thus manifest both on the familial level and in immediately felt social realities. As we will see, they are foundational to the 1980s youth-cultural quandaries faced by Wheatle's protagonists.

Importantly, Rastafarianism deviates from Christianity in that it does not advocate a patient waiting for the return of the Messiah, but an active recovery of the history that has been effaced by millennia of oppression, an active overturning of white supremacy and an active restoration of African glory. It celebrates those traditions that have survived the Middle Passage, slavery and further dispersal around the world, coalescing around the tri-colour red, gold and green of the Ethiopian flag, consumption of marijuana as a spiritual as well as a cultural practice and embrace of blackness as a source and guarantee of authenticity. Finally, it emphasizes community over individuality, and a rejection of exploitative practices – whether economic, personal or political – in favour of a restored paradise on earth in which black people will ascend to their rightful place of equality and deliverance.

Reggae carries with it all of this and more. If soul is the locus of inauthenticity for Wheatle, then reggae is the site of an historically rich black identity, one that is set against soul's superficial integrationism. Musically, this opposition manifests in terms of reggae's preference for the offbeat in its rhythms, a bass-line defiance of mainstream rock's four-on-the-floor beat. The music lopes along rather than being driven, and presents a stripped-down musicality against the big-band echoes of soul's use of brass. Lyrically, reggae breaks with soul's romance and gospel influences to present a politically sharp outlook that advocates for redemption in this world rather than a quietist attendance of it in the world to come. As Wheatle put it in his Afterword to *Brixton Rock*, 'for my peers and myself, reggae was the only thing that kept us going through those dark days of early Thatcherism. It spoke of our plight and our struggles and that is why I referred to certain reggae tracks in the text of *Brixton Rock* and even more so in *East of Acre Lane*. My way of paying homage if you like' (*Brixton* 252). Reggae's use of talk-over, where either the singer or a dub poet speaks over the background music rather than singing to a tune, likewise presents a voice of resistance enabled by the music rather than fighting against it or drowned out by it. Much of the time in Wheatle's novels, reggae is characterized in terms of menace, as well. It is 'rabble-rousing', 'full of menace' and 'relentless' (9, 11–12, 64), adding rude boy danger to the Rastafarian long view. Many of the chapter titles in *East of Acre Lane* are the names of reggae songs, providing a steady bassline to the narrative (e.g. Stir it Up, There She Goes and Ring the Alarm). The novels likewise bristle with the names of reggae artists, for example, 'Johnny Osbourne, The Twinkle Brothers, Gregory Isaacs, Dennis Brown' (*Brixton* 139). Anticipating rap's virulent celebration of violent heteronormative masculinity and nihilist/anarchistic politics just as the Lyceum's all-night dance party anticipated rave culture, reggae aligns itself with a strong masculine identity anchored in a quasi-military activism that celebrates tribal roots. In this, it is explicitly roots music, invoking the Old Testament vision of history acclaimed by Rastafarianism.

In a replay of a manoeuvre we have seen more than once already, reggae makes its way into mainstream white youth culture when it is separated from its Rastafarian backing and appropriated merely as a sonic style. Such appropriations go back at least to Teddy boy borrowings from gospel and early R&B. Reggae in particular had been appropriated even more recently in its ska version by the skinheads, and as an activist backing for one stream of punk. Rude boy style had formed the backbone of mod fashion throughout the 1960s, though separated from the rudies' reggae affiliations. With the 1980s, though, reggae influence on the white youth-cultural mainstream expands by an order of magnitude. Already '*The Specials*' deeply political *Ghost Town*, released in the summer of 1981, was one of the year's biggest selling records' (Afterword 252), marking a decided shift towards embracing reggae music on its own terms – at least among young black members of the underclass. When The Police upped the ante on their use of reggae in their early albums with their 1983 release *Synchronicity*, though, reggae went platinum. *Synchronicity* was such an enormous hit that The Police were, by the middle of that year, acknowledged to be the biggest band in the world. Interest in reggae spiked among white teenagers, and artists like Bob Marley and the Whalers suddenly found themselves globally popular across lines of class, race and nationality as they never had before. In a sharp turn away from the earlier mod borrowing of rudie style, white kids began adopting the signifiers of reggae cool, including the Rastafarian black nationalist regalia of the red, gold, and green colours, dreadlocks and of course the consumption of marijuana. Such adoptions work on a logic of equivalence, eliding race with class so that simply being economically disadvantaged equates to a long history of slavery and oppression – and that's at their best. At their worst, such adoptions are ignorant appropriations of reggae in a blithe pursuit of cool that cares not a whit for the historical, religious and political contexts in which it originated. Crucially, though, such appropriations seem – at least in the early 1980s – not to have been problematic for the young blacks in Wheatle's novels. Though they clearly respond to reggae as roots music that speaks to their racialized experience and the long history of slavery and dislocation out of which it emerges, they bear no resentment towards white people who listen to reggae, dress and style themselves in the Rasta aesthetic, attend the all-night reggae parties or even participate in the riots alongside their black peers. When it comes to reggae, Wheatle's characters are willing, it seems, to let race and class function as two sides of the same coin, forming a bond of solidarity that must have driven the racist members of the National Front nuts.

In both *Brixton Rock* and *East of Acre Lane*, the primary figure of Rastafarianism is Jah Nelson, a one-eyed reggae man who apparently fears no one and leaves his door open to all who would come to hear him teach the Rastafarian gospel. 'Jah' is an honorific, derived from Jaweh, and used in Rasta circles to designate a teacher or elevated wise man. 'Nelson' is a fascinating counterpart to this honorific, since it identifies Jah Nelson with no one more immediately than Admiral Horatio Nelson, perhaps the most famous commander in British naval history. The link ties Jah Nelson to British imperialist history, and directly to British activity in Africa, given Admiral Nelson's active service in Egypt, fighting during the Napoleonic wars. He was a key defender of British interests in north and northwestern Africa. Both Nelsons are one-eyed, Jah having lost his at the hands of the Jamaican police in his youth (*East* 158), and the Admiral having lost his in battle in 1797. Jah Nelson's single eye carries a metaphorical resonance as well, solidifying his role as the wise man in Brixton: In the kingdom of the blind the one-eyed man is king. Finally, Jah Nelson's blind eye likewise ties him into a very long tradition of the blind man who has insight, the missing eye serving as a visible guarantee of his wisdom.

And indeed, Jah Nelson is the only person who stands up to Terry Flynn – in Flynn's own apartment, no less – by demanding to know why he preys upon his own people and helps to keep them oppressed: '"if you're for your own people, why do you rob dem?" the rastaman asked, peering through the smoke and noting the gasps from the multitude of sinners inside the room' (BR 191). Flynn responds with 'a hot hatred' (192) and tries to bully Nelson into leaving, but Nelson pushes harder, asking why Flynn is so quick to stab other blacks when he has even less respect for whites. The conflict is generational, with the elder Nelson squaring off against the younger Flynn, but it's also ideological: People respect Nelson, while they only fear Flynn. 'Every ghetto yout' respected [Nelson]. Jah Nelson wasn't a man of violence' (192), which makes it all the harder for Flynn to kill him: 'Flynn knew that in his environment it was easier to ratchet-sketch another violent man' (192). Things get really interesting as the script flips. Flynn goes after Nelson's Rastafarianism, while Nelson becomes the man of menace. Flynn starts it: '"Why should I listen to a man who gives praises to a dead African Emperor who made his own people starve to death? [...] Emperor Haile Selassie I, fockin crook who 'ad whole 'eap ah money inna Swiss bank account an' made his people starve. Don't talk to me, dirty dread"' (192). Fascinatingly, Nelson doesn't spring to Selassie's defence, but effectively calls Flynn a coward: 'Remember dis, [...] those who induce fear are only hiding their own fears. Jah know!' (193). When Flynn leaps out of his chair and holds a blade to Nelson's one remaining eye, Nelson assumes an even more menacing tone: '"you'd better mek a good job of it. Cah if you leave me standing an' alive, in Jah's name I will tek 'way your life. You better believe it!"' (193). It's a direct confrontation between Rasta/reggae and rudie/reggae, in which the two streams are both starkly juxtaposed and shown to be remarkably similar. Only Jah Nelson is sufficiently respected to get away with such impudence, but in the end he descends to the same level of menace and bravado as Flynn. The distance between the two closes dramatically, exposing the extent to which they are in fact just two different kinds of the same outcome. The only reason Jah Nelson is in the apartment is to buy marijuana, suggesting that he, too, depends upon the violent gangster even as he strives to adopt the high ground.

Even so, it seems clear that Wheatle sees the Rastaman option as preferable to the rude boy option, presenting Jah Nelson as a beacon of wisdom and learning in the community, the only viable father figure in sight. By the time we get to *East of Acre Lane*, around a year after the action in *Brixton Rock*, Jah Nelson seems to have outgrown his lingering bad bwai tendencies. His criminal past is re-cast here as politically motivated and non-violent, and though the penalties are harsh, it sends a clear message about history and empire:

Apparently, Nelson had been arrested at the front door of Westminster Abbey with a 'disciple' of his, both of them carrying pick-axes. Defending himself and his disciple in court, Nelson told the magistrate that since European man had continually desecrated the tombs of ancient Egyptian royalty and got away with it, he didn't see no reason why he couldn't destroy the tomb of an English monarch. The magistrate sentenced him to six months in prison. (*East* 42)

Fresh out of prison, Nelson takes to 'delivering lectures on racial pride in Brockwell Park', earning him multiple arrests as 'a stirrer of racial hatred' (44). When he protests his harassment on the steps of the Brixton police station, he gets another month in prison for 'disturbance of the peace'. This shift, away from his prior presentation as a potentially violent man unafraid to challenge 'Terror' Flynn in his own apartment and into a figure of political protest, sets the stage for the riots that will conclude *East of Acre Lane*. More importantly, though, it presents Nelson as perhaps the only grown-up among a bevy of physically mature but emotionally stunted 'bwais' – whether

168   YOUTH CULTURE AND THE POST-WAR BRITISH NOVEL

sweet or rude. Biscuit, whom Jah Nelson singles out for some education, is always referred to as 'the youth' or 'the teenager' in relation to him. This language is reserved for Biscuit's encounters with Jah Nelson and does not appear elsewhere in the book. Their relationship is generationalized, if you will, articulated in terms that explicitly engage with the problematics of generational tension, continuity, and (mis-)understanding. Biscuit finds Jah Nelson to be almost impenetrably cryptic in his utterances, impatiently enduring his lessons so he can finish buying his dope. Nelson, for his part, is infinitely patient with Biscuit, adopting the long view of both history and the individual's maturation process that identifies him as both an extra-historical wise-man figure and a patient father figure for all the young men who lack real fathers in Brixton (and that is almost all of them). In this respect, Nelson represents a fully achieved masculinity that no longer needs to establish itself through domination of other men by violent means, or to show off its social standing. He presents a viable alternative to the rude boy culture that has captured so many of the young men.

That alternative locates Nelson in a long lineage going all the way back to Africa, a lineage of responsible men who understand their situation in Babylon and know the necessity of freedom from bondage. More, he understands fully how white culture foments tensions within the black underclass to keep it from coalescing into a revolutionary force. Against these forces, he stands, almost alone, for roots, history, political engagement and above all authenticity. As such, he represents an historical alternative to the quagmire of the present: The last chapter of *East of Acre Lane* is entitled 'Redemption', and features Nelson beginning the long process of educating Denise into an awareness of black history. It's the first step in helping her cultivate the requisite self-respect to move beyond her abuse by Flynn and enforced period as a prostitute:

> 'But let me tell you dis. You are ah strong African woman, first an' foremost, let no one tek dat 'way from you.'
>   Denise managed a half smile. Jah Nelson resumed. 'An' when you realise dat, you will rise from your pit of low esteem.' The dread's features changed from a smile to the countenance of a historian. 'Fe dat reason alone you should walk proud. Great men an' women 'ave come fort' from your loins an' history is blessed wid dem.' (305)

Nelson launches into a prepared inventory of great figures in black history, going back to the Egyptian goddess Isis and concluding with the recently deceased Bob Marley himself (305). Nelson urges education on Denise as the key to overcoming her own grief and guilt, and to rising up to build a strong foundation for the next generation, perhaps the generation that will finally redeem history. 'Denise, fully understanding the parable, smiled and nodded' (307). So ends the novel, with the suggestion that there is a return from the *East of Acre Lane/Eden*, the land of Nod, the curse of Cain, a deliverance from Babylon just out of reach (for now).

There is a fundamental problem with this conclusion, though, in that it places the burden of such a redemption upon Denise, a woman and victim of deranged masculinity, without taking up the problematics of masculinity per se as they continue to ravage the young men who form the novel's primary focus. In terms of the generational logics at play here – and of the formation of youth culture in this increasingly complex environment – Jah Nelson's status as a viable alternative to the arrested adolescence of the other 'bwais' in the novel is key. As I have suggested, Nelson serves as the primary, if not the only, father figure in the novels. But there is a problem with this: Nelson has no family, no wife, no issue. When he is asked about whether he has a wife, Nelson admits that he has never even had a girlfriend, that he has instead devoted all his time to his studies and to spreading the Rastafarian gospel. In this total repudiation of romantic sexual intimacy, he represents the polar opposite of all that soul stands for, the polar opposite of the perverse path down which both Brenton and Juliet (incest) and Denise (prostitution) wander. As the quintessential rasta man, he is all politics, community, history, wisdom – but he is utterly hollow as a father figure. He can only function as a father *figure*, an image or trope of fatherhood. Instead, he represents an interestingly monocular figure looking to the past. With his one good eye, he can see history, the past and the authenticity that resides there. But his blind eye, presumably the eye turned towards the future, can see nothing. He can suggest no way forward other than a dogged return to past greatness: regress, not progress. He instructs young men and women in their heritage but himself models no viable futurity.

The power of the irony Wheatle thus encodes manifests with devastating clarity in the call and response of the reggae parties in *East of Acre Lane*. At those parties, dub street poets are invited on stage to recite their verses, earning the crowd's response, '"FORWARD!"' (278). One such poet, Yardman Irie, takes the stage at a party the day after the 1981 riot with which the novel culminates:

> Yardman Irie grabbed the mic and addressed the revolutionaries. 'In tune to de great boss sounds of Crucial Rocker. Dis one is special request to all de revolutionary foot soldier, so flash up your lighter if you der-ya inna de uprising. From de murder of Blair Peach in 1979, to de eleventh of April, 1981. An' if you was der-so, bawl FORWARD!'
> 'FORWARD!' the crowd cried. (278)

The ensuing poem rehearses complaints about the current political and economic situation, referring to the riot as an 'uprising', threatening to 'riot inna friggi' Buckingham Palace', and concluding with an admonition/threat:

So listen Maggie T'atcher an' William Whitelaw
You better do somet'ing fe de needy an' de poor
Fe de ghetto suffferer you don't open any door
If you carry on dat way den we declare WAR. (279)

The way 'FORWARD' through armed insurrection is quickly dropped, though, and the crowd readily embraces the next poet, who introduces instead a narcotizing rhyme that celebrates lightweight diversions instead of open rebellion:

Swing an' Dine, dance all the time
Swing an' Dine, dance all the time
That's how we do it 'pon de Front Line
Yes, that's how we do it 'pon de Front Line. (279–280)

The reference to the 'Front Line' echoes with the call to '*declare WAR*', but since 'Front Line' is just the vernacular name for the strip of road which hosts most drug deals, record shops, and violent crime, the resonance dissipates rather quickly – the energy is lost. Instead, where a moment before the crowd of 'revolutionaries' had shouted 'FORWARD!', now they robotically repeat the second poet's inertializing couplets:

SWING AND DINE, DANCE ALL THE TIME
SWING AND DINE, DANCE ALL THE TIME
THAT'S HOW WE DO IT 'PON DE FRONT LINE
THAT'S HOW WE DO IT 'PON DE FRONT LINE. (280)

No revolution is in the offing. Instead, Biscuit, Floyd and some others stage a risky raid upon Terry Flynn's brothel to liberate Biscuit's sister Denise from his clutches. They succeed, opening the way for Denise to visit Jah Nelson in the final chapter and begin to recover her self-respect and respect for her black heritage, but it is a far cry from storming Buckingham Palace to bring about a revolutionary future. The utopian potential so often located in youth culture is defused almost as soon as it is envisioned in concrete political terms, giving additional heft to Jah Nelson's inability to see anything but the past. Even the street poets on stage at the rave cannot see a clear path forward. Like Jah Nelson, they can see into the past, but not the future.

This troubled futurity – directly tied to Jah Nelson's failure to become an actual husband and father, to be in fact only a father *figure* rather than an actual father – marks a new stage in the development of generational tensions as we have seen them engaged so far. In *Saturday Night and Sunday Morning* and *Absolute Beginners*, the parental generation represented official history, the self-aggrandizing war narrative, and above all tradition: conformity, in a word. Youth culture emerged as a defiant

FIGURE 4.2 *March Against Apartheid in Trafalgar Square, 2 November 1986.*
Contributor: Janine Wiedel Photolibrary/Alamy Stock Photo.

break with that context, rejecting the world that had brought about two
world wars and the Holocaust, and demanding a new world with a new
set of priorities. In *A Clockwork Orange*, the generational break was in
full swing, manifesting in the newspaper editorial's hand-wringing over
the problem of 'Modern Youth', and culminating in the humiliation of
the parent culture's institutions of government, punishment, education,
and art. With *The Rachel Papers* and *The Buddha of Suburbia*, youth
culture crossed a certain Rubicon, facing up to the fact that the parent
culture was now irreversibly made up of those who had previously forged
the youth-cultural frontier. The result was both a kind of meta-stasis of
youth culture – a self-ironization on all levels – and a profound shift in
how the parental culture was understood. As erstwhile rebels themselves,
the parents in *The Rachel Papers* and *The Buddha of Suburbia* tended to
regress rather than stay grown up. They divorce and begin dating, have
affairs, take drugs, pursue mysticism and continue the hedonistic habits
they had cultivated in their youth. The resulting chaos and confusion
over generational authority drives much of the narrative of *The Rachel
Papers* and *The Buddha of Suburbia*, both of which feature young men
who deplore not their fathers' conservatism or quietism, but their fathers'
irresponsibly adolescent conduct. Both Charles and Karim fantasize
about taking their fathers to task for their self-indulgence and actually
make plays for the moral high ground at key points in their respective

narratives. In the end, though, the generational tension is resolved with the conventional *Bildung* as each young man comes to understand his father as a flawed individual who nonetheless continues to occupy the mythic psychic space and role of *pater familias*.

In Wheatle's novels it is otherwise. *Brixton Rock* and *East of Acre Lane* present us with a parental generation that has never achieved full adulthood, let alone indulgently taken the decision to regress to an earlier developmental stage. Instead, Wheatle presents us with a parental generation that is itself in crisis, facing structural obstacles to full maturity themselves. The independence, autonomy and self-sufficiency long associated with even working-class adulthood elude most of the grown-ups in Wheatle's Brixton. Cut off from becoming a source of tradition and stability against which their children can rebel, the mothers, fathers, aunts, uncles and neighbours in *Brixton Rock* and *East of Acre Lane* are likewise pushed hard from behind as their offspring themselves grow up. The results are twofold: First, both the adults and their children find themselves in rebellion against the system that blocks their access to maturity and generational renewal; second, we find a bottleneck, an adolescence-jam in which some simply vanish, others leapfrog to play roles for which they are not prepared, and yet others simply keep trying different blocked routes, blindly seeking a way forward where there is simply none to be had.

Exemplary in this regard is Biscuit and Denise's mother who, though she tries to do the right thing, nonetheless finds herself with three children by different fathers – all of them now absent – and unable to support her family on her own. She regularly accepts money from Biscuit to cover bills and buy food; Biscuit even provides money to Denise so she can buy a new dress. Though she claims not to want to know how Biscuit earns his money, his mother must be aware that it is ill-gotten, primarily by selling drugs. This economic relationship places Biscuit in the traditional role of the husband and father as bread-winner, though he is neither a father nor a husband and can only fulfil his traditional role by operating outside the system of respectable legality. He wields economic control over the family, but also bears enormous responsibility for them as a result:

> He knew it all came down to money; that was the bottom line. He wouldn't have to wake up to family debates so often if there was more of it around. Maybe he could give Denise the money for the dress if he sold a decent amount of herb in the next few days. That would get her off her mother's back. Perhaps he could even buy Royston his much-needed new shoes for school if things went alright. Biscuits mother had mentioned to him a few days before how she had had to box the young bwai for kicking stones. He knew it was a hint he couldn't ignore. How much is dat? He asked himself. A pair of new shoes might cost a tenner – and a new dress? Maybe twenty notes for a decent one. (*East* 21)

Biscuit's disjointed position manifest subtly here in his reference to getting Denise off '*her* mother's back', rather than *their* mother's back, or even just Mummy's back. Hortense is mother to both of them, though they have different fathers, but in this moment of 'weighing up his financial position' (*East* 21), Biscuit is something other than Denise's sibling: He is her provider. He feels the full pressure of the household bread-winner, allocating funds for school clothes, luxury items, food, laundry, rent, gas bills and so on (*East* 57).

The quandary of Biscuit's situation manifests in the fact that despite the economic responsibility he bears, he lacks the authority to discipline or control how the family members behave. His privileged status is constantly challenged by Denise in a dynamic of sibling rivalry that is further complicated by the fact that Denise and Biscuit, and even their younger brother Royston, all have different fathers:

> 'Don't frig me 'bout, Denise.' He raised his voice, pointing a finger at his sister. 'I told you already not to deal wid [Nunchaks]. You carry on an' see dat pure tribulation don't lick your behind.'
> 'An' since when you become my daddy?' Denise replied. (*East* 199)

The ironies proliferate: Denise caught Nunchaks' eye in the first place because she was wearing the dress Biscuit paid for, and Biscuit is completely right about Nunchaks, who will quickly turn Denise from his girlfriend into one of his prostitutes. This topsy-turvy situation presents an intense double-bind for Biscuit. He is trapped in a generational time-warp of sorts, in effect having to perform the role of his own father and his mother's husband before he has grown up. It's a role he has neither chosen nor can easily escape, leaving him no choice but to continue selling drugs if he is to have any chance at all to achieve a mature masculinity. That is, he must remain a 'bad bwai' on the Front Line of *Brixton* in order to sustain his family, as even his mother recognizes: 'Hortense looked at the cash [for Denise's dress] for five seconds before opening her left palm. "Y'know Lincoln, yu 'ave ah 'eart. Like I said before, me nuh waan to know weh yu get your money from. But yu 'ave ah 'eart. God bless"' (East 54). He has no time for a girlfriend, let alone *Bildung*. Instead, his only prospects are to follow in his father's (and Denise's father's and Royston's father's) footsteps: to disappear. Whether he does this by simply walking out, as his neighbour Frank does temporarily, or by being sent to prison, or by being killed in the course of his criminal activities – the novel begins with this very real prospect – is irrelevant. He will simply become another young man acting *like* a father for but a brief time before he vanishes from the scene like so many others before him. Though she struggles to provide security and consistency for her family, their mother has in fact created a precarious situation in which no one is quite sure of their place, and each person has good reason to feel that the others are benefitting disproportionately.

Crucially, Biscuit can only act *like* a father – or rather, like what he imagines a father acts like – because he has no template. The only fathers on show in the novel are struggling or inadequate, so the image of fatherly authority and care Biscuit tries to live up to is entirely imaginary. It's a mixed product of the volatile masculinity he imbibes on the streets and his own sense of what he would have liked in a father for himself. That is, it draws upon youth culture to generate a passable performance of adulthood, measured against an imaginary – and therefore idealized – standard. Recursively enforcing this pattern, the lack of a father makes the choice of joining the rude boy youth culture more or less inevitable for Biscuit: He becomes trapped in a loop where the absence of a father forces him into the rudie youth culture, and that youth culture's forms of masculinity circle back to inform the model of mature masculinity by which Biscuit charts his role as *pater familias*. It gives entirely new resonance to the old saw that 'the child is father to the man'. This is uncharted territory for us. Previous young men chose their youth-cultural affiliations in some sort of clearly *generational* relationship with the parental generation, whether of rebellion, disregard, scorn, mimicry, or what-have-you. Here, though, we have a young man who is forced into a particular youth-cultural affiliation by the *lack* of a sufficient parental generation to define himself against. The result is a closed circuit of reduced possibilities that can have only a handful of possible outcomes – none of them very good.

This generational turmoil illustrates a wider youth-cultural anxiety that perhaps the preceding generations have exhausted all possibilities. The future, it would seem, has an expiration date, and the young people in Wheatle's novels appear to have been born both too early and too late. They are out of time in more ways than one. They lack sufficient leeway to forge their own identities by pushing back against their parents' values (even if in the end they accept or reaffirm them). They are also historically disjointed, suffering the misfortune of being teenagers in a moment characterized by an unprecedented lack of socio-economic opportunity and a preceding generation unable in key ways to move into its respectable middle age. In this respect, Biscuit and his like provide a powerful correlative to the larger sense of the 1980s as bringing about the end of the post-war consensus – the decade concludes with exclamations that the end of History itself is nigh. The utopian energies, however misdirected, that animated post-war youth culture for three full decades seem finally to have run into a stone wall. If the immediate post-war youth cultures sought a decisive break with history and their parents' generation, then the youth cultures of the 1980s finally achieve it, though the resulting panorama is not quite what had been envisioned.

Brenton's family situation in *Brixton Rock* is even more complicated. Having been given up by his parents in early infancy, Brenton has grown up without any family at all, so the generational tension we are tracing has remained almost entirely mythic. Until he meets his mother, Brenton's parents are both, for all intents and purposes, imaginary. They form the key poles in a mythos where he is permanently an infant, but also, by the time of the narrative, a nearly-grown man. The frequency with which events in his adult life, particularly after he remakes contact with his mother, are juxtaposed with memories or dreams of his childhood in care homes illustrates this simultaneity. As he is slowly integrated into Juliet and Cynthia's household, memories of his childhood in care flood back regularly, providing a powerful counterpoint to the promise of relief held out to him. This juxtaposition also presents him as a figure who has been wrenched out of time, at once re-living a traumatic childhood he has certainly not left behind and struggling for a mature identity. As with Biscuit, the result is a generational time-warp in which traumatic past, confusing present and undefinable future commingle. Hanging like a pall over it all is a sense of generational betrayal, of a failure to provide the conditions for thriving on both the personal and social levels. Brenton tells Juliet in clear terms:

I don't think I'll ever forgive my mother, or my paps come to think of it', he told her flatly. 'I suppose you can call it deep emotional scars or what you like. Even now I still have nightmares about when I was a kid. Me and my mother, in time, will probably get on and be polite to each other. But don't ask me to forgive. Not while the memories are still so clear. (*Brixton* 106)

Reversing Biscuit's use of 'her' to designate Denise's mother, excluding himself from identification as one of her children, so Brenton here uses 'my mother' to describe Cynthia, excluding Juliet from the relationship. The implication is clear: The mother who abandoned her child is *his* mother, while the mother who loved, kept and raised her child is *her* mother. Brenton splits her into two figures, associating the bad mother with abandonment and betrayal, intermixing that foundational trauma with the abuse he suffered in various care homes. His anger with his mother is thus simultaneously a social anger, a generational resentment that misrecognizes the circumstances of his placement in care as evidence of his mother's selfishness. More importantly, it conditions his masculinity as a fragile construct forged in the absence of *both* a viable father figure and a valid maternal model.

The complexity this generates for Brenton as he attempts to leave childhood and accede to mature masculinity manifests in his memories of the one mother figure Brenton *did* have as a child: The powerful matron of the care home, known only to the children as 'The Belt'. The Belt is sadistic, cruel and authoritarian; 'She was a short, squat white woman with long straggling brown hair. Aged in her mid-forties, she smiled rarely and had a feverish hatred for anyone under the age of eleven' (94). Many of Brenton's worst memories of his time in care involve her arbitrary and excessive punishments. Brenton's understanding of himself, and especially of the mother who abandoned him, is conditioned by the Belt. His anger towards his mother must be understood simultaneously as rage at having been abandoned *and* as transferred fear and loathing for the Belt, now directed at his mother. That is, Brenton's generational angst must be understood as a product of both insufficient attention and superabundant attention: Insufficient in terms of tenderness and care and superabundant in terms of violent enforcement of arbitrary rules. I suggest that he blames his mother for both of these facets of his childhood and struggles to overcome them in his rude boy persona.

As evidence for this, consider the intensity of his anger towards his mother versus the relative equanimity he displays towards the Belt. Though Brenton clearly thinks of The Belt as evil, he also accepts her as a fact: 'The young Brenton Brown was summoned downstairs, dressed only in his striped pyjamas. He knew what his fate was' (*Brixton* 94). Resigned to his fate, Brenton seems to accept the Belt as an objective element of his personal history, instead transferring all his anger and pain onto his mother. His reaction to The Belt's beating him for lashing out at a teacher who had called him '"a nigger"' is wilting understatement: 'Adults are sometimes so unjust to children [...] and you don't know who to trust' (95). By contrast, whenever he gets the chance, Brenton charges his mother with the crime of placing him in care, and holds her responsible for the anger and pain he feels:

> 'You could never begin to know what the feeling's like when you are a kid in a children's home', he told her slowly. 'The friends I had went to various relations to spend some time over the Christmas holidays. And me? Well, no relation for me to go to, was there? That time I spend on my own, I used to do a lot of thinking, you know what I'm saying? Yeah, I used to think nuff. I thought about my mother, and shit, I hated her badly; I still hate her.' (*Brixton* 106)

The logic at work excuses The Belt for being who she is, while it condemns his mother for behaving unnaturally and even transfers his childhood sense of outrage at the Belt's injustice onto his mother. Even more interestingly, Brenton thinks very little if at all about his father – 'I don't think I'll ever forgive my mother, or my paps *come to think of it*', he tells Juliet, including his father only as an after-thought. Focussing on his mother's unnatural abandonment of a son by his mother, Brenton appears to accept his father's parallel abandonment as normal, if not natural. His anger over being abandoned, and the generational resentment that goes along with it, is fascinatingly specific.

As I've suggested, that anger derives in no small part from a fundamental misunderstanding of the circumstances surrounding his abandonment. This misunderstanding determines how Brenton navigates the generational tensions that manifest with increasing clarity as he re-establishes contact with his mother. It also illuminates the crisis of masculinity that finds renewed impetus in that navigation. The origin story Brenton constructs for himself on the basis of a very few very vague bits of information is anchored in error, and deviates tellingly from the facts of the case. It is a fantasy of abandonment designed to justify his sense of anger and frustration, and thus to ratify his choice of masculinity. According to the story he has told himself, Brenton's mother got pregnant with him and, preferring to keep her options open and to continue her youthful pursuit of pleasure, placed him in care rather than accept the adult responsibility of caring for him: '"While you've been living a cushy life, I have been fighting and struggling just to stay alive, and sometimes, believe me, I didn't think it was worth it"' (*Brixton* 60). He thus lays the blame for all the violence and abuse he suffered consequently while in care on his mother. In this rendition, Brenton's choice of a rude boy identity appears rational, as does the sense of independence and rugged masculinity it encodes. The path of sweet bwai was never open to him in large part because his imaginary back-story precludes such emotional openness, with its hope for acceptance, love and libidinal release. Keep in mind that his good friend Floyd, who was raised by his mother, is an aspiring sweet bwai by contrast. Though he is in constant conflict with his father, Floyd nonetheless understands his masculinity as related to femininity rather than utterly isolated. Moreover, he stands in a solid and recognizable generational relationship to his mother: 'he thought the generation gap between his mother and himself had grown the length of the Brixton dole queue' (*Brixton* 216). Though the gap is perhaps sad, it is at least consistent with generational renewal and proper allocation of subject positions. Deprived of this clarity, Brenton follows the rude-boy path of almost exclusive homosociality, either keeping to himself or mixing only with other rudies on the make. Even when Floyd brings girls around to their half-way house, Brenton must be coaxed into joining them in Floyd's room and soon enough makes excuses to leave – this despite Carol's clear attraction to him. His romantic entanglement with his half-sister Juliet only illustrates the dangers of his self-defeating approach to masculinity and generational tension: Unable to accept his mother's love but driven by his instinctive need for affection, Brenton fuses the filial with the libidinal in a perverse short-circuit. His incestuous relationship with Juliet is precisely the negative version of what he needs: He simultaneously achieves mature masculine heterosexuality and accepts his mother's love (at one remove) in a transgression that threatens to place both permanently out of reach.

The irony undergirding Brenton's fate derives from the fact that he is entirely mistaken about the story of his abandonment, and consequently about the shape his life has taken as a result. The real story doesn't necessarily make things simpler, though, instead adding some important depth to Wheatle's rendering of the youth-cultural impasse in which young people like Brenton, Biscuit, Denise, Floyd, Sharon and the rest find themselves.

Brenton believes that his mother is the one who put him into care, and the records appear to bear out this belief until Mr. Lewis digs deeper and discovers that it was actually Brenton's father who signed him over. As the details of the story emerge, reality shifts for Brenton as both the actual conditions under which he was abandoned are clarified, and his relationship to those conditions changes.

So, here's the story. Brenton's mother, Cynthia, had come '"over to England in 1961 [...] to study nursing"', part of the first wave of West Indian immigrants taking advantage of the 1948 British Nationality Act (*Brixton* 52). She was already married and had a child, Juliet, with her husband Dwight back in Jamaica. In England, she fell in love with a white man, Gary, and soon found herself pregnant by him. When Dwight turned up unexpectedly in England '"just before Christmas 1962"' he and his family demanded that Cynthia break off her relationship with Gary and give up the infant Brenton for adoption (*Brixton* 52). Here's where things take an unexpected twist: Rather than see Cynthia put the infant up for adoption, Gary offers to raise him on his own: 'Gary promised Cynthia that he and his family would look after their child and give Brenton a decent start in life' (*Brixton* 110). Cynthia finishes her nursing studies and returns to Jamaica, believing that Gary is raising their son. But Gary finds the going tougher than he expected. His family and friends turn on him and he finds no support from any quarter in his effort to raise a mixed-race child in the 1960s: 'Gary's family were fiercely against him rearing a mixed-race child, and were not prepared to help in any way. So, ultimately, feeling desperate and at his wits end, Gary had placed Brenton in care, feeling unable to give his son the proper upbringing he deserved. Even the people Gary had thought of as friends let him down when he most needed them, refusing to look after the infant Brenton while he completed his studies' (*Brixton* 110). In the end, unable to carry on, Gary places Brenton in care and signs the papers to give him up.

As we can see, Brenton initially has things almost precisely the wrong way around. He has spent his life resenting his mother for selfishly abandoning him, while his father was the one who put him in care. He hates his mother for choosing her own comfort over raising him, when she was in fact faced with an impossible choice: She was forced to choose between her two children, since if she stayed in England she would be blocked from ever seeing Juliet again. Choosing what she believed to be the lesser of two evils, Cynthia left Brenton with the man she loved and returned to protect her daughter from the extended family she did not trust to care properly for her. Brenton's resentment of his mother is misplaced, belonging more properly with Gary who – tellingly – has disappeared so completely that there is no question of ever tracking him down. Cynthia, by contrast, has returned to England and though she has not sought out Brenton, has not hidden from him either; she is quite easily located by Mr. Lewis the social worker. Both the actual conditions under which he was abandoned and his relationship to them shift for Brenton: The discovery of the truth places him on a false footing and complicates his previously easy stance of moral condemnation of his mother. It also challenges his rude boy identity, insofar as the model of masculinity he has adopted is based upon a false origin story and a psychological profile for which he is at least partly responsible (as the one who created the story of the evil mother in the first place). It presents him with an alternative account of himself, one which has class as well as gender and sexual implications. An alternate history carries with it the potential for an alternate future as well, a chance to move ahead through healing, regeneration and optimism.

The acrobatics Brenton must go through to navigate these revelations greatly complicate both his own psychological state and the novel's vision of generational responsibility, betrayal and progression. As he gets re-acquainted with his mother, Brenton enters a topsy-turvy generational situation that mirrors Biscuit's relationship with his mother. The difference is that where Biscuit cedes the moral high ground to his mother but holds the power of economic agency, Brenton struggles to hold the moral high ground, while lacking – and resenting the lack of – economic power. Brenton's rebellious reggae-based values license him to hold on to his false belief that his mother abandoned him to gain comfort: Personal resentment over abandonment morphs smoothly into socio-economic resentment that carries with it generational overtones. From his place as an oppressed member of the underclass, Brenton is able to convert his lingering anger over his mother's abandonment into a complex class-based rage at her relative material prosperity. Her home, always filled with the smell of home-cooking, at once represents a tempting fantasy of comfort – the maternal sphere concretized as bourgeois stability – and a capitulation to the white, capitalist values of the very Babylon that holds him in check:

> 'What's the matter?'
> 'I know I shouldn't, but shit, look at this. Bwai, am I jealous! Nice bedroom, nice yard, you got a job and t'ing, know what I mean? And what have I got? I'll tell you what I've got – one pair of decent trainers and my brethren's old suitcase. Yeah, I envy you nuff.'
> Juliet gazed into her brother's eyes, suddenly feeling guilty about possessing her material luxuries. (*Brixton* 113)

As the messy reality of the trans-generational social structures that effectively kept his mother from living up to the ideal by which he has judged her for seventeen years becomes harder and harder to ignore, Brenton is himself driven into two profoundly untenable situations: an escalating conflict with Terry Flynn and a romantic entanglement with his half-sister Juliet. I will turn to the former of these in my discussion of masculinity, just below, concentrating instead on the latter for the present.

Brenton's relationship with Juliet captures the deformation of libidinal and generational energies manifest outwardly in the social stagnation of the ongoing recession of the 1970s–1980s, and exploding on the streets in the riots of 1981 and 1985. Brenton and Juliet are children of the same mother but two different fathers: Gary and Dwight, respectively. They have never known each other, or even about each other, until Brenton turns up at Cynthia and Juliet's house one evening. Their parentage bears historical import, fusing the domestic realities of an historically white country with the legacy of its centuries-long imperialism. In terms of social condemnation, Wheatle presents miscegenation as the mirror image of incest, the one an exogamous violation of taboo, the other an endogamous violation. The imperialist legacy of mixed blood itself triggers social proscriptions that see Brenton orphaned while his fully black sister is raised in a loving home. Their incestuous relationship is in a key way then a return of the repressed in inverted form. Like her Shakespearean namesake, Juliet is one of a pair of star-crossed lovers whose two houses are so implacably set against each other that their only children must die rather than consummate their love. In *Brixton Rock*, though, the two houses are fused into one and sublimated into a rhetorical opposition between the mixed-blood, underclass, man and the pure-blood, bourgeois, woman. The family torn apart by social pressures – and, importantly, masculine concerns over lineage – fuses when the two lines reconnect, giving a new resonance to the notion of the nuclear family. Just as Dwight and his family's, and Gary's friends', condemnation forced a separation of mother from child, so the return of the 'Prodigal Son' (209) flips the script into an unnaturally close bond between siblings. Just as Biscuit runs into problems by attempting to play the father to his sister Denise, so Brenton faces a near-impossible situation in playing the lover to Juliet – and being barred from playing the father to their child. Careening wildly from one extreme to the other, the children of Windrush replay on an intimate level the dynamic of welcome, repudiation and grudging acceptance already lived in public and historical terms by their parents.

Brenton and Juliet's relationship generates plenty of difficulties to be overcome, including hiding it from Cynthia and Floyd, and managing the guilt that attends knowingly sleeping with one's half-sibling, but easily its single most important element is the child it produces. We may be tempted to read this child as redemptive, a sign of a hopeful futurity along the lines of the only other baby we have seen so far, Leila Kollontai – Jamila and Simon's offspring in *The Buddha of Suburbia*. But Wheatle undercuts any such hopeful possibility by underlining the persistent taboo on racial mixing, at least among black Brixtonians (recall Denise's sneering at romantic racial mixing in her rejection of soul clubs), and adding incest to the mix to ensure that Juliet and Brenton's child faces a difficult prospect. Wheatle underlines the social disapproval of racial mixing by timing the news of Juliet's pregnancy to coincide with Brenton's final battle with Flynn – a battle that has its origins in Flynn's calling Brenton 'a liccle half-breed' (19). As the fight escalates, Brenton increasingly risks his life to defend his honour against Flynn's articulation of the persistent social disapproval of racial mixing, a minor key repetition of the racist politics driving the 1980s vicious skinhead revival (the return of the 'bovver boys' sometimes known simply as 'Oi!') and the perennially resurgent National Front. Given the traumatic history surrounding Cynthia and Gary's abandonment of Brenton because of social disapproval of miscegenation, still resonating in insults like those Flynn tosses about, it is clear that even if miscegenation were its only handicap, Juliet and Brenton's child would already face an uphill battle.

Wheatle doubles down on this particular baby's marginal position by compounding racial with familial mixing. The fact that the child is also a product of incest ironically provokes Cynthia to visit the same sort of condemnation upon Juliet as was visited upon her by her family and friends a generation before. Soon enough, though, she voices precisely the point I'm trying to outline here: 'Cynthia continued: ' "Sometimes, t'ings in life work out funny. An' sometimes people don't 'ave no control over dem destiny, y'understand?" Brenton nodded impassively. "It seem like history repeat itself"' (*Brixton* 247). Perhaps because of his experience as a mixed-race child, Brenton feels no guilt or remorse at all for his relationship with Juliet, simply embracing love where he finds it, while Juliet torments herself and ultimately breaks off the relationship because she cannot lie to her mother any longer. This difference tellingly illustrates the extent to which Juliet has imbibed moral norms through her stable familial and social upbringing, where Brenton has come to view all such norms as mere exercises of power. Moreover, as an aspiring rude bwai, Brenton is predisposed to reject social norms and to take what he wants when he sees it. He's grown up in a setting dominated by abuse at the hands of people with power, and his confused moral-political consciousness has no room for nuance beyond rudie assertiveness and menace – even if they are anchored in profound insecurity and confusion. As a more or less constant object of various such exercises, Brenton views the norms that encode and naturalize them with suspicion if not outright scorn. He is painfully maladapted to the kind of normativity that has so irreversibly shaped Juliet's subjectivity, not because he has been excluded from it, but because he has been shaped as its other. He is a rude boy reggae man stranded in Babylon and awaiting delivery back to a land of promise and equality. In this respect, he is, no less than Shakespeare's Romeo and Juliet, condemned in advance to choose among a series of impossible options – just as Cynthia was forced to do a generation earlier. Had the problem been simply that of racial mixing, perhaps there would have been a viable futurity in *Brixton Rock*; racial mixing was gradually becoming acceptable in the 1980s, as the sudden rise of bands mixing black and white musicians (e.g. UB40) indicates. But Wheatle closes down this possibility decisively by adding incest to the mix. In 1980, as today, incest remained not only deeply unacceptable, but outright illegal. As a symbol of the future, an emblem of hope, then, Brenton and Juliet's child manifests a form of impossibility, a future that starts out foreclosed.

It begins life with a potentially crippling deficit, one that parallels the historical deficit faced by the orphaned mixed-race infant Brenton, and facing a lifetime of having to overcome not only a heritage of mixed race but also the shame of being the product of an incestuous coupling.

Wheatle thus invokes structural constraints upon human potential in a way that practically forces Brenton to repeat history by abandoning his own child. In their final conversation, Brenton asks Juliet, '"So what you gonna do?"' (*Brixton* 248). When Juliet confirms that she will keep the baby and keep living with Cynthia, both she and Brenton make it clear that he will *not* be centrally involved in raising the child, much less acting as a father to it. Juliet says, '"After all that's happened I hope you keep in touch"', to which Brenton replies only, '"Don't worry about that; I will. This family is all I've got"' (*Brixton* 248). Brenton will 'keep in touch', but his romance with Juliet is over, he has permanently damaged his relationship with Cynthia (ironically – and legitimately – earning her disapproval just as he had initially believed she had earned his by abandoning him), and he will remain a part of their lives (perhaps), but only peripherally. Importantly, in *East of Acre Lane*, Brenton has a picture of a baby – presumably *this* baby – in his apartment, but there is no mention of his relationship with Juliet and Cynthia, or of his being a father. Wheatle strikingly creates a situation in which Brenton both becomes yet another in the epidemic of absentee fathers, and illuminates the sorts of social and structural pressures that lie behind that epidemic. The key point here is that it is not the fact of incest, or even the fact of miscegenation, that drives the stifled development of a viable parental culture but a long history of familial disruption, cultural prejudice and multi-generational dysfunction. Evidently, Wheatle sees no easy resolution to the problem, either: Brenton and Juliet's child will grow up without a father, battling against social pressures she had no choice in facing. The anarchic utopian energy by which post-war youth cultures initially defined themselves has, it seems, at last been recontained decisively.

If the generational chaos captured in the relationship between sons and their mothers represents one side of this culmination, the other is captured by the troubled relationships between fathers and sons in the novels – when the fathers are present at all. As we have seen, Brenton has no father, though his mother has had one husband and one lover; Biscuit's mother has had three husbands and a child by each of them; even Aunt Jenny, Biscuit's mother's sister, is a single mother despite belonging to the church-going lower-middle-class. Equally telling, virtually none of the young men is a father in any responsible way, though one or two are credited with having had children with women they then abandon. The only exception to this rule would seem to be Brenton, and we have already seen how complicated that situation is, and how he is de facto barred from fatherhood, pre-empted as it were by his status as the baby's uncle.

Indeed, there are only a tiny handful of fathers present in either novel: In *Brixton Rock* Floyd's father still lives with his mother though Floyd has been in care for several years. In *East of Acre Lane*, Biscuit's neighbour Frank still lives with his wife and children though he is just as subject to structural blockages and economic hardship as anyone else. Floyd's conflict with his father has created an abyss between them that is every bit as bad as having no father at all. As we have seen, Jah Nelson, who has no wife or children, represents the most viable father figure in the novels, though he remains simply that: a figure. Even so stalwart a character as Frank, who ultimately kills Nunchaks, at one point abandons his family for several days, ironically returning only after a chance encounter with Jah Nelson in the park: The figurative father counsels the actual father into reassuming responsibilities he himself has avoided. The fact that Frank is both white and a close friend of Biscuit's family illustrates the structural nature of the generational blockage facing Wheatle's Brixtonians: This is not about race, but about socio-economic status and a significant log-jam in the inter-generational dynamic. The result is an epidemic of arrested adolescence, as young men push into their twenties and beyond without being able to accede to full manhood. As Royston puts it, '"So, when people been looking for a job for a long time, and they can't find one, do they do what Frank done? Just go somewhere and go missing?"' (*East* 53). Frank's disappearance highlights the intense pressure placed upon underclass parents in Thatcher's England, playing out a drama of paternal abandonment for his family – however temporarily – that virtually every other character has already experienced, some of them multiple times. That drama itself resonates with the increasing sense/realization that the larger caretaker of social welfare, the government, is itself in the process of walking out on its charges, leaving them to fend for themselves even as it places the means of doing so out of reach.

Nowhere is the psychological impact of absent fathers and the larger social implication of that absence more profoundly manifest than in the story of Mr. Brown. Mr. Brown is the name Brenton gives to a dilapidated scarecrow he finds in the shed of his care home, and which he lovingly restores. Importantly, though the home has various adults acting as housefathers and housemothers, it is dictatorially run by the Belt. The home is thus an institutional parallel to the fatherless homes we see everywhere we turn in Wheatle's Brixton, with a strong woman holding everything together in the absence of a masculine counterpart – though the Belt's sadism decisively separates her from the mothers in the novels, who clearly care deeply for their children even if they often make poor choices or face insuperable barriers to providing ideal home situations for them. Brenton's desire for a father is manifestly acute, and he clearly restores the scarecrow to meet that need, as its name indicates: Brenton's last name is Brown, and he privately dubs the scarecrow Mr. Brown, though he keeps this information entirely to himself. Even the Belt approves: 'she thought it was encouraging that Brenton displayed an interest in constructing something' (*Brixton* 226). It is at once an aesthetic object Brenton creates, something he can care about and in which he can invest himself, and a fetish of his absent father.

I mean fetish here seriously: It is a material object created by a person and then endowed with powers that in no way inhere in the materials or their combination themselves. Mr. Brown is constructed out of a pumpkin, toilet paper roll, broomsticks, tree branches, cast-off clothing and sandals and a flower garland (226). Assembled from junk, he is endowed by Brenton with all the tender power of an actual father, a fact that eludes the grown-ups around him: 'Social workers, psychiatrists, child experts all tried to unravel the mystery of Brenton's traumatised mind regarding his love for Mr Brown, telling him gently that the scarecrow was nothing but bits of wood and old clothes. But', the narrator continues, 'no one ever understood' (*Brixton* 227–8). Assembled with the help of Uncle Georgie, 'the housefather from next door' (*Brixton* 226), Mr. Brown provides a stable point of sympathetic parental reference for Brenton, who rushes to see him immediately upon returning home from school: 'Today, Brenton reached the outhouse, ready to tell Mr Brown how school had gone that day' (*Brixton* 227). At a crucial developmental stage, as Brenton is beginning to understand himself as a proto-young man, and desperately in need of an ideal to guide that development, Brenton fashions a father to stand in for the total absence of family. It is a version of an imaginary progenitor who also – in its fetishized form – represents what Brenton himself might become.

When Mr. Brown is destroyed, Brenton reacts in a manner that is out of all proportion to the destruction of an assemblage of bits and bobs in a cold shed, but completely consistent with the loss of a father figure. As he takes in the split pumpkin, smashed sticks and torn clothing, Mr. Brown's 'body hacked into three parts', Brenton

> scream[s] a scream to end all horror flicks [...] Housemothers and housefathers raced to the scene, believing a child had fallen off a drainpipe and cracked its skull. His belly-mangling shrieks only subsided after half an hour or so, when even The Belt's heart was boxed by the wanton brutality of the killing of Mr Brown. The display of Brenton's hysterical emotions moved Georgie himself to tears. Never in his life did he witness such a heart-battering scenario. (*Brixton* 227)

Even the Belt seems to understand that the destruction has struck more deeply at Brenton than the usual run of cruelty, and Brenton is not punished for his effusions, nor required to perform his other duties. The moment bears traumatic currency for Brenton, haunting his dreams with the kind of immediacy associated with the unconscious record of formative – ego-shattering – moments. It affirms the impossibility of fathers for Brenton, naturalizing their absence as an inevitable feature of human society, at least for the likes of him. More to the point, it normalizes violence and the necessity of detachment in order to survive. Brenton learns important lessons from this experience: Love nothing; all ends in violence. They are lessons that lock him into a pattern of perpetual adolescence, a permanent drift towards the rude boy ethos of criminality, violence, self-aggrandizement and emotional deformity.

Small wonder, then, that neither Brenton nor any of his cohort seem troubled by the lack of a father while they hold their mothers to such stiff accounting much of the time. Indeed, as I've already mentioned, this double standard itself animates Brenton's more or less whole-cloth mythic account of his own origins, blaming his mother for what was in fact his father's abandonment, and actually unable – even if willing – to correct his sense of things even when the facts are brought to light. In a lineage of systematic disruption of familial continuity that extends back to slavery, Brenton and his peers are inured to the absence of fathers in their lives. They register that absence as a fact of life consistent with the withdrawal of government, and even more amorphous social, support. They face instead a generational model in which precedents are not simply impossible to emulate, as they were for the first post-war youth-cultural men like Arthur Seaton, but missing altogether. By the same stroke, they are deprived of models for developing into a future generation that can sustain both continuity and change. Crucially, Wheatle portrays this blockage as a social structural operation, as a register of how youth culture's anarchic utopianism – however we have seen it undercut, ironized or withdrawn – has lost momentum and succumbed to powerful forces of recontainment. Just as the reggae call and response, 'FORWARD!' too quickly gives way to a bread-and-circuses chant in the rave on the night of the riot, so the impetus for political change and youth-cultural renovation of a world the parental generations have run into a dead end too quickly dissipates across Wheatle's novels.

As we might expect, given the centrality of fathers – or, rather, the centrality of their absence – in *Brixton Rock* and *East of Acre Lane*, these generational tensions manifest in a crisis of masculinity. The overwhelming masculinity of the novels – almost all the main characters are young men – manifests in the narrator's repeated use of 'brethren' to refer to them (it first appears in *Brixton* 31, but permeates both novels). The term recalls to mind Alex's refrain, 'O my brothers' in *A Clockwork Orange*. As in these other cases, the term establishes an exclusive community for the young men, dependent upon their sex. *Brixton Rock* and *East of Acre Lane* build upon these resonances, and supplement them with a touch of the religious, linking the term 'brethren' to Rastafarianism's Zionist politics. This usage also adduces an element of tribalism to the term, marking out one's own group of young men as righteous, sympathetic and figuratively if not actually related to one: We are a family extending across space and time within the context of the black diaspora. In these terms, though, the use of 'brethren' is fully as much a form of wishful thinking – an imaginary solution to a real problem – as it is a statement of loyalty and affiliation. It bespeaks a fundamental anxiety about one's status as belonging to a community that is palpably at war with itself and with those outside it, and about the terms upon which one can convincingly establish one's masculinity. It elevates masculinity as perhaps the key locus of anxiety and tension in the novel, isolating and amplifying the ambivalence circulating around it even as it rather desperately tries to assert masculinity as the basis for community.

I have touched on several key aspects of this crisis in Wheatle's novels already, but there remain one or two points to draw out. Deprived as they are of a stable set of men who can model mature masculinity rather than brazenly (and violently) arrested adolescence, Brenton, Biscuit, Floyd, Frank and so many more pass through their teenage years within a radically narrow horizon of possibilities. The main categories of articulation available to them are participation in the bad bwai world of criminal activity and reputational sweepstakes and peripheral participation in the criminal world in the role of sweet bwais who are more focused on having sex than on establishing their authority among other men. For the rude boys intent on either affiliating themselves with – or even becoming – Bad Men, everything comes down to establishing a totalizing, normative and violent masculinity. Even for the sweet bwais, the world of criminality and masculine reputation-building is inevitable since a life of gratifying promiscuity can still run you afoul of 'bad men' – as when Floyd discovers that the girl he's been crubbing with at a dance is one of Flynn's girlfriends (*Brixton* 187). There is no question, either, of falling in love and settling down since '"der is over fifty per cent of young blacks unemployed [...] It's like de Government jus' kinda forget 'bout us –"' as Floyd notes (*East* 84). Female characters such as Carol and Sharon both resist sexual activity with their boyfriends in an attempt to pressure them into leaving off criminal activity and finding regular work, but this tactic only criminalizes Floyd and Biscuit's libidinal drives, placing an impossible demand on them that they go straight in a world where there is no straight path, if they want sexual gratification (*East* 57). The resulting frustration on both the economic and libidinal fronts only pushes them more forcefully into a life of crime.

Indeed, all signs seem to direct the young men in Wheatle's novels down a one-way road towards entry into the fraught world of masculine credibility – street cred – that presents an increasingly narrow horizon of possibilities. The realm of reputational conflict is anchored by Terry 'Terror' Flynn and Nunchaks, the 'bad men' who dominate *Brixton Rock* and *East of Acre Lane*, respectively. In *Brixton Rock*, Flynn is the nemesis with whom Brenton has a series of increasingly violent confrontations, progressing from insults to Brenton glassing Flynn's leg, to Flynn stabbing Brenton in the neck, and finally to the battle royale in which Brenton is hospitalized and Flynn's hand is severed by a train pulling into the Tube stop where they are fighting. Symbolically, the fight progresses through a series of symbolic castrations, beginning with the symbolic castration of the 'liccle half-breed' insult through the wound to the upper leg, thence to the neck-stabbing and finally to the actual severing of a limb. With each escalation the masculinity stakes go up and the victor's reputation on the street likewise rises. By *East of Acre Lane*, Brenton is an acknowledged apex predator in *Brixton*: No one messes with him. And though things do not quite reach the pinnacle of actual homicide in *Brixton Rock*, Flynn has killed before, and kicks himself for not finishing off Brenton when he had the chance. Moreover, *East of Acre Lane* establishes clearly that death is well within play in the effort to establish supremacy as a man not to be antagonized, beginning as it does with Nunchaks and his henchmen taking Biscuit to the top of a building and threatening to throw him from the roof if he does not return some items mistakenly stolen from Flynn's sister-in-law's apartment.

Again, only Jah Nelson presents a viable alternative to the destructive masculinity in which Wheatle's characters are trapped, though even he is wary enough of Flynn not to push him too far. What's more, Nelson only seems able to kick against the toxic masculinity all around him because he has a source of income that is not bound up with the criminal world of Brixton in the novels. He buys drugs from Flynn and then from Biscuit, but does not sell them or participate in the rude-boy theft economy that sustains or supplements those who do not sell drugs. And, participating in either of these aspects of Brixton's economy seems inevitably to bind young men either to Flynn or to someone equally deranged: If you buy or sell drugs, or steal or buy stolen goods, you will invariably end up working for one of the kingpins in the neighbourhood. In effect, this process channels and consolidates individual masculinities into a super-masculinity of reputation, violence and menace that, regardless, has no proper line of development past adolescent reputational politics enhanced with guns. It remains critically important that even at the pinnacle of this ecology of manifold toxic masculinities, containment and abrupt terminus are the only options: Not even Flynn can transcend the solipsistic generational impasse in which masculinity is so powerfully deformed. When Brenton tries, he violates perhaps the only universal human taboo and ends up abandoning his intention of attending college, formulated mid-way through *Brixton Rock*. He resurfaces in *East of Acre Lane* as simply one of the baddest of the 'bad bwais'. Nelson represents an alternative, but it is an alternative dependent upon economic independence and an alternative reputational economy that values education, political savvy and hard-earned wisdom. Even here, though, it matters a great deal that Nelson has lost his eye to police violence – he is still in the Brixtonian ecosystem even if he tries to sit above it. Moreover, as we have seen, his independence presents only a backward-looking alternative to the present impasse; even when it does gesture towards potential generational renewal, it promises that renewal to Denise, not Biscuit or indeed any of the other young men trapped around him.

The crisis in masculinity that has driven youth-cultural adaptation from the immediate post-war to the 1980s (so far) reaches something of a turning point in itself in Wheatle's novels. In *Brixton Rock* and *East of Acre Lane*, the crisis of masculinity finally falters in its quest for alternative forms of manliness, turning back on the fluidity and openness of masculinity in *The Rachel Papers* and *The Buddha of Suburbia* to reassert a retrograde toxic masculinity that is not only rigidly heterosexual but also openly violent, competitive and above all dangerous. It is concentrated in generational discontinuities, especially between fathers and sons, and compounded by the intense double-bind his young male characters face as they struggle to achieve conventional forms of mature masculinity. For Wheatle, masculinity is shaped and intensified by the ongoing economic crisis of the 1980s. As a result, he presents a variety of young men facing tremendous pressure to live up to conventional forms of masculinity that are either structurally out of reach or achievable only in perverse forms (i.e. as the father of your own sister's child, or as a pimp who gets sexual release by raping his own prostitutes, as does Flynn).

In the historical context, the extremity of this absurdly difficult situation manifests perhaps most cruelly of all in the Carlton Club's elevation of Margaret Thatcher to the status of honorary man so that she can join its ranks (Saunders n.p.). The 1950s problem of an absence of role models for achieving mature masculinity outside the clear-cut parameters of armed conflict and/or physical labour seems almost quaint by comparison. The decayed model of traditional masculinity presented to us by Sillitoe has indeed been cast aside, though not all the challenges we have seen have been of equal valence. Arthur Seaton's extramarital shenanigans and contained sexual violence towards Brenda, Winnie and Em'ler are part and parcel of a clear – if deplorable – path to mature masculinity in *Saturday Night and Sunday Morning*. MacInnes' Teenager's easy friendship with Big Jill the Les and the homosexual Fabulous Hoplite, not to mention his erotic view of Mr. Cool present alternative possibilities, even if he ultimately asserts heteronormative privilege by capturing and containing Suze in a highly traditional relationship. And if *A Clockwork Orange*'s Alex finds himself bored because there's 'Nothing to fight against, really' (12), perhaps he should count himself lucky in the option of softening into acceptance of life as a father to his own little hellion, however deterministic that option ends up being. Charles's willingness – even desire – to record his own 'queer period' en route to his promiscuous antics, and in tandem with his conventionally effete bookishness and physical weakness, similarly encodes a relatively wide-open realm of possibility for masculinity in *The Rachel Papers*, if we can ignore the possibility that he has left Rachel unwittingly pregnant at the novel's conclusion. Karim's fluid sexuality, embrace of the theatre, and easy comfort with polymorphous promiscuity, taken along with Charlie's exploration of multiple identities – some much more effeminate than others – marks out *The Buddha of Suburbia* as perhaps the high-water mark of post-war youth culture's responses to the crisis of masculinity precipitated by the end of the war and unprecedented peace and prosperity. As that prosperity degraded into an extended recession, though, the pendulum appears to have swung back all the more violently to the regressive models of toxic masculinity with which the era began. Experimentation with masculinity is now blocked, it would seem, forced into ever narrower channels with ever less promising and ever more depressing outcomes.

As this catalogue indicates, we have indeed come a long way, baby. While each of the preceding decades has yielded up for us novels that try to articulate some mode of utopian or anarchic possibility, and our readings have shown them to be compromised in that effort, the 1980s present us with novels that seem instead to accept youth culture as something stuck in the present, pressed on one side by an idealized distant past of authenticity and on the other by a series of insuperable obstacles to progress into the future. The youth cultures corresponding to this shift – rude boys, sweet boys and Rastafarians – have a great deal in common with the stable of youth cultures we've seen so far. Like teddy boys, rockers, skinheads and punks, they emerge from the working class and articulate frustrations around identity, masculinity and generational tension. In their specific racial affiliation, though, they also inflect the problems of history and empire distinctly. They present one line of descent from the Windrush generation, whose arrival in England in 1948 heralded a dramatic shift in concepts of Englishness. Continuing the line of literary treatment inaugurated by the likes of James Berry, George Lamming, Samuel Selvon, C. L. R. James, V. S. Naipaul and Wilson Harris, Wheatle both thinks *about* contemporary youth cultures and uses them to think *with* as he engages with the emergent issues of 1980s England. His angle of approach, through the youth cultures predominant among descendants of the Windrush generation, lends urgency and cogency to his mode of thinking *with*. It makes the larger, potentially overwhelming, problems specific and comprehensible even as it gives them allegorical and symbolic heft.

If I may borrow a phrase, the 1980s were in many ways a 'low dishonest decade', as W. H. Auden wrote of the 1930s. A key difference of course is that race was a factor in the 1980s as it was not in the 1930s. Nonetheless, Wheatle insists that economic depression trumps racism as the chief source of discontent and futility facing young men. His rude bwais and sweet bwais understand the police to be inherently racist, but locate the real source of their problems in economic hardship and lack of opportunity. Rasta men such as Jah Nelson take a longer view, linking the situation of all blacks in England to the history of slavery, and inflecting that history with the promise of religious redemption. And indeed, racial tensions are surprisingly muted in *Brixton Rock* and *East of Acre Lane*, as Wheatle keeps the focus closely on the intimate lives and psychological challenges faced by young Brixtonians. The Thatcher government's shadow falls dark across both novels, as it did the entire decade, and particularly across those struggling to survive in the underclass during a time of intense economic pressure. The result, among black youth culture of the decade at least, is a darker view, but also one that is more explicitly engaged with history, politics, race, identity and empire than its predecessors. As we move from the 1980s to the 1990s, happily, the darkness lifts and the mood lightens considerably. We will pick up the thread in the next chapter by back-tracking slightly to account for the rise of post-punk new wave through the 1980s, preparing the ground for a discussion of rave culture, and moving on to our focus there: heroin chic and Irvine Welsh's *Trainspotting*.

5

Rave and Heroin: *Trainspotting*

Trainspotting marks something of a terminal point for post-war youth culture in the UK, by shifting away from an aesthetics of rebellion, utopian projection and independence towards what I will be calling an *anaesthetic* youth culture. Where previous youth cultures sought to express themselves through their stylistic ensembles (clothes, music, stimulants, modes of transportation, argots), the youth cultures represented in *Trainspotting* do so through numbness, evacuation of the self, and retreat from the social and political. Where the early 1980s had been dominated by political rock, including the revolutionary Rastafarianism of black British youth culture, the late 1980s and early 1990s quickly turned away from the world and focused inward instead. The high age of political rock quickly gave way to techno, house and electronic dance music (EDM)'s trance-inducing beat-focused music. This shift away from engagement with the outside world provided the soundtrack to the two main anaesthetic youth cultures that inform *Trainspotting*: rave and heroin cultures. In their emphasis on anaesthetics, rave and heroin cultures differ from all preceding youth cultures in their total abdication of authenticity and withdrawal from the world. They mark those cultures' culmination and exhaustion, enfolding all previous youth cultures and squeezing the last breath out of them.

Perhaps unsurprisingly, then, *Trainspotting* presents us with a smudgy temporality in which (a) aspects of all the post-war youth cultures from Teddy boys forward bleed together and (b) the novel's 1980s, early 1990s publication, and mid-1990s film adaptation are overlaid and fused. Between them, the 1993 novel version and the 1996 film version of *Trainspotting* – what I will call the *Trainspotting* phenomenon – manage to cram in explicit appearances of Teds, mods, hippies, punks, goths and new wavers. To these, it adds ravers and junkies. The music mentioned in the novel and the soundtrack to the film borrow music going back half-way to the war. They juxtapose Lou Reed with Underworld, and David Bowie with New Order in a manner that is at once truly postmodern, and yet historically specific. It is postmodernist in its disregard for historical specificity, and historically specific in its embrace of the early 1990s mix-n-match youth-cultural ethos – which is to say that it is historically specific precisely in its postmodernism. This blurriness informs the other aspect of the novel's smudgy temporality: The slippage back and forth between the 1980s setting and the early- to mid-1990s moment of its publication. As Welsh's online biography puts it, *Trainspotting* originated when, 'Energised by the rave scene', Welsh dug out 'some old diaries' and 'did a draft of what would become *Trainspotting*. Welsh published parts this from 1991 onwards' (irvinewelsh.net). Emerging from Welsh's diary accounts of life in Edinburgh in the 1980s, *Trainspotting* was reworked around 1990 into stories that begin to see publication in 1991. It appeared as a (semi-)coherent volume in 1993, got reworked again into a film script shortly thereafter and appeared on screen in 1996. *As with Saturday Night and Sunday Morning, The Buddha of Suburbia, Brixton Rock* and *East of Acre Lane*, this time lapse produces some anachronisms and blurs the novel's relationship to its moment. As Welsh himself put it, ' "If you're being pedantic about it, you could say [*Trainspotting*] was set in Edinburgh between 1982 and 1988, but the issues of drug addiction and drug abuse and the on-going HIV issues are as pertinent as ever" ' (qtd. in Stalcup 120–121). Though it is set in the 1980s, then, *Trainspotting* is inevitably informed by the decade that followed, as we see in aspects of its treatment of rave culture and its role in popularizing heroin culture. The novel both thinks *with* and *about* the state of youth culture in this oscillation. To those ends, it generates an *an*aesthetic anchored in cynicism that articulates the true legacy of the Thatcher years and the end of the post-war consensus better than any political critique ever could.

Most broadly, that thinking with and about youth culture takes place against the backdrop of the end of the Cold War. Born in the terrifying onset of the Nuclear Age, post-war youth cultures seem to reach a point of exhaustion as the Cold War concludes, though of course echoes and after-images of both persist well into the new millennium. On a global scale, we may think of post-war youth cultures as in fact Cold War youth cultures, and to consider them as various articulations of the same complaint against a parental culture that seemed barely able to control its newfound power to annihilate all life on earth. The initial reaction against the parental culture that had allowed the Holocaust to take place (e.g. in *Saturday Night and Sunday Morning*) morphed regularly into rebellion against the war generation's sanctimonious self-regard (e.g. in *Absolute Beginners* and *A Clockwork Orange*), bourgeois complacency (*The Rachel Papers* and *The Buddha of Suburbia*), and the racist and classist underpinnings of British imperial self-regard (e.g. in *East of Acre Lane* and *Brixton Rock*). For five decades, the Cold War had beat a steady rhythm by which successive youth cultures rehearsed the perennial dramas of generational tension and crises of masculinity, history, cultural institutions, nation, ethnicity, empire and belonging. With the fall of the Soviet empire, this steady beat fell silent, though many of the same concerns persisted as the new, more frenetic and disoriented rhythms of techno and house took over.

For late 1980s and 1990s youth cultures, the end of the Cold War at times furnished a triumphalist horizon against which to measure their potentials, successes and – more often than not – failures. With the fall of the Berlin Wall, the UK found its feet, and rediscovered something of its previous influence on the world stage. The country played a vital role in bringing about the end of the Cold War, at the same time as it finally addressed itself to the task of re-inventing itself in a post-imperial frame. The formation of the EU under the Maastricht Treaty of 1993 afforded the UK the chance to assert its independence from the continental powers by declining participation in the shared currency of the Euro, and yet to assume a leadership role in how the new political reality would be configured. Having been a central player in the European Common Market since its advent in 1958, the UK thus reasserted its importance to the European political and economic system. Things were likewise improving at home. On surer international footing than it had been for decades, the UK cemented its new direction with the 1994 IRA ceasefire and the 1998 Good Friday Agreement, putting an official end to hostilities – and, ostensibly, the Troubles – in Northern Ireland. No longer divided quite so drastically along that front, and having dramatically reduced the risk of terrorism on domestic soil (for the time being), the UK consolidated its pivotal role in the formation of the EU with a new attitude of collaboration.

If it may be said of a nation as old as England, the country seemed to shake off an awkward post-war adolescence and to be on the verge of coming into its own (again). Though things were far from perfect at home, as the bitter struggle of the 1984–1985 miners' strike demonstrates, the UK was nonetheless back in place as a global force to be reckoned with. The election of a New Labour government under the youthful and charismatic Tony Blair in 1997 promised the end of nearly two decades of hard-bitten policy and coincided with the widespread re-branding of the UK as 'Cool Britannia'. This out-with-the-old ethos assumed directly generational proportions, both as relatively young Blair replaced the elder Thatcher and as that hoariest of all English institutions, the monarchy, faced up to the need to modernize. Princess Diana's death in the same year as Blair's election provoked a critical reassessment of the monarchy, leading to relaxed attitudes, eased rigidity and – eventually – the ascension of a new generation: Diana's sons, Princes William and Harry. The old, imperialist, arrogant and hidebound Britannia celebrated in James Thomson and Thomas Arne's 1740 anthem, 'Rule, Britannia' had changed course dramatically.

It wasn't all sunshine and roses, though. The 1970s and 1980s were hard on the UK. Though there was a mid- to late 1980s economic recovery, it was followed by another recession. Economically, the Cold War's end didn't deliver a capitalist utopia so much as more of the same challenges that had characterized the 1970s, though without the looming threat of nuclear extinction for a change, which was nice. The economy did not suddenly improve, terrorism did not disappear, and jobs were no more readily available than they had been for at least a decade before. The nation continued to be plagued by violence both home-grown and globally inspired, and faced ongoing economic and political woes that undercut the triumphalism of capitalism's emergence as the clear winner of the post-war's ideological battles. Domestically, much of this was focused on the IRA's continued bombings and killings of civilians and British soldiers alike, and the retaliatory strikes back the other way. The IRA's mortar attack on 10 Downing Street in 1991 marked perhaps the peak of the ongoing tensions, though multiple cases of abduction and murder on both sides of the conflict were persistently and deeply unsettling as well. Globally, the triumphalism of the end of the Cold War was undermined as tensions in the Middle East made themselves felt on British soil in the 1988 bombing of an airliner over Lockerbie, Scotland. Aberdeen suddenly became the focus of the world's grief and anger over this escalation in airline-based terrorism. The Libyan leader behind the attacks, Muammar Gaddafi, continued to defy Western powers and openly supported Iraq when it seized British hostages in retribution for England's involvement in the 1990 Gulf War over Iraq's invasion of Kuwait.

Adding to these political problems dogging the country was a further mixture of uncertainty and concern over biological crises. The AIDS/ HIV pandemic struck in the mid-1980s, and soon dominated the news, particularly in the early days when no one was quite sure what the syndrome was, how it was transmitted or if it could ever be treated effectively. The casual, anonymous fluid interactions among people at raves seemed to be a high-risk breeding ground for the spread of the syndrome, and it soon became glaringly obvious that sharing needles among intravenous drug users was undeniably a Very Bad Idea. Though it never really did catch on with a wider audience, the punk practice of spitting on one another at gigs suddenly seemed even less appealing, and maybe even terminally unwise. The mass popularity of rave culture and the increasing spread of IV drug use already gave AIDS/HIV all the impetus of a moral panic, but when it turned out that the NHS had unwittingly provided HIV-tainted blood to haemophilia patients – and that in principle anyone who had received a blood transfusion at all was at risk – the government found its most basic competence called into question. Following closely on the AIDS/HIV crisis was the discovery of Bovine Spongiform Encephalopathy (BSE, or 'mad cow disease') across much of the British beef industry; 4.4 million cattle were slaughtered as a preventative measure, causing untold millions of pounds of damage to the British economy. European nations' bans of British beef only compounded the psychological shock of widespread uncertainty about how transmissible the disease was from cattle to humans, how long it incubates after consumption and whether it is possible ever to be sure of having eradicated it.

On the cultural front, the UK was likewise in the global spotlight, though not necessarily for the right reasons. Oh, sure, the 1980s and 1990s had generated a spate of world-class writing by the likes of V. S. Naipaul, Penelope Lively, Kazuo Ishiguro, Pat Barker and Graham Swift (to name just Booker Prize winners). William Golding had won the Nobel Prize for literature in 1983, and Seamus Heaney took it for Ireland in 1995. And, of course, Hanif Kureishi, Martin Amis and Anthony Burgess continued to publish as the millennium neared as well. But, all this wonderful writing and so much more was instantly blotted out by the lethal circus that took place around Salman Rushdie's *The Satanic Verses* (1988). That novel features what some deem to be an unflattering portrayal of the Prophet Muhammad and quickly became the focal point for precisely the sort of 'clash of civilizations' Samuel Huntington would delineate in 1996. Even as Iraq was still parading its British hostages on international television, Iran's Supreme Leader, the Ayatollah Khomeini, issued a *fatwa* calling for Salman Rushdie's death. The *fatwa* was the real deal and cast a decided chill over the myth of frictionless multiculturalism that seemed so necessary to the smooth advance of globalization. Rushdie had to go into hiding for nearly a decade following the decree, as the space opened up by the end of the Cold War was rapidly filled by globally creeping sectarian violence. Hanif Kureishi, who fictionalized the episode in *The Black Album*, wrote in the *Guardian* in 2012 that it was 'one of the most significant events in postwar literary history' (Kureishi 2012, n.p.). Small wonder, then, that sizeable portions of the nation's youth cultures preferred retreat over engagement.

In Scotland, things were much worse. Even with a new recession in the offing in the 1990s, the unemployment rate in the UK at large remained well below 10% – in fact below 7% – from about 1988 to 1990, and peaked at just under 11% in 1993. In Scotland, however, it hovered around 16–18% for those aged 16–25, with a breathtaking 25% showing up as 'economically inactive': Those who are 'deemed to be outside the labour market and often are looking after family members, unable to work (usually due to disability), are in full time education or have declared they have no commitment to job search' (Cook 7). The recession of 1981 had hit the industrial north of England, and Scotland – especially its youth – particularly hard, and the recovery of the mid- to late 1980s had been dampened by the regions' over-reliance on now outmoded industries such as steel production. The rebound felt in much of the rest of the UK thus barely moved the needle in Scotland before a second round of recession arrived with the new decade.

It's perhaps no surprise, then, to find that the 1980s end with a resurgence of Scottish nationalism and a reinvigorated movement for Scottish independence – or at least for devolution and the re-opening of the Scottish parliament (closed since the 1706–1707 Acts of Union). Young people were not the only ones seeking independence and testing out their autonomy. In 1988 the Scottish National Party (SNP) won a by-election in Glasgow Govan and nearly repeated the act in Glasgow Central the following year.

That same year, 1989, the Claim of Right, a document proclaiming Scottish sovereignty, was signed by all but one of the Labour and Liberal MPs in Scotland, as well as many other prominent politicians and groups. Though it had no legal status, it served notice of a groundswell of support for Scottish separation from the UK, and began laying the groundwork for devolution, finally achieved in 1999. In the general election of 1992, Labour once again won a clear majority in Scotland, though the SNP made significant inroads, indicating a growing tendency to see the independence achieved by Ireland as an incentive to struggle for greater autonomy at home.

The *Trainspotting* phenomenon doesn't merely take place against this backdrop; it plays a vital role in it. It both helped make Scotland cool again (contra the ersatz Scottishness of the tourist industry) and highlighted the massive problems of drug addiction, poverty, unemployment, despair, and AIDS in the region. The heroin epidemic found fertile soil in

> a peculiarly Scottish cocktail of risks. Firstly there's an underlying issue of self-esteem. 'Englishness is the norm', says [Irvine] Welsh. 'Scottishness is increasingly seen as a second-class thing. There's always been an idea of two types of Scots – those who went to London and made it big, and the second-raters who stayed home. It's a very negative thing.' In Thatcher's Britain 'Scots were losers, young people were losers, the unemployed were losers.' (Edemariam and Scott n.p.)

The flood of cheap heroin into Scotland in the late 1980s provoked a full-on epidemic of drug addiction, exacerbated by the Thatcherite NHS's withdrawal of the most effective treatment methods in favour of low-success measures such as methadone outpatient therapy. Welsh's novel thinks about this incredibly bleak situation explicitly in terms of youth-cultural participation – and withdrawal (chemical, social and otherwise). It measures the difference between the Scottish and English youth-cultural modes and thinks with them as it engages the perennial problems of masculinity, generational tension, and historicity, all now doubly (perhaps even more) inflected with the problematics of a halting nationalism.

The different contexts and moods in England versus Scotland may be usefully summed up by England's popular cultural output of the two during the late 1980s and early 1990s. In England, the years are dominated by the Big Four bands with one-word names: Blur, Suede, Pulp and Oasis. Dominated, that is, until the advent of the Spice Girls in 1994, with their history-making release of *Spice!* in 1996. Taking the second British invasion of America global, the Spice Girls almost immediately became the biggest selling female group of all time with the release of the single 'Wannabe' and the biggest British pop phenomenon since the Beatles. They simply overwhelmed the world of pop music through the middle of the 1990s. Geri Halliwell's iconic Union Jack mini-dress lent their pop stylings a retro-mod nationalistic dimension, though the group's fashions as a whole were so eclectic as to defy easy identification – just as *Trainspotting* itself mixes and matches styles. Nevertheless, mod was among the most influential style revivals of the period, informing the northern soul resurgence as well as the speed-fuelled dance pace of raves in general. Cinematic tributes such as the Austin Powers films, which literally depended upon bringing late-mod Swinging London into the present; *Bend it Like Beckham*, which re-cast England's imperialist past as the source of its positively charged multicultural future; and romantic comedies illustrating that Britons really do have heart (and humour) such as *Truly Madly Deeply* (1990) and *Four Weddings and a Funeral* (1994), provided hip contemporary ballast to a spate of period films set upon recuperating the mahogany past: *A Passage to India* (1984), *A Room with A View* (1985), *Chariots of Fire* (1981), *Gandhi* (1982), *The Remains of the Day* (1993) and *Sense and Sensibility* (1995).

In Scotland, the popular cultural output was decidedly more dour. On one side, the cinematic experience balanced muddy nationalist epics such as *Braveheart* and *Rob Roy* with the gritty – profoundly anti-nationalist – *Trainspotting*. As Grant Farred has put it, '*Trainspotting* is the voice of the disaffected, the postmodern, postindustrial Scottish junkie-as-critic who rejects the romance of his nation's history in favor of a scathing attack on Scotland's historic anti-Englishness. No contemporary commentator has ridiculed his people's desire to maintain their difference as much as *Trainspotting*'s chief protagonist, the heroin-using Mark Renton' (217). There is likewise a marked dearth of romantic comedies, elegant period pieces, or cheeky hipness. Musically, where England rode high on the Britpop invasion, Scotland produced darker, edgier bands such as The Simple Minds, The Jesus and Mary Chain, Big Country, Belle and Sebastian, and The Flowers. Even where the music took on regionally specific tones – as in Big Country's signature bagpipe-resonant guitar riffs – both the content and the sound of the songs were often bleak, wistful or simply despairing. Moreover, as we see when Renton and Dianne have their first argument, when bands such as The Simple Minds achieved popularity it was often perceived as at the expense of selling out, of adopting a cynically opportunistic political activism driven more by the desire to sell records than to enact real change in the world. Renton dismisses Dianne's taste for The Simple Minds precisely *because* they have become political: 'The Simple Minds huv been pure shite since they jumped on the committed, passion-rock bandwagon of U2. Ah've never trusted them since they left their pomp-rock roots and started aw this patently insincere political-wi-a-very-small-p stuff. […] Aw this Mandela stuff is embarrassing puke, he rants' (Welsh 136). Likewise, Sick-Boy, when considering which T-shirt identity to put on to seduce a random backpacker rejects his Free Mandela T-shirt as simply out of date (335). What some might think of as a characteristically Scottish mood of dour grimness pervades the musical output as well as the cinematic output of these years, positioning the entire country in terms roughly consonant with standard teenager fare: marginalized, misunderstood, rebellious, self-conscious and resentful. If England was shaking off its awkward stage, Scotland was fully immersed in sullen rebellion.

Thus, though the mid-1980s looked pretty good on balance for the UK at large, with falling inflation and unemployment numbers, and though the Cold War was over and Thatcheresque neo-liberalism seemed to have carried the day in History's last great ideological clash, there remained challenges aplenty. Appearing to snatch defeat from the jaws of victory, the UK approached the end of the millennium not with a full head of utopian steam, but instead with a dodgy economy, political problems on all fronts, and multiple emerging biological threats to manage as well. And while the BritPop youth-cultural reaction to the advent of 'Cool Britannia' was one of excitement, optimism, and even euphoria, there was an equally influential counter-reaction of exhaustion and withdrawal. This is the youth-cultural mood that gains the greatest purchase in the literature of the period, feeding into the twin anaesthetics of rave and heroin cultures. In this line of youth-cultural development, the political outrage of the 1980s was largely abandoned in favour of insulation from the shocks of the world and a desperate quest for the kind of numbness that can only come from either heroin's opium dreams or rave's mindless 'celebration of celebration' (Reynolds 1997, 86).

The young people who came of age at the end of the 1980s had matured under Margaret Thatcher's neo-liberal regime, and it shows. Popularly known as the 'iron lady' and famous for declaring that 'there is no such thing as society' Thatcher promoted a particular brand of rugged individualism that challenged each and every child of Britain to make his or her own way, and to consider the welfare state an enfeebling crutch. Her decade-long assault on organized labour was only matched by her efforts to privatize or cut back any and all public services. Children growing up under her tenure lived in a country led by someone who believed that poverty was the suitable consequence of laziness or insufficient application to the task at hand. Making one's own way without social support was a sovereign good, and clearly many of the rules that had applied to limit or constrain individual success were no longer being enforced. The communal 'can-do' attitude that had won the war was given notice in favour of a Hobbesian war of all against all. Simon Reynolds has written that these conditions produced a generation of outlaw entrepreneurs who took their cue from Thatcher's ideology and began making their way by thievery, piracy, and other illegal means:

'We're Thatcher's children', Shaun Ryder, Happy Mondays' singer, was wont to claim. The Conservative leader's assault on the welfare system and the unions was intended to instill in the working class the bourgeois virtues of providence, initiative, investment, and belt-tightening. But a significant segment of British working-class youth responded to the challenge of 'enterprise culture' in a quick-killing, here-and-now way, becoming not opportunity conscious but criminal minded. Eager to participate in the late-eighties Thatcherite boom but excluded by mass unemployment, these kids resorted to all manner of shady money-making schemes: bootlegging (fake designer clothes, pirated records and computer games), organizing illegal warehouse raves, drug dealing, petty theft, and fraud of all kinds (benefit, credit card). It was from this lumpen-proletarian milieu that Happy Mondays emerged. The truth was that the band and its ilk were Thatcher's *illegitimate* children – unintended, and operating on the wrong side of the law. (Reynolds 1999, 95–96)

The youth cultures that formed in the transition from the 1980s to the 1990s were Thatcher's progeny. They are in a very real sense just the inevitable logical conclusion of her long assault on the welfare state.

From this perspective, we can see that the Thatcher generation responded to her anti-social politics in two key ways: The first was to indulge in a chemically induced fantasy version of the kind of community she had declared obsolete (i.e. rave culture), the second was to embrace the isolation and individualism she had promoted, but without the economic prosperity she had promised would come with that individualism (i.e. heroin culture). Both alternatives are *anaesthetic* youth cultures organized around withdrawal rather than engagement, driven by commitment to particular drugs: Ecstasy and heroin. Though they seem to be polar opposites in their effects on the people who take them, the settings in which they are taken, and the cultures they fuel, Ecstasy and heroin are really two sides of the same ethic of withdrawal, capitulation, and isolation. Each assumes centrality as the core around which style circulates, chemically inducing a sense of authenticity, whether of community or of exclusion that ultimately collapses into inauthenticity – physical illness in both cases – and an increasing experience of deadening: an anaesthetic existence.

Let's begin with rave culture, which precedes heroin culture's full-blown arrival at roughly the same moment *Trainspotting* is published. Though Simon Reynolds offers a more nuanced and expansive origin story for the emergence of rave culture among white youth in the UK, it seems clear that it is in many ways yet another instance of borrowing from immigrant cultural practices. All-night dance parties in abandoned warehouses, featuring DJs spinning records, had been a mainstay of immigrant youth for years before white youth added sampling and mixing into the equation, and took the competitive aspect out of it, to create rave culture. Among youth like those depicted in Wheatle's novels, such raves featured competing sound-systems that would set up in opposite corners of a huge open space like a warehouse and then take turns competing to see who could rev the crowd up the most. Prestige, street credibility, and popularity were the payoffs, though of course there was also money at stake since the winning sound-system would take home most or all of the house receipts. When raving caught on among white youth in the mid-1980s, many of the same elements were kept in place, though the music departed from reggae and dub in a decidedly techno-oriented direction, and the dances not infrequently took place outdoors (see Reynolds 1999, 194 on dub Reggae versus Techno). They are also much, much larger, at least at the peak of the rave scene, and the moral panic that attended it.

White rave culture is characterized by a very particular clothing style that evolves into a recognizable caricature of itself within a very short time. For women, it entails close-fitting Lycra outfits that combine ease of movement with breathability and moisture-wicking to keep them cool. Bright colours, preferably in shades that will glow under black lights or are already neon, are the order of the day to enhance the psychedelic, feel-good vibe of the rave. White gloves, childish iconography and glow-sticks complete the outfits. For men, rave style means baggy pants and t-shirts, or no shirts at all, to maximize ventilation and ease of movement. Again, childish iconography such as giant happy faces and cartoon animals play a key role. As rave culture gained momentum, and its adherents developed methods of combating the dehydration and dry-mouth caused by long-term intense dancing combined with the amphetamine in Ecstasy (or just plain speed), accessories such as soothers made their appearance. Practically, soothers aided ravers in keeping their mouths moist while they danced, and helped prevent the teeth-grinding that can be an irritating side-effect of speed. Aesthetically, they tied into the childlike aspect of rave culture, which Reynolds links to Ecstasy's tendency to produce a distinctly asexual experience of pleasure, one that mimics pre-adolescent enjoyment. Uninterested in libidinal release, whether through orgasm or violence, 'rave instead locates *jouissance* in the pre-pubescent childhood or pre-Oedipal fantasy' (Reynolds 1997, 88). Begbie puts this aspect of rave culture in his own inimitable way when he trashes Renton's suggestion that they skip the plan to find a tourist to beat up and rob, and instead visit a rave club:

> Wir huvin a barry crack here. Wuv goat the speed n the E. Let's jist enjoy oorsels, mibbe go tae a rave club, instead ay wanderin aboot the fuckin Meadows aw night. Thuv goat a big fuckin theatre tent thair, n a fuckin fun fair up. It'll be crawlin wi polis. It's too much fuckin hassle man.
> – Ah'm no gaun tae any fuckin rave clubs. You sais yirsel thit thir fir fuckin bairns. (Welsh 153–154)

The childishness and simplicity of popular conceptions of rave culture manifest in *Trainspotting*'s close association of Spud – the animal-loving, easy-going, somewhat dense, sweetheart of the gang – with it.

The clothing aspects of rave culture, however stylized and attention-getting they were, were emphatically secondary to the music and the drugs that shaped them. Techno, house, and all their variants, departed dramatically from the album- and artist-based musical standards of all post-war youth cultures so far. 'Rave music is only "about" its own sensations.

Instead of the rock notion of "resonance" (with its psychological/sociological connotations), rave is about frequencies; it's music that's oriented toward impact rather than affect' (Reynolds 1997, 91). In a manner utterly in keeping with the ego-dissolving anonymity of the rave experience, rave music made a virtue out of repetition, rapidity, and indistinction: 'There was a liberating joy in surrendering to the radical anonymity of the music, in not caring about the names of tracks or artists. The "meaning" of the music pertained to the macro level of the entire culture, and it was much larger than the sum of its parts' (Reynolds 1999, 4). The aim of the music was to provide a soundtrack for dancing, not to articulate or express an authentic emotional truth, a political viewpoint, or even a means of discovering selfhood: Raves generate 'a series of heightened here-and-nows – sonically, by the music's repetitive loops, and visually, by lights, lasers, and above all the strobe (whose freeze-frame effect creates a concatenated sequence of ultravivid tableaux)' (Reynolds 1999, 246). The traditional topics of popular music went by the wayside in favour of the beat, and the beat alone. As the narrator of *Trainspotting* puts it at one point, 'Spud turns and says something to Renton, who can't hear him above a song by The Farm, which, Renton considers, like all their songs, is only listenable if you're E'd out of your box, and if you're E'd out of your box it would be a waste listening to The Farm, you'd be better off at some rave freaking out to heavy techno-sounds' (137). For Renton, rave music like that he associates with The Farm is only enjoyable if you are already chemically prepared for it – amped up on speed and MDMA – and if you are, you should be listening to hardcore techno in an actual rave rather than trying to pick up girls in a club. In keeping with the pre-adolescent affect produced by Ecstasy, rave clearly separates the two sorts of activities, marking the rave itself out as a space antithetical to the sexualized cruising zones of the typical nightclub, and subordinating sexual pleasure to the sheer physical enjoyment of movement and camaraderie. The beats per minute of rave tracks steadily increased as electronic means allowed DJs either to sample and accelerate live percussion recorded in studio or simply to programme their own percussion at the rate they wanted. The effect was one of timelessness, numbness to any outside influences, and oceanic continuity with the entire crowd – all humanity – in the life-affirming beat. The sincere engagement of 1980s political rock was unceremoniously shoved aside. Reynolds quotes DJ Alex Paterson: '"Our music doesn't reflect the times, it ignores them... . Society today is so suppressed, you can only make music that is escapist"' (1999, 194). The music as often as not sought to induce a trance-like state that dissolved egoic self-interest, sublating the opposition between individual and society into a homogenous sludge of pleasurable flows.

Absolutely essential to the power of rave music to produce such an overwhelming affect – a short-cut to nirvana – was Ecstasy, or MDMA: 'the intransitive, go-nowhere aspects of rave culture are almost chemically programmed into MDMA itself' (Reynolds 1997, 87). A class of

FIGURE 5.1 *IBIZA, SPAIN, 1999: Clubbers dancing during the matinee at Space night club in Ibiza, Spain, on 20 July 1999. (Photo by Dario Mitidieri/Getty Images.)*

amphetamine, Ecstasy combines the rush of speed with the hallucinogenic effects of LSD. Its key effect is an overwhelming sense of well-being and connection to others. It triggers an oceanic sense of community that is often, as we have seen, characterized as a return to childhood. Antagonism is banished in a mental regression to an earlier developmental stage, one safe from the risks and responsibilities of mature adulthood. As Reynolds notes, 'Generally speaking, Ecstasy seems to promote tolerance. One of the delights of the rave scene at its height was the way it allowed for mingling across lines of class, race, and sexual preference' (1999, 238). It generates intense physical pleasure, but in a purely pre-sexual sense: 'E may be the "love drug", but this refers more to *agapē* than to *eros*, cuddles rather than copulation, sentimentality rather than sticky secretions' (Reynolds 1997, 88). Witness the loveable Spud's Ecstasy-fuelled stream of consciousness:

> Sick Boy brings oot some E. White doves, ah think. It's mental gear. Most Ecstasy hasnae any MDMA in it, it's just likesay, ken, part speed, part acid in its effects ... but the gear ah've hud is always jist likesay good speed, ken? This gear is pure freaky though, pure Zappaesque man ... that's the word, Zappaesque ... ah'm thinkin aboot Frank Zappa wi Joe's Garage n yellow snow n Jewish princesses n Catholic girls n ah think that it wid be really great tae huv a woman ... tae love likesay ... no shaggin

likes, well no jist shaggin ... but tae love, cause ah sortay feel like lovin everybody, but no sortay wi sex ... jist huvin someboday tae love ... [...]
Renton's shirt's unbuttoned n he's sortay tweakin his nipples, likesay ...
  – Spud ... look at ma nipples ... they feel fuckin weird man ... nae cunt's goat nipples like mine ...
  Ah'm talkin tae him aboot love, n Rents says that love doesnae exist, it's like religion, n likesay the state wants ye tae believe in that kinday crap so's they kin control ye, n fuck yir heid up ... some cats cannae enjoy thirsels withoot bringing in politics, ken ... but he doesnae bring us doon ... because, it's likesay he doesnae believe it hissel ... because ... because wi laugh at everything in sight ... the mad guy at the bar wi the burst blood-vessels in his coupon ... the snobby English Festival-type lemon whae looks like somebody's just farted under her nose. (Welsh 156–157)

Even Renton's cynicism cannot bring Spud down as he talks idealistically about 'lovin everybody, but no sortay wi sex'. What might be read as homoerotic here takes on a childlike innocence, as Renton sings the praises of his nipples with genuine wonder (later, they will be an erogenous focus as Renton pairs off with Kelly, whose primary mode of foreplay seems to be to tweak his nipples in public). Ecstasy removes Spud and Renton not only from the everyday cares that trouble them when they are not high, but even from their own cynicism. Renton's demystification of love falls flat 'because, it's likesay he doesnae believe it hissel'. Renton's attempt to bring politics into the mood simply disappears: They laugh it away. As Leanne McRae notes, in using Ecstasy, 'individuals numbed themselves to the ever expanding and extending realms in which dominant ideologies asserted their supremacy' (McRae 127) – they anaesthetized themselves against the harsh realities of Thatcherite rule. Though Ecstasy provokes intense bodily and mental pleasure, it is ultimately part of an anaesthetic style, one that values numbness and a buffer from reality over any quest for authenticity or identity.
  However central Ecstasy was to rave culture, it remained only one part of a stylistic ensemble that included a particular way of dressing and a particular musical genre, however; with heroin it is distinctly different. The distinctive feature of heroin culture – the thing that marks it out as both fundamentally different from any preceding youth culture and a fitting conclusion to the 'teenage epic' we began with Sillitoe – is that it is entirely organized around the drug. Though a specific look emerges in the mid-1990s as a result, in part, of *Trainspotting* and certain *haute couture* fashion lines' embrace of the gaunt, wasted, waif look, heroin culture is not characterized by a style of dress: heroin chic. I've chosen not to use the term 'heroin chic' precisely because it is not a mode of self identification but a fashion label, *haute couture* getting its own back forty years after the Teds first commandeered Savile Row styles for their own youth-cultural purposes. Though the fashion style is a key element of heroin culture, it is

far from the whole story, and risks at once minimizing and glamorizing the complex youth culture at hand. Still less is heroin culture identified with a particular musical genre, though as we will see it has a decided preference for the ragged sounds of Iggy Pop, Lou Reed and David Bowie. Where all previous youth cultures had multiple aspects to them – clothes, music, slang, modes of transportation, as well as stimulants of choice – heroin culture is only about one thing: heroin. The drug produces a particular look in its users, and induces specific kinds of behaviour, but these are not mannerisms adopted in the performance of a particular identity so much as they are predictable side-effects of heavy use of the drug. And while certain precursor movements also folded drug side-effects into their stylistic ensembles, such as the mod's speed-induced stutter immortalized in The Who's 'My Generation', none had come to be defined solely in relation to its narcotic or stimulant of choice in quite the same way as heroin culture does. This all-encompassing grip, this totalizing reach and singular focus gives heroin culture its distinctiveness, and is also key to its allure, as we will see shortly. This all amounts to heroin culture producing its adherents rather than being chosen and performed by them, which likewise accounts for the fact that it is the only one of the post-war youth cultures whose label is not self-generated or embraced by its members.

So: about heroin. As an opiate, heroin is the opposite number of the amphetamine Ecstasy and in fact has a medical history of use as an anaesthetic. In terms of the physical pleasure they afford, Ecstasy generates

FIGURE 5.2 *Heroin Chic Stock image. (Getty/iStock Images).*

an experience of pre-sexual synthetic *bonhommie*, while heroin generates an experience of what we might call supra-sexual chemical isolation. Where Ecstasy thins the walls of the ego to produce its signature oceanic experience, heroin thickens them to let the user drop out of the social into a hermetic realm of self-referentiality. 'The use of heroin can be described as a voluntary withdrawal from the outside world in order to avoid dealing with it' (Quabeck 296). If Ecstasy generates a sustained sensation of diffuse pre-orgasmic intensity that never reaches resolution, heroin produces an intensely orgasmic but insular release. It induces a concentrated physical pleasure that renders any outside contact or influence not only unnecessary but repugnant. Where Ecstasy allows the user to revisit a pre-pubescent innocence of desire and pleasure without sexual overtones, heroin simply overwhelms sexuality in its intensity, rendering it superfluous: 'That beats any meat injection ... that beats any fuckin cock in the world ... Ali gasps, completely serious' (Welsh 9). Ali's characterization of her hit in explicitly sexual terms humorously unsettles Renton, – 'It unnerves us tae the extent that ah feel ma ain genitals through ma troosers tae see if they're still thair' (9) – though he readily admits that she is not wrong: 'Ali wis right. Take yir best orgasm, multiply the feeling by twenty, and you're still fuckin miles off the pace' (11). The pre-orgasmic tension associated with the Ecstasy high has nothing, it would seem, on the fully orgasmic release of the heroin rush. And though being high does not actually stop the junkies in *Trainspotting* from having sex (except when the men are too high to get erections), sexual activity is clearly secondary to the pleasure afforded by the drug: It is an accident of proximity rather than a product of connection. It removes others from the equation so that even when sex occurs there is, still, no relationship. In its most elemental effects, heroin isolates its users, providing an insular experience that they do not want to share with anyone else, and which they will readily sacrifice friendship to guard for themselves. It is a drug of insularity, selfishness and egotism fully as much as Ecstasy is a drug of sociality, generosity and community.

Trainspotting is perhaps the central cultural document in the advent of heroin culture. The combination of the novel and its film version, together with a hugely popular sound track, placed it at the epicentre of both the establishment of heroin as a central element in 1990s youth-cultural cool and the moral panic over it. On the one hand, it highlighted an existing problem with drug addiction, particularly in Scotland, following the sudden availability of cheap heroin in the UK in the mid- to late 1980s. On the other hand, it undoubtedly glamorized the junky life through the standard poses of flinty-eyed realism, dark romanticism and tragic fatalism. Mark Renton is the key spokesperson for this new anaesthetic, voicing all the sentiments that would find such fertile soil in the popular imagination that some bookstores had to keep the novel behind the counter because it was so frequently stolen. In all of his pronouncements, and in his characterizations of heroin, Renton constructs the style of heroin culture as a latter-day form of tragic romantic individualism, a funhouse mirror version of the rugged Randian individualism Thatcher had sought to encourage. As Lewis MacLeod puts it, 'Renton and his friends often duplicate the self-serving, highly privatized cultural logic of Thatcherism' (105). The ensemble of affects and beliefs Renton cobbles together in his effort to rationalize and justify his addiction is fundamentally incoherent, but such incoherence is in fact a defining feature of late-stage post-war youth culture.

Renton understands the self-absorption of heroin to be key to its appeal: It is, for him, an honest drug that simplifies life into a crystal clear relationship of need and gratification. It strips away all else, including friendship, reducing all human relationships to little more than means to the end of scoring heroin. Renton values this aspect of heroin's effects so much that he grants oracular status to Johnny Swan's declaration that there are 'Nae friends in this game. Jist associates' (6). It's a sentiment echoed by non-fictional addicts as well: ' "You try and keep away from people," says David. "You just want to be left alone to do heroin. Even if someone overdoses, your first thought is not, 'Oh, are they OK?' Your first thought is to seek out where they got the heroin from – that's how sad it is. Everyone uses everyone, and if you do build relationships it's for a common purpose, to get what you need. It's dog eat dog" ' (Edamariam and Scott n.p.). The novel famously opens with exactly this mood, as Renton describes his resentment of his best friend Sick Boy for insisting that they go out to get more heroin. Renton is comfortably high, though 'the sweat wis lashin oaf Sick Boy', who is going into withdrawal, and Renton wants nothing more than for Sick Boy to disappear so he can enjoy his high: 'Whereas the piss-heid in the pub wants every cunt tae git as ootay it as he is, the real junky (as opposed to the casual user who wants a partner-in-crime) doesnae gie a fuck aboot anybody else' (Welsh 7). Renton only finally gets up and goes with Sick Boy to score drugs because he knows that he is also out of the drug, and will soon enough be feeling sick as well: 'it's in the fuckin post, that's fir sure' (4). In a perverse version of Thatcheresque self-interest, Renton embraces heroin's capacity to remove the individual from social commitment, placing selfish need above any form of empathy or communal obligation. He resents anyone who stands between him and his high, and sees others strictly in terms of two camps: Those who provide access to heroin and those who block access to heroin. Because of its chemically addictive element, heroin thus makes selfishness and self-interest into physiological imperatives.

Renton justifies his selfishness through a tortured logic that presents heroin as a means of heightening reality rather than fleeing from it. The argument is complex, and moves through four stages: (1) an objective account of the conditions of existence, (2) heroin as a positive influence, (3) the crash and its revelation of the true state of affairs, and (4) a return to step 2, taking heroin to escape the misery of reality. Wash, rinse, repeat. In the first stage of his rationalization, Renton tells Tommy that heroin 'kinday makes things seem mair real tae us' (89). The 'things' that heroin helps elucidate manifest as a pseudo-nihilist coffee-house cool philosophizing: 'Life's boring and futile. We start oaf wi high hopes, then we bottle it. We realise that we're aw gaunnae die, withoot really findin oot the big answers. [...] Basically, we live a short, disappointing life; and then we die' (89). Reprising Arthur Seaton's bleak summary of life nearly forty years previously, Renton adopts the perspective of the wise-beyond-his-years young rebel who understands the cosmic emptiness of existence. It's a sloppy popular rendition of existentialist philosophy, hinging upon the speaker's access to an objective understanding of the nature of human existence: This is, according to Renton, *how things really are*, though only he among a handful of others has the moral courage to face it. As part of this bleak vision, Renton writes off all the rest of philosophy, human enterprise, family and relationships as so much self-delusion, designed by those lacking in sufficient moral courage to avoid having to face the reality he has a hold of: 'We develop aw they long-winded ideas which jist interpret the reality ay oor lives in different weys, withoot really extending oor body ay worthwhile knowledge, about the big things, the real things. We fill up oor lives wi shite, things like careers and relationships tae delude oorsels that it isnae aw totally pointless' (89–90). Philosophy, careers and relationships are little more than anaesthetics, means by which we deaden our awareness of the cosmic emptiness of human existence. They are comforting illusions that allow us to live dishonestly, to avoid confronting the truth. Up is down, good is bad, reality is fiction. Importantly, at this stage of his rationalization, Renton speaks of a 'we' who fall prey to these illusions, including himself and Tommy in a community of benighted fellow sufferers.

In the second and third stages of his rationalization, Renton presents heroin as the antidote to this false consciousness: 'Smack's an honest drug, because it strips away these delusions. Wi smack, whin ye feel good, ye feel immortal. Whin ye feel bad, it intensifies the shite that's already thair. It's the only really honest drug. It doesnae alter yir consciousness. It just gies ye a hit and a sense ay well-being. Efter that, ye see the misery ay the world as it is, and ye cannae anaesthetise yirsel against it' (Welsh 89–90). First, there is the glaring shift in pronoun use. Renton now uses the impersonal 'you' to generalize to all who have ever taken heroin, identifying himself with the enlightened user of the drug, and universalizing his experience. It's a crafty rhetorical move, one that subtly excludes Tommy from the community of those who have seen the truth and establishing that community as a Kantian in-group. He makes himself and heroin together the measure of all things. Insisting that heroin does not alter your consciousness, Renton nonetheless details several ways in which heroin has altered his consciousness. First, he allows that the high of heroin makes 'ye *feel* immortal' (my emphasis), emphasizing affect over consciousness, and a feeling over reality. The high he spends so much of his time chasing and indulging gets but a single short sentence to describe it – and a far less eloquent sentence than the one about its orgasmic force used earlier. No doubt motivated in part by a desire to put Tommy off using any of his reserve, Renton minimizes the incredible high heroin provides him, and instead focuses on the come-down as the locus of its true value. After the hit and the 'sense ay well-being' it provides (this may be the understatement of the novel), Renton specifies the honesty of heroin in its revelation of 'the misery ay the world as it is'. Having separated the high from the drug's 'honest' effects by identifying it as simply something you 'feel' and a 'sense' you get, Renton claims that the real value of the drug experience is that it removes the blinkers of false consciousness. Ironically, he claims that heroin thus awakens the user to reality and makes it impossible to 'anaesthetise yirsel against it'. That is, he claims that heroin is anti-anaesthetic, a stimulant rather than an opiate, and yet truth resides not in its high, but in its after-effects. In keeping with a long-established romantic notion of suffering as authenticity, Renton insists that only the bad is real; the good is false. So profound is this experience, for Renton that he equates the use of heroin with the discovery and experience of the authentic self: 'Rehabilitation means the surrender ay the self' (Welsh 181). To return to the everyday world is to relinquish the crystalline clarity of vision and the moral courage that lets one face up to the emptiness of existence.

Renton's rationalization for his addiction partakes of what is by 1993 a long-established tradition of the uncompromising teenager in the adult world, the rebel who sees through the dulling effects of bourgeois complacency, and who calls out the hypocrisy around him with a revolutionary fervour. It is of a piece with every declaration of youth's impatience with age we have seen so far, and many more besides, going all the way back to Plato's cave. What's different here is that Renton locates the power to see through the deadened lives of those around him not in his youth, historical innovation, or unprecedented intellect, but in a drug. Like a good capitalist, he saves time and energy by out-sourcing the youth-cultural work of generational tension and counter-cultural rebellion that used to be done in-house. Unfortunately, this move misses out two key points that quickly expose cracks in his view of heroin and undermine his defence of it.

The first of these is the question of why anyone would take heroin in the first place. Circularly, Renton argues that the world is bleak and pointless, and that 'we' anaesthetize ourselves against this knowledge with such fripperies as love, family, career and relationships, *but* that he has only come to see the 'misery ay the world as it is' because of heroin. Why, then, take heroin in the first place, if the anaesthetic power of human interaction and industry is powerful enough that the majority of people simply fail to notice the emptiness of it all? No doubt there is a vestige of the tragic romantic genius buried here, an after-image of the voice in the wilderness, the sensitive soul who intuits the unreality of the everyday and sets out to discover its true essence, but it's a vestige well buried: Renton never makes any gesture towards a self-conception along these lines, giving heroin all the credit for his higher consciousness. The second point Renton elides is why he continues to take heroin once he has achieved his insight. If heroin is 'the only really honest drug' because it clarifies and amplifies the truly bleak nature of human existence, of 'the world as it is' then what call is there to continue using it, if not to escape the truth it exposes? Renton's logic suddenly inverts itself, as he unwittingly admits that heroin's anaesthetic effects, the high he passes over so quickly and lamely, is precisely what makes it so attractive. Its honesty has precious little to do with its draw, compared to its power to dull your sense of misery, and to hide your complicity in the miserable state of affairs around you. It absolves its users of responsibility for ameliorating the misery they see, let alone for finding a lasting remedy for their own misery. The anaesthetic function Renton claims is provided by philosophy, family, career, relationships and so on turns out to belong to heroin rather than to human intercourse. Heroin is at once the anaesthetic, a prosthetic consciousness, and an outsourced subjectivity. Behind the blinding insights it supposedly enables, the drug hides – and thus makes it possible to avoid – personal responsibility and communal obligation. In this, it both fulfils and cancels out Thatcherite individualism with a total sense of impotence and freedom from obligation.

Welsh thus manages to use heroin as indeed 'a brilliant metaphor for our times', though in ways Renton likely does not envision, particularly for Scottish youth after a decade of neo-liberalism. By 1993, the utopian energy of previous generations of youth cultures has stifled in its crib under Thatcher. The death of baby Dawn, Lesley and Sick Boy's child, in the novel concretizes this fact as a direct consequence of neglect, chemical dependency, and an inability to mature. (The) Dawn dies, foreclosed by the bleak horizon it should properly illuminate. Though teenagers such as Renton can clearly see the real conditions of existence, they feel powerless to change them; they simply do not believe in the possibility of a youth-cultural revolution bringing about a new world, as previous generations had (e.g. the Teenager in *Absolute Beginners*). Instead, they disassociate, locating identity, subjectivity, insight, moral courage and truth itself in a drug whose effects are precisely to numb, immobilize and isolate. The teenage dream is in tatters by the time we get to *Trainspotting*, and that's not all.

As Renton's abortive university career and demonstrated interest in philosophy illustrate, much more is at stake in the throttling of youth-cultural utopianism than simply neo-liberal preservation of the market as a site of free enterprise safe from disruption. Having won a scholarship to Aberdeen university, where he found the course 'easy' (147), Renton also finds the history of Western thought to be dull and unrelated to the material conditions of existence of Scotland in the 1980s. Losing interest in his studies, Renton instead seeks the anaesthetic of cheap sensation, spending his grant money on prostitutes and drugs before returning home without his degree. That this failure is not down to a lack of intelligence becomes clear when Renton and Spud face trial for shoplifting books. Mocked by the judge for his claim that he intended to read the volume of Kierkegaard he had stolen, Renton voices a glib but insightful justification of his interest in the Dane's philosophy:

> I'm interested in his concepts of subjectivity and truth, and particularly his ideas concerning choice; the notion that genuine choice is made out of doubt and uncertainty, and without recourse to the experience or advice of others. It could be argued, with some justification, that it's primarily a bourgeois, existential philosophy and would therefore seek to undermine collective societal wisdom. However, it's also a liberating philosophy, because when such societal wisdom is negated, the basis for social control over the individual becomes weakened. (165–166)

Briefly put, Renton cites Kierkegaard as justification of his determination not to 'choose life', but to choose heroin instead. He also shows how a little knowledge of Kierkegaard can make him sound proto-Ayn Randian, offering a philosophical justification for Thatcher's cynicism. Wryly, Renton invokes the larger questions of ethics which underpin the notions of justice that ideally animate the criminal justice system. At the same time, he mocks the judge for both believing in such high-faulting notions and assuming that they would be of no interest to a junky. The irony here cuts in multiple directions, as Renton simultaneously mocks the tradition of Western philosophy he has previously lumped together with family and career as anaesthetic to the real conditions of existence, and yet admits not only that he is interested in it, but that he has read some of it and understood it quite well.

This irony points to another aspect of Renton's twisted rationalization of heroin as an 'honest' drug: Many of the core ideals Renton uses in his defence of heroin belong precisely to the philosophical tradition he runs down as 'they long-winded ideas which jist interpret the reality ay oor lives in different weys, withoot really extending oor body ay worthwhile knowledge, about the big things, the real things'. These ideals include honesty, of course, authenticity, objectivity, truth, the self, choice and freedom. We have already seen that Renton treats honesty and authenticity as sovereign values, even if they are outsourced to a drug to afford him sufficient ironic distance. His emphasis on 'life as it is' implies a reverence for objective truth as well, and his reference to rehab as threatening the loss of the self indicates that he values notions of a stable identity and core subjectivity too. Finally, and most famously, Renton values choice and believes unquestioningly in free will. He presents this belief in a layered rant which deplores 'social control over the individual':

> Society invents a spurious convoluted logic tae absorb and change people whae's behaviour is outside its mainstream. Suppose that ah ken aw the pros and cons, know that ah'm gaunnae huv a short life, am ay sound mind etcetera, etcetera, but still want tae use smack? They won't let ye dae it. They won't let ye dae it, because it's seen as a sign ay thir

ain failure. The fact that ye jist simply choose tae reject whit they huv tae offer. Choose us. Choose life. Choose mortgage payments; choose washing machines; choose cars; choose sitting oan a couch watching mind-numbing and spirit-crushing game shows, stuffing junk food intae yir mooth. Choose rotting away, pishing and shiteing yersel in a home a total fuckin embarrassment tae the selfish, fucked-up brats ye've produced. Choose life. (Welsh 187)

Charging 'society' with using 'a spurious and convoluted logic' much like his own, Renton in effect objects to the illegality of suicide. He begins with suppositions that are by no means easily granted: That you can be 'ay sound mind' and still want to pursue an addiction to heroin. He then projects an irrational motivation for this social control: 'it's seen as a sign ay thir ain failure.' It's an elaborate deflection from a much more likely seeming option: Heroin addiction alters the brain chemistry so that addicts are *de facto* no longer capable of freely choosing to use or not to use the drug. Holding the humanist notion of free will out as an incorruptible and permanent feature of all sane humans (sanity being another of the humanist values Renton sneaks into his logic), Renton ignores heroin's capacity to undermine an individual's capacity to exercise free will. He overlooks the fact that heroin use literally makes its users insane by damaging the organic integrity of their bodies and minds. Despite his special pleading earlier, heroin clearly does 'alter yir consciousness', casting the whole question of freedom of choice into doubt. Finally, the litany of imperatives to 'choose' Renton runs through here bring a decidedly more mundane element to his earlier condemnation of family, career and so on but once again does so in terms that simultaneously undermine the very category of choice and cast him as a romantic outlaw, one who can preserve the integrity of choice only by choosing 'tae reject whit they huv tae offer'. The spurious alignment of 'life' with the list of consumer goods and sordid realities contributes yet again to the idealized pose of the teenage rebel, but it can only do so by aligning real choice with the very drug Renton himself admits is virtually impossible *not* to obey. His cut-rate Nietzschean pseudo-philosophizing works well for him – and apparently for legions of young readers as well – as a justification for heroin use as a legitimate means of social protest, but it is intellectually incoherent, a scrambled reaction to an impossible set of circumstances.

Trainspotting thus establishes heroin as a massively overdetermined signifier that ironizes, dislocates, outsources and yet preserves a desperately sincere faith in youth-cultural potential. Its function varies depending upon who is using it, who is speaking about it, and what effects it has most immediately produced. Crucially, though heroin is not uniformly presented as a positive force in the novel by any means, its negative impacts are dramatically mitigated. No one in the novel dies from using it, for example. Tommy dies of toxoplasmosis because he has HIV, Matty dies of HIV, baby

Dawn dies of neglect, but no one dies from injecting heroin directly. The closest we come is Renton's overdose at Johnny Swan's apartment, and that episode only results in Renton being forced by his parents to get clean, though he apparently wastes no time in reacquainting himself with the drug before the novel's ending. In the terms of this study, heroin *is* the youth-cultural style of the novel, a death-driven *modus vivendi* for a bleak world. It organizes and determines how virtually all the characters live their lives, and provides the an-aesthetic articulation of how they understand their specific situation as young people living at what looked every bit like the end of history.

Second only to the drug itself in terms of youth-cultural an-aesthetics in *Trainspotting* is music. The soundtrack to the film version was hugely popular – perhaps more so than the film itself – and presents a fusion of late 1980s and early 1990s dance tracks, mixed together with key heroin-related tracks from much earlier. These heroin-related tracks are telling, as they align heroin culture in the novel with a specific line of authenticity and masculinity. Balancing out the techno and dance tunes that hold the film's soundscape together are songs by Iggy Pop, Lou Reed and David Bowie. Notably, the novel, film and soundtrack all avoid the predictable use of such druggy classics as Pink Floyd, apparently preferring Pop, Reed and Bowie's ragged authenticity over slick production. In contrast to the indulgent stoner ethos of Pink Floyd, moreover, Iggy, Reed and Bowie all present conflicted attitudes towards heroin in particular.

First, very early in the narrative, Renton notes with distaste that Raymie has put on Reed's 'Heroin' while the junkies are getting their fix, breaking 'the junky's golden rule' (8). The song's variable tempo takes us from lugubrious despair through the rush of the hit and its high, and downward into the nihilistic death-drive of the incurable junky. It presents heroin in precisely the same terms Renton uses to describe it to Tommy – it makes you feel immortal, then takes away everything you had and more – and no doubt has come to inform Renton's thinking about the drug over many repetitions. Its concluding lines achingly voice the total surrender of the junky to the habit, and the sense of helplessness attendant upon being in its grip. The song's honesty may be why it is in poor taste to play it among junkies, though it captures better than most other such songs (barring perhaps Burt Jensch's 'Needle of Death') the inescapable push-pull of the drug and the paradoxical mental and affective states it provokes.

The film version of *Trainspotting* opens with Pop's 'Lust for Life' providing the soundtrack to Renton and Spud running from the police, and paradoxically sets up their heroin habits as part of an elemental *joie de vivre*, a jokey bit of lads' fun rather than a life-destroying response to an ostensibly hopeless life situation. When Tommy attends the Iggy Pop concert – effectively choosing the event over his girlfriend and nearly missing it altogether because he is so high and drunk – he experiences an epiphany when Iggy looks right at him and intones ' "America takes drugs in psychic defence"; only he changes "America" for "Scatlin", and defines us mair accurately in a single sentence than all the others have ever done' (75). Of course, this epiphany reverses Renton's claim that heroin 'makes things seem mair real tae us', instead declaring the truth that the drug provides a barrier against reality, a means of defending the mind from full engagement with difficulty. Moreover, 'Lust for Life' articulates the quandary of the junky deciding (no doubt not for the first, or the last, time) to kick the habit. In a key sense, Iggy's song – sung by someone who has authentic experience of heroin and of kicking the habit – articulates the 'lust for life' as the cause of both dabbling in 'liquor and drugs' and, more urgently, for kicking the habit. As with Reed's song, though, Iggy's is overlaid with the ironic veil that is by now standard issue for any aspect of youth culture. The transposition of serenades to heroin from twenty years previously to the context of 1990s Scotland itself establishes a sort of historical distance that challenges the effectiveness of any effort to move beyond it. Iggy and Reed's songs remain every bit as relevant as when they were first released, indicating the terminal holding pattern that takes over when youth-cultural drug experimentation becomes a permanent way of being in the world.

Rounding out the trio of music icons the novel, film and soundtrack present is David Bowie, every one of whose releases Renton owns (17). Instantly, this claim establishes Bowie's pre-eminence as a cultural reference point for the novel. With his constant re-invention of himself, and experimentation with identity on all fronts – including experiments with drugs – Bowie presents a glimmer of hope: A survivor who has maintained contemporary relevance in the world of youth culture for decades. His fluidity and capacity to morph with the times, to discover alternatives to established patterns where none appeared possible, is in itself utopian. It articulates possibility and promise where so many see only grey impossibility. 'Above all –' as Michael Bracewell puts it, 'above his influence on fashion and music – David Bowie was a unifier of pop youth: he brought together a massive faction of lost romantics and disbelievers in the rock orthodoxy; he built a bridge between the sexes that inspired mutual identification and adoration from boys and girls, in a way that neither the Beatles nor the Rolling Stones had ever achieved' (192). In precisely this vein, the only song of Bowie's that gets mentioned in the novel is Golden Years, its lyrics even quoted directly: *'Don't let me hear you say life's taking you nowhere'* (17). Importantly, the song itself articulates something of a time-warp, demanding that its addressee recognize that the present will soon enough appear sepia-tinged with nostalgia, that the today is always already the 'golden years' of youth. Ironically admitting that it is difficult to recognize the present in as positive a light as it will one day appear, 'Golden Years' nonetheless insists upon a wilful optimism that apparently stands in stark opposition to the bleakness and despair that governs so much of the rest of the novel.

Only apparently, though. As I've suggested is one of the key functions of using 'Lust for Life' to open the film, 'Golden Years' here helps create an aura of hipness and light-hearted cool around heroin culture in the novel. It is one of the representational strategies that make the *Trainspotting* phenomenon complicit in the emergence of heroin chic, buffering the devastating impact of heroin use by associating it with cool characters engaged in youthful hijinks. There's a self-awareness here that helps us understand youth culture in *Trainspotting* as aware of itself *as* youth culture; it knows that however bad things really are, and however many people's lives are destroyed, the past will inevitably become the locus of nostalgic longing. The novel thus allows its characters to perform youth-cultural identity and experimentation from a distance. They can both live the moment and understand it as always already having taken place, as both happening and receding into the past at the same moment.

The ambivalence towards heroin, the very real hardships of youth-cultural identity formation, and the inevitable transformation of those hardships into the stuff of wistful memory mirrors another key aspect of Reed, Iggy and Bowie's inclusion in the novel: their sexual and gender fluidity. Though there is a decided dearth of fluid or alternative masculinity in the novel, the invocation of these three preserves such possibilities in amber: They belong to the past, anchored in heroin culture's ersatz history. And yet, the novel is obsessed with the latest iteration of the ongoing post-war crisis of masculinity: 'Welsh writes about social exclusion and individualism; the local, national and global; neoliberal economy and the commodification of drugs; but maybe, above all, about the dissolution of patriarchy and the de(con)struction of masculinity, about the erosion of gender categories and the family' (Herbrechter 109). The connection *Trainspotting* charts between heroin and alternative masculinities helps us untangle the representation of masculinity in this novel, and understand heroin's role in the crisis of masculinity we have been tracing.

As the pastness of Reed, Iggy and Bowie illustrates, the challenges to conventional styles of masculinity undertaken by glam, punk and the new romantics have changed very little, and a traditionalist backlash was well under way by 1990. As we saw with *East of Acre Lane* and *Brixton Rock*, the 1980s witnessed the pendulum swing away from the experimental ethos of the 1970s, and back towards traditional forms of masculine heteronormativity. This reversal took place in the second-generation immigrant culture Wheatle traces, but it was equally part of the skinhead resurgence of the 1980s, and of the working-class xenophobia tacitly licensed by a decade of Conservative rule. In Scotland in particular, it helped reaffirm the tradition of the 'hard man' – what Welsh calls 'manhood Ecosse' (Welsh 198): The drinking, fighting, fucking lad for whom anything smacking of deviance is itself provocation to a beating. *Trainspotting* outlines this resurgence of hardcore traditional masculinity, though it adds an ironic spin to its representation and introduces heroin itself as a dead-end alternative. It presents the return of Arthur Seaton in an intensified form, with the *bonhommie* and confidence gone, replaced by a belligerent and disproportionate promiscuity and wanton violence. The resulting vision is every bit as bleak as that in *East of Acre Lane* and *Brixton Rock*, with a radically narrowed horizon of possibility for achieving mature masculinity in which virtually every permissible option is already overcoded with futility and death. Most obviously, *Trainspotting* establishes two lines of potential for mature masculinity, falling precisely along the same sweet bwai/bad bwai binary Wheatle introduced: Sick Boy and Begbie.

Something of a sexual wonderkid, Sick Boy is seductive, careless and manipulative – even sociopathic – and representative of the 'lover' ideal of mature masculinity. Evidently capable of bedding any woman on whom he sets his sights, he is characterized as a 'sexual aristocrat' (131) in comparison to his mates. 'Sexual jealousy is an in-built component in a friendship with Sick Boy for men', while 'It seemed, for women, that fucking was just something that you did wi Sick Boy, like talking, or drinking tea wi other punters' (131, 13). This easy ability to seduce women comes with its risks and penalties, though, as Sick Boy is less than meticulous in his use of birth control: He is the father of Lesley's baby, Dawn, and extraordinarily lucky that he has managed not to contract HIV given his enormous promiscuity, particularly with drug addicts. In one of the very few sections of the novel where we get inside Sick Boy's head, he meditates on precisely this point:

> That reminds us, ah must buy some flunkies. .. but there's no way you can get HIV in Edinburgh through shagging a lassie. They say that wee Goagsie got it that way, but I reckon that he's been daein a bit ay mainlining or shitstabbing on the Q.T. If ye dinnae get it through shootin up wi the likes ay Renton, Spud, Swanney n Seeker, it's obviously no got your name on it ...still ... why tempt fate ...but why not. (31)

This attitude is immediately related to a fundamental nihilism at the heart of Sick Boy's exemplary masculinity, and implicates it directly in his sociopathic tendencies: 'at least ah know that ah'm still here, still alive, because as long as there's an opportunity tae get off wi a woman and her purse, and that's it, that is it, ah've found fuck all else, ZERO, tae fill this big, BLACK HOLE like a clenched fist in the centre ay my fucking chest' (31). First of all, Sick Boy's promiscuity is re-framed here in terms of money as well as libidinal gratification, linking the difficult economic situation facing young men in Scotland circa 1990 to a primal physical need, and perverting both. The assertion of masculine prowess that attends sexual conquest is undermined by the equal need to steal money from women. The style of masculinity on display here is more complex than simple phallic bravado, and in fact indicates a fundamental lack – a 'BLACK HOLE' – at its core.

The inessential nature of Sick Boy's masculinity, its structuring around a basic lack and total dependence upon female support, manifests in detachment, manipulation and the gradual take-over of sociopathy. Sick Boy's promiscuity belongs to the long tradition of the male Lothario, the lady-killer whose capacity to divine any given woman's weakness and cater to it is key to his success. When Sick Boy decides to seduce a backpacker on the bus from Edinburgh to London this capacity manifests explicitly in terms of style. Observing the backpacker and categorizing her stylistically, Sick Boy then changes his style to chime with hers:

> He pulls off his *Italians Do It Better* t-shirt, exposing a wiry, tanned torso. Sick Boy's mother is Italian, but he wears the t-shirt less to show pride in his origins, as to wind up the others at his pretension. He pulls down his bag and rummages through its contents. There is a *Mandela Day* shirt, which was politically sound and rock enough, but too mainstream, too sloganistic. Worse, it was dated. He felt that Mandela would prove to be just another tedious old cunt once everyone got used to him being out of the jail. He only gave *Hibernian F. C. – European Campaigners* a cursory glance before rejecting it out of hand. The Sandinistas were also passe now. He settled for a Fall t-shirt which at least had the virtue of being white and would show off his Corsican tan to its best effect. Pulling it on, he moved over and slid into the seat beside the woman. (335)

The chapter is entitled 'Station to Station' – the title of Bowie's 1976 album featuring 'Golden Years' – and it appears that the lesson Sick Boy has learned from Bowie is not just that masculinity, like all gender and sexuality, is merely performative. He has additionally extrapolated from that lesson that given its inauthenticity, identity can be used to manipulate others to fill your need: 'Renton observes, with a mixture of admiration and distaste, the metamorphosis of Sick Boy from waster into this woman's ideal man. Voice modulation and accent subtly change. An interested, earnest expression comes over his face as he fires seductively interrogative questions at his new companion' (335). Tellingly, Sick Boy is just as motivated by the chance to steal the backpacker's money as he is by the prospect of having sex with her – Begbie clues in to this and warns Sick Boy that robbing her would jeopardize the day's mission, which is to sell a quantity of heroin down in London. The value of the money over sexual release for Sick Boy manifests clearly here, as Sick Boy admits the truth of Begbie's point and abandons the pursuit (337).

The fusion of sex and money in Sick Boy's increasingly incoherent style of masculinity-as-sociopathy culminates in his entry into the world of pimping. Driven by a fundamental lack of identity, and decreasingly satisfied by the superficial triumphs of bedding women, Sick Boy turns the tables and begins selling sex to other men in a final assertion of total independence from the social. As Reynolds earlier said of the 1990s youth culture more broadly, Sick Boy responds 'to the challenge of "enterprise culture" in a quick-killing, here-and-now way, becoming not opportunity conscious but criminal minded':

Ah couldnae believe ma ears. Sick Boy wisnae jokin. He wis gaun tae try tae set up Planet Ay The Apes wi wee Maria Anderson, this junky he'd been fucking on and oaf for a few months. The cunt wanted tae pimp her oot. Ah felt sickened at what he'd come tae, what awe'd aw come tae, and started tae envy Spud again.

Ah pull um aside. – Whit's the fuckin score?

– The score is ah'm looking eftir numero uno. Whit's your fuckin problem? When did you go intae social work?

– This is fuckin different. Ah dinnae ken whit the fuck's gaun oan wi' you mate, ah really dinnae.

– So you're Mister fuckin Squeaky Clean now, eh?

– Naw, bit ah dinnae fuck ower any cunt else.

– Git ootay ma face. Tell us it wisnae you thit turned Tommy oantae Seeker n that crowd. His eyes wir crystal clear and treacherous, untainted by conscience or compassion. (174)

As the Wizard had done in *Absolute Beginners* before him, Sick Boy chooses a grotesquely disfigured masculinity over friendship and community. As illegitimate a child as Thatcher ever produced, cornered by the homophobic configuration of masculinity that mocks all forms of same-sex tenderness, and in full flight from existential crisis, Sick Boy illustrates the utter sterility of sweet-bwai masculinity in its Scottish iteration.

That Sick Boy consciously constructs his style of masculinity over the other alternative – the hard-man style we are about to explore – manifests with crystal clarity in the one case where we seek him get violent. In this episode, Sick Boy sights with his pellet rifle a skinhead with a pitbull in a nearby park: 'Ah ... the enemy ish in shite, as the old Bond would have said, and what a fuckin sight the cunt looks as well. Skinheid haircut, green bomber-jaykit, nine-inch DMs. A stereotypical twat; and there's the woof-woof trailing loyally behind. Pit Bull, shit bull, bullshit terrier ... a fuckin set ay jaws on four legs' (178). His imagination invokes specifically the Edinburgh-native Sean Connery version of James Bond, which Patricia Horton associates with 'a masculinity grounded in "self-reliant and competitive individualism"' (229). From this vantage, Sick Boy focuses on the skinhead with homoerotic intensity: 'Ah then travel up and doon his body, up and doon, up and doon ... *take it easy baby ... take it one more time* ... nobody has ever given the bastard this much attention, this much care, this much ... yes, love, in his puff' (178). Pain, pleasure, love, power and authority intermingle fluidly for Sick Boy as he contemplates this 'stereotypical' figure of violent masculinity.

As is his habit, Sick Boy shoots the dog, provoking it to attack the skinhead, and then runs to the rescue. As he twists a baseball bat in the dog's collar, slowly strangling it to death, Sick Boy feels a perverse elation: He is both punishing the dog 'for the shite you've done in the parks' (178-179) and masculinely dominating the skinhead. His victory over the hard-man style of masculinity leaves him feeling extraordinary, 'as high as a kite and horny as a field of stags. It's been a fucking beautiful day' (181). The oblique violence of the episode, all executed by phallic proxy – the rifle, the bat – and without any hint of direct physical contact between him and his skinhead nemesis, amounts to foreplay for Sick Boy, further illustrating the toxicity of his masculinity. As the representative of one stream of traditional masculinity in *Trainspotting*, Sick Boy is compromised in virtually every respect. Even if similar levels of sexual prowess were within the reach of characters like Spud or Renton, the trade-offs that come with them clearly prove that path to be utterly sterile.

While Simon's skinhead victim promptly recedes from view, his legacy is taken up and articulated with great force and clarity by Begbie, *Trainspotting*'s second entry into the masculinity crisis sweepstakes. In Renton's words, 'Begbie, total fuckin crazy psycho Beggars, is held up as an archetypal model of manhood Ecosse. Yes, there may be poor bastards picking bits ay beer glass oot ay thir faces when Franco goes on the rampage, but the laddie works hard and plays hard etcetera, etcetera' (Welsh 198). Begbie is perpetually angry, violent, touchy, and belligerent. He epitomizes the tradition of the 'hard man the working-class male who knows hard labor and though not necessarily physically imposing, is tough beyond reckoning'. As Renton notes, he works hard and plays hard holding to a notoriously simple credo of 'sticking by your mates' that really amounts to asserting his status as the alpha male, governing a pack of followers who must be defended and disciplined with equal vigour: 'a slight shift in the cunt's perception ay ye wid be sufficient tae change yir status fae great mate intae persecuted victim' (75). Like heroin, he is an addiction for his mates – he has no *bona fide* friends – a habit they cannot quit in large part because doing so would invite physical suffering much like the suffering of withdrawal. Unable or unwilling to think in depth about his own situation, his beliefs or his conclusions about life, Begbie values only unquestioning adherence to a barren code of conduct that leads him frequently into contradiction and incoherence.

Perhaps the best instance of this simplistic and rigid mentality manifests at Matty's funeral:

> Franco Begbie felt angry and confused. Any injury to a friend he took as a personal insult. He prided himself on looking after his mates. The death of one of them confronted him with his own impotence. Franco resolved this problem by turning his anger on Matty. He remembered the time that Matty shat it off Gypo and Mikey Forrester in Lothian Road, and he had to have both the cunts on his puff. Not that it presented him with any difficulty. It was the principle of the thing though. You had to back up your mates. He'd made Matty pay for his cowardice: physically, with beatings, and socially, with heaps of humiliating slaggings. Now he realised, he'd not made the cunt pay enough. (Welsh 293)

Initially angry and confused not over the loss of a friend, but because his standard operation of punishing violators with a savage beating has been stymied, Begbie pursues a meandering set of associations that allows him to revive an old anger with Matty. The move illustrates the anaesthetic effect of Begbie's hard-man masculinity, since it allows him to transmute sadness and confusion, personal hurt ('any injury to a friend he took as a personal insult') into anger. The regret he feels at Matty's death is over not having made Matty 'pay enough' for getting Begbie into a fight with two other tough guys. It is precisely the inverse of what we might expect: That he regrets having made Matty suffer for his error. Having backed up his mate by defeating Mikey Forrester and Gypo in a fight, Begbie turns around and makes Matty pay for his transgression both physically and socially. He bullies him, in short, for the rest of his short life, and only regrets not having done it more. His persistent anger bespeaks not so much fidelity to a principle, whatever Begbie might want to think, as a transmuted fear over finding himself alone and outmatched. Though Begbie won the fight this time, the dynamic of provocation and abandonment clearly strikes a chord. His anger is a form of anaesthetic, the physical violence a means of damping down the emotional turmoil he experiences. Begbie's sense of being under threat is so profound that he sees provocation at every turn. Ultimately, he can only assert his masculinity through '"the discipline ay the basebaw bat"' (172). His insistence on a pack mentality that is constantly policed for loyalty and subjected to discipline is a means of holding at bay the certainty that he in fact has no friends, nothing like a real community, and no genuine affiliations.

At the heart of this anaesthetic hard man style of masculinity is a fundamental crisis of authority, in which Begbie teeters perpetually on the brink of mature masculinity, unable ever to achieve it. In this respect, he captures an elemental truth facing many of the young men coming of age in Thatcher's Britain, unable to find the independence and autonomy necessary to making the transition from adolescence to adulthood. 'Seen in perspective, Welsh's male psychos come at a time when masculinity has been forced out of its hegemonic silence. Feminism, the gay, lesbian and transsexual movements and postcolonial and postmodern theories have been attacking the hegemonic model of the white heterosexual patriarch as masculinity's natural "norm"' (Herbrechter 119). This situation of perceived attack is why Begbie flirts with authority as he does, never finding the right balance to allow him to settle into a sense of power that is not constantly under threat or in need of defence. Most viciously, this tendency manifests in his mugging of an American in a pub toilet. Begbie pulls a knife and the American refuses to hand over his wallet. The result is predictable, though bad enough that Spud (who narrates it for us retrospectively) is lastingly affected by it:

Begbie went fucking crazy, goat that carried away likesay, wi the bladework, ken, we nearly forgoat the wallet likes. Ah goat intae the guy's poakits and fished it oot while Begbie wis bootin um in the face. Blood wis flowin intae the latrine, mixin wi the pish. Ugly, ugly, ugly man, likesay, ken? Ah still shake thinkin aboot it. Ah lie in bed n likes, shudder. (155)

When the American tourist ignores Begbie's authority – guaranteed by his knife, his role as gang leader, and his status as local – Begbie snaps. In such a situation, the hard man has only one option: To be so hard that no one will ever again challenge his authority. So resounding is his victory in this regard, so effective his assertion of toxic masculinity not only over the American (who is hospitalized, but lives) but his mates as well, that Spud characterizes it in terms of rape. 'The Beggar, dear old Franco, he raped us likesay, raped us aw that night, sort ay shafted us up oor erses n peyed us oaf, like we wir hoors man, ken likes?' (155). Begbie anaesthetizes his fragile sense of masculinity by buffering his vulnerability with the traumatized psyches of those who pass for his friends.

As we might expect of a novel so anchored in drug use, *Trainspotting* does offer one alternative to the abortive Sick Boy and Begbie styles of masculinity: opting out. Keeping alive Bowie's legacy of fluid gender and sexuality, aided by the power of heroin to anaesthetize against social disapprobation and the more urgent promptings of desire, the novel navigates a third option between hyper-sexual conquest and violent domination. This option depends upon nullifying heterosexual desire in the first place, and then creating a space for expressions of same-sex tenderness and care. In doing so, *Trainspotting* sounds a possible version of masculinity in a conventionally feminine key – though even this option is held at an aesthetic distance. Moreover, it plays a key role in the global popularity of heroin chic, linking it to a broad increase in acceptance of non-normative gender and sexuality even in the midst of a Scotland pervaded with fear over the twin epidemics of AIDS/HIV and heroin use.

Crucial to this operation is an opening gambit where the novel feminizes its junkies: The more serious a person's habit, the more feminized he is. According to this line of thinking, the feminization of men transforms activity, strength, continence, and energy into the opposing values of passivity, weakness, bodily excess, lassitude and helplessness. The novel opens with Renton and Sick Boy loafing in Renton's room, watching an action movie on video. The contrast between the hyper-masculine action hero on the screen and the two junkies – one effectively inert, the other pacing in growing hysteria as his symptoms of withdrawal worsen – clearly indicates the distance between their actuality and the idealized masculinity they passively consume. Their need finally motivates them to leave on a quest for more heroin, not like two plucky heroes heading out on an adventure but like two wounded victims crying out in distress for relief. Think Beckett rather than Tolkein. Like Beckett's Molloy and late-stage Moran, Renton and Sick Boy lack agency, power, self-control and reason – all values commonly associated with masculinity. Instead, they avoid confrontation with another group of young men by stealing their taxi and heading to see the dealer: Johnny Swan. Though Renton informs us that Johnny Swan is only called the 'Mother Superior' 'because ay the length ay time he'd hud his habit' (6), his presentation as a feminine figure of succour matters in terms of how the novel configures its understanding of conventional masculinity, and any possible deviation from it. The ironies multiply on both the linguistic level, punning on 'habit' and on the levels of morality, abstinence, purity, dedication, transcendence and so on.

As the 'Mother Superior' Johnny Swan offers an experience of transcendence that depends upon chemically inducing a sense of beatitude which, however, can only lead back to even greater need. It's a cycle that continually turns up the degree to which the junkies are rendered dependent, passive and supra-feminine – in need of rescue not by a man, but by a female hero. As Renton puts it, his 'dry, cracking bones' are only soothed by his 'beautiful heroine's tender caresses' (11). The 'e' on the end of 'heroin' here signals the link between the drug and Renton's place as a person in distress, needing rescue and receiving it not from a male action hero but from a heroine whose super-power is 'tender caress' rather than the capacity to kick some ass. Masculinity-as-activity, the long-standing conventional view, is simply banished from the scene in favour of Renton as ultra-passive, rescued from distress by a heroine who soothes rather than acting. Begbie has no power here. Thus personified, heroin soothes by inducing an even deeper level of passivity than had obtained before the sickness of withdrawal set in: Renton and Sick Boy thus sink further into passivity, embracing their heroine and welcoming its feminizing salvation.

As the designation of Swan as the 'Mother Superior' also indicates, a heroin habit brings with it a tendency to abstinence, though that abstinence must be put down to the direct physical effects of heroin rather than self-control and piety. Simply put, heroin emasculates its male users in *Trainspotting* by making them superfluous to the women junkies and by obliterating the pleasures of sex with the pleasures of its chemical beatitude. As we noted earlier, when Ali takes the first hit of heroin after Renton and Sick Boy arrive at Swan's place, she disconcerts Renton with her intensely sexual reaction. Ali's orgasmic response, and her declaration that it is better than sex with a man could ever be, makes Renton feel as though he has literally been emasculated: He actually checks to see if he still has his genitals (9). Disconcerted as he is, though, Renton immediately affirms Ali's exclamation, adding, 'Ali wis right. Take yir best orgasm, multiply the feeling by twenty, and you're still fuckin miles off the pace' (11). If her initial comment caught him off guard and troubled his sense of the indispensability of his genitals, his own hit leads him to escalate the claim. Sexual pleasure suddenly becomes dispensable; the heroin rush is supra-sexual – that is, before it returns the user to a state of passivity verging on death itself: After the initial rush, 'users usually will be drowsy for several hours; mental function is clouded; heart function slows; and breathing is also severely slowed, sometimes enough to be life-threatening' (National Institute on Drug Abuse). Of course, sex remains on the menu, though it is really only appealing or viable for 'sexual aristocrats' such as Sick Boy, and then only because his habit is not as serious as Swan's or Renton's. After they have had their hits, Ali and Sick Boy eventually do go through to the next room to have sex, though they do it as a matter of course, a business transaction rather than an act of passion or even desire. As Renton has said, 'for women, [. . .] fucking was just something that you did wi Sick Boy.'

Even where heroin fails to extinguish desire altogether, though, its physiological effects can simply rob the male junky of sexual function. Leaving Swan's place, Renton contemplates going over to see Kelly, whom he has just learned is attracted to him, but decides instead to return to his action video rather than attempt masculine function: 'The truth ay the matter is, ah'm a bit too skaggy-bawed tae fuck n a bit too fucked tae jist talk. A number 10 comes, n ah jump oan it back tae Leith, and Jean-Claude Van Damme. Throughout the journey ah gleefully anticipate the stomping he's gaunnae gie that smart cunt' (Welsh 13). Incapable of either sexual function or conversation, Renton quits the field, opting instead to indulge in the prosthetic masculinity of watching an action hero 'stomp' a 'smart cunt'. Though it is so common as to have lost much of its meaning, the formulation here nonetheless seems to carry additional significance in this context. The violent sexual imagery provides a fantasy release for Renton, an imaginary masculinity he not only lacks sufficient desire to perform, but couldn't if he tried. Sexual conquest is now purely stylistic – it is a skeuomorph preserved in the junkies' language rather than part of their lives.

Nor is Renton alone in suffering the affliction of being 'skaggy-bawed'; Swan later confesses that he missed out on the chance to bed Ali when he was dealing drugs to her, though he tries to claim this was due to honour and self-restraint rather than physical incapacity:

– The White Swan wid nivir take advantage ay a damsel in distress though, he smiles.
   – Aye, sure, ah sais, totally unconvinced.
   – Too right ah widnae, he stridently contends. – Ah didnae, did ah? The proof ay the puddin's in the fuckin eatin.
   – Aye, only because ye hud skag in yir baws.
   – Uh, uh, uh, he goes, touchin his chist wi the can ay coke.
   – The White Swan disnae fuck ower his mates. Golden rule number one. No fir smack, no fir nowt. Nivir question the integrity ay the White Swan oan that issue, Rents. Ah wisnae skaggy-bawed aw the time. Ah could've hud her cunt oan toast if ah hud've wanted it. Even whin ah wis skaggy-bawed; ah could've pimped her oot. (313)

Tellingly, Swan re-activates the language of the 'damsel in distress' suggested by Renton and Sick Boy's dire situation at the novel's opening, positioning himself and his heroin as both Ali's persecutor and her saviour. His heroin has turned her into a damsel in distress in the first place, just as it reduced Renton and Sick Boy to desperate supplicants at the doors of his infernal convent. By the same token precisely, though, he proclaims himself her saviour. He claims that his failure to have sex with her demonstrates an heroic code of honour. But Renton quickly counters with the observation that he is retroactively gilding his behaviour to give an honourable sheen to the fact that he could not have had sex with Ali if he had wanted to because he 'hud skag in [his] baws'. This leads to Swan's strange effort to preserve his fantasy of masculine sexual effectiveness by proxy: Such was his command over Ali's body at one point that he could have made it available to other men even if he could not have used it himself:

> Easy fuckin meat. Ah could've hud the bitch doon Easter Road in a short skirt n nae keks; gave her a jab tae keep her quiet, n stuck her oan the flair ay the pish-hoose behind the shed. Could've hud the whole fuckin home support oan a line-up, wi the White Swan standin ootside chargin a fiver a skull. Even wi a flunky thrown in, the margins wid be astro-fuckin-nomical. Then doon tae Tyney the next week, let aw they infected Jambo bastards go in eftir the boys hud hud thir fil. (313)

The economization of Ali's body here illustrates once again both the toxic level to which masculinity has sunk in *Trainspotting* and the superfluity of sexual contact. As Renton had done earlier, opting for a prosthetic experience of potent masculinity over the possibility of real intimacy with Kelly, so Swan here preserves a fantasy of his own sexual effectiveness by deflecting it into a fantasy of dominance utterly bereft of sexual pleasure. The point is not that sex is mobilized in an economic context, or that it is supplanted by prosthetic forms of masculinity, but that it goes by the wayside. The displacement of sex by heroin is literally true for Swan, who has lost his leg due to injecting heroin into arteries rather than veins, and whose penis is covered in scabs because he began injecting into the veins there when he ran out of viable options in his arms and legs. And though he assures Renton that the amputating doctors did not take his 'middle leg' (311), the fact remains that they need not have since heroin has done it for them. He has, in the end, been emasculated by his habit (ha!).

In contrast, heroin use enables a style of masculine tenderness, even if that style is restricted to a homoerotic/homophobic expression. In this context, it buffers the characters against the homoeroticism they express, furnishing a pretext for contact and anaesthetizing them against the fallout of any sincere tenderness. Again, Renton and Sick Boy's opening visit to Swan's provides our initial glimpse of this possibility. As Sick Boy positions himself next to Ali, who is preparing a shot, establishing his place in the queue, Raymie first mocks the lot of them by putting on Lou Reed's 'Heroin and then kisses Sick Boy':

> Raymie pulled Sick Boy's face tae him, and kissed him hard oan the lips. Sick Boy pushed him away, trembling.
>   – Fuck off! Doss cunt! (8)

Everyone else laughs, except Renton, who is by now too sick to join in. The kiss, and Sick Boy's rather lame response to it eroticizes the situation, though in an unwonted key, as is clarified after Sick Boy takes his hit: 'Sick Boy hugged Swanney tightly, then eased off, keeping his airms aroond him. They were relaxed; like lovers in a post-coital embrace' (10). The kiss and its explicitly erotic aftermath anticipate the later assertion that the need for heroin both makes sex superfluous and opens it up to exploitation. Just as Swan claims he could have pimped out Ali, Raymie reveals that Sick Boy can be sexually taken advantage of when the promise of heroin is on the horizon. And yet the kiss remains deeply ambiguous as well; it is not the preamble to a more aggressive sexual come-on, let alone to sex itself (at least between Raymie and Sick Boy), but an ironic expression of simultaneous tenderness and mockery. In this, it is of a piece with Raymie's improvised rap, belted out just before the kiss: 'Stick in the boot, go wi the flow, shake it down baby, shake it down honey … cook street, spook street, we're all dead white meat … eat the beat … Raymie burst intae an impromptu rap, shakin his erse and rollin his eyes' (8). The situation – a shooting gallery – is deadly serious, but Raymie is just plain silly. He's enjoying himself, and exploiting the situation to have some fun at his friends' expense. The heroin – Sick Boy's need for it, Ali's preparation of it, Swan's provision of it – is such a powerful diversion from what such a kiss might mean that it simultaneously opens the way for expressions of masculine tenderness and keeps them on an uncertain footing. Such acts can never be taken as straightforwardly sincere, but nor can they be written off simply as jokes; they express tenderness, but may also be acts of aggression.

A similar dynamic manifests when Renton and Spud express genuine affection for each other. The pair are out on the Meadows with Sick Boy in tow, and all three are drunk and high on Ecstasy. Spud has just made himself terribly vulnerable by showing real concern for a squirrel Sick Boy is encouraging Renton to kill. Spud's authentic concern touches Renton, provoking mutual declarations of affection. Renton 'grabs a haud ay [Spud] n hugs' him, then says, 'Yir one ay the best, man. Remember that. That's no drink n drugs talkin, that's me talkin. It's jist thit ye git called aw the poofs under the sun if ye tell other guys how ye feel aboot them if yir no wrecked' (161). Renton's expression, and his meditation on the conditions of its possibility, limn clearly the role played by drugs in opening up the possibility for genuine expressions of same-sex masculine tenderness. Almost before he finishes saying what he feels, Renton has to clarify that it's 'no drink n drugs talkin' – that his sentiments are sincere. At the same time, he confesses that they are the condition of possibility for expressing those sentiments: If you are not 'wrecked' then you get called gay for such expressions. The drugs, then, make possible a style of masculinity that is otherwise foreclosed by social pressures and – especially circa 1990 – haunted by the spectre of AIDS. At the same time, they cloud any expression of that style because by definition they alter consciousness, affect, and capacity for communication. The awkwardness and ambiguity of the situation is summed up in Spud's response: 'Ah slaps his back, n it's likesay ah want tae tell him the same, but it would sound, likesay, ah wis jist sayin it cause he sais it tae me first. Ah sais it anywey though' (161). Spud shares Renton's tenderness, but worries that he will seem to be insincere if he reciprocates, and yet does so anyway. In this, he risks the appearance of inauthenticity and the corollary danger of appearing not to take Renton seriously: 'I love you man!' – 'Yeah, I love you too, buddy.' Even when their effect is explicitly disavowed, drink and drugs afford plausible deniability for such expressions, at once making them possible and couching their authenticity in reference to altered states of consciousness.

Lest we be tempted to view this moment on the Meadows as too utopian, however, Sick Boy is on hand to bring us back to earth. Witnessing this exchange, he promptly snaps it into homophobic focus and re-asserts the rigid distinction between acceptable heterosexual masculine interaction and homosexual sex: 'We hear Sick Boy's voice at oor backs. – You two fuckin buftie-boys. Either go intae they trees n fuck each other, or come n help us find Beggars n Matty. Wi break oor embrace n laugh. Wi both ken that likesay Sick Boy, for aw the cat's desire tae rip open every binliner in toon, is one ay the best n aw' (161). Asserting his heterosexuality and invoking his sexual prowess, Sick Boy impatiently dismisses the possibility of non-sexual same-sex tenderness among men. Despite the open homoeroticism of his attack upon the skinhead and his dog, and despite being included in the transient homosocial community of tenderness established by Spud and Renton – 'Sick Boy [...] is one ay the best n aw' – Sick Boy cannot let down his guard. Less susceptible to the addictive powers of heroin than Renton, and simply more together than Spud, Sick Boy is also more beholden to social standards of acceptable masculine tenderness and desire. Where drugs license a freedom of affect and expression for Spud and Renton, anaesthetizing them against Sick Boy's homophobic barbs, they lack sufficient hold on Sick Boy to let the moment develop. The utopian possibility of openly expressed same-sex masculine tenderness mooted by Renton and Spud is thus quickly foreclosed – the episode ends and the next section begins with Renton and Spud standing before a magistrate, facing charges of shoplifting. The narrative thus ratifies Sick Boy's mockery by reintroducing the disciplinary apparatus of social order, punishing Renton and Spud for petty theft while the properly (read: conventionally) masculine Begbie's violent crimes go unpunished.

This gesture of recontainment is hardly final, though, and the narrative preserves the possibility of homosocial/homoerotic tenderness explicitly as an element of style. Tellingly, this episode occurs when Renton – whose nickname, 'Rent-boy' identifies him as a gay prostitute – is temporarily clean. He makes a trip to London and, unable to contact his friends, falls in with an Italian named Giovanni. Giovanni's sexual advances lead Renton to ask himself, with eminent reason and equanimity,

> How the fuck dae ah ken ah'm no a homosexual if ah've nivir been wi another guy? Ah mean, really fir sure? Ah've always hud a notion tae go aw the wey wi another guy, tae see what it wis like. Ah mean, yuv goat tae try everything once' (233). And though he quickly walks this back a bit – 'Huvin said that, ah'd huvtae be in the drivin seat. Ah couldnae handle some cunt's knob up *ma* erse. (233)

Renton not only remains open to the possibility that he is gay, but divulges a past homosexual experience. He informs us that 'One time ah picked up this gorgeous young queen in the London Apprentice. Ah took um back tae the auld gaff in Poplar' (233). The fact that Renton can allow the gorgeousness of the 'queen' he picked up is one thing, but he further informs us that he and the young man perform oral sex on each other. The sex is boring (when he is performing fellatio) or laughter-provoking (when he is being serviced) for Renton, but both he and his date achieve orgasm, though Renton is only able to do so by imagining that his partner is a girl he used to date. Caught in the act, Renton takes 'a real slaggin' from his friend Tony, but that seems to be all – he is not dogged by rumours of homosexuality or disowned by his circle as a result. He is, however, located in the realm of the feminine, earning approval from Tony's girlfriend Caroline, who 'thought that it wis cool, n confessed tae us this she wis as jealous as fuck. She thought the guy wis a honey' (234).

Despite this underwhelming experience, Renton remains open to gay anal sex, noting that his objection is aesthetic before anything else: 'Anywey, ah widnae mind gaun aw the wey wi a gadge, if it felt right. Jist fir the experience. Problem is, ah only really fancy birds. Guys jist dinnae look sexy. It's aw aboot aesthetics, fuck all tae dae wi morality' (234). Interestingly putting his own lack of attraction to men down to aesthetics rather than morality, and thus making desire a sub-category of aesthetics, Renton proclaims a shocking open-mindedness, especially in the face of a prospective sexual encounter with a gay stranger at the very height of the AIDS/HIV epidemic. His assertion to Giovanni that, 'Ah'm no a buftie pal [...] No homosexual' (233) is thus less definitive than he makes it sound, and his acceptance of Giovanni's offer of a place to sleep at least a little bit ambiguous.

No doubt Renton is at least partially aware of this ambiguity, since he reacts surprisingly calmly when he wakes up to find that Giovanni has masturbated and ejaculated on Renton's face:

Ya dirty auld cunt! ... wankin ower us in ma fuckin sleep ... ya fuckin mingin auld bastard! Ah felt like a dirty hanky, just used, just nothing. A rage gripped us n ah smacked the wee cunt in the mooth n pulled um oaf the bed. He looked like a repulsive, fat gnome wi his bloated stomach n roond heid. Ah booted um a few times as he cowered oan the deck, then ah stoaped as ah realised he wis sobbin. (235)

Vitally, Renton is angry not because what Giovanni has done implicates him in homosexual activity, but because he feels he has been used. His anger manifests a fundamental self-respect that goes beyond sexual identification, and quickly exhausts itself when he realizes how tortured and pathetic Giovanni is. Articulating perhaps the one truly utopian moment in the novel, Renton stops beating Giovanni and begins comforting him, taking him out for breakfast and letting him tag along to a party where he finally locates his friends. This is a genuine scene of homosociality, of one man caring for another in an extra-sexual way, providing physical comfort as well as emotional support and social integration. It illustrates the continuum of homosocial behavior from homosexuality to tender care initially mooted by Eve Kosofsky Sedgwick in relation to women's same-sex relationships, and indicates a possible escape from the crisis of traditional masculinity that has plagued young men since the end of the Second World War. That it remains inconclusive, dropping out of the narrative altogether, preserves its possibility even as it fails to imagine a fully realized alternative to the logic that otherwise structures masculinity in the novel. As was the case in Wheatle's novels, the options for mature masculinity are dead-ended in *Trainspotting* as well. The historical crisis of masculinity inaugurated at the end of the war, having tried a range of different solutions, lapses once again into sterile traditional channels. Male teenage Ecosse presents a terminally arrested adolescence as the only viable option – definitively short-circuiting the utopian drive to generational renewal.

Trainspotting's inability to see a clear way out of the various quandaries faced by its characters, including social regression, economic hardship, Thatcherite neo-liberalism, restrictive models of national and sexual identity, and of course chemical dependence manifests perhaps most clearly of all in its depiction of generational tensions. In *Brixton Rock* and *East of Acre Lane* these tensions were articulated in terms of how sons relate to their mothers; in *Trainspotting*, *Absolute Beginners*, *Saturday Night and Sunday Morning*, *The Rachel Papers* and *The Buddha of Suburbia*, however, we are back to the conventional opposition between fathers and sons. This opposition is articulated in *Trainspotting* along the axis of generation, regeneration, and sterility. It manifests in two directions: Young men as fathers and young men as sons of fathers. In terms of the first of these, earlier novels had imagined their young men as either avoiding fatherhood altogether or abandoning pregnant lovers. Wheatle's novels had envisioned but a single child on the horizon – and that one doomed to a life of difficulty if not social persecution for being the product of both incest and miscegenation. In *Trainspotting*, various young men become fathers, and yet true regeneration is nowhere to be found: Even though there are progeny, sterility remains the overarching atmosphere. In terms of the second line of development, young men as sons of fathers, we find many of the same generational tensions we have seen in operation all along rehearsed in a new setting, but with little in the way of evident progress. Perhaps surprisingly, Begbie furnishes the most fully articulated engagement with both of these lines, though the results are far from heartening.

The most immediately devastating instance of sterile generational dynamics centres around the infant Dawn, who dies in a shooting gallery while the adults around her are high. As her name indicates, Dawn ought to represent something of a new beginning, a new world ready to unfold, but there is no new day on the horizon here. Her mother, Lesley, is a junky, and though she feels intense remorse for her daughter's death, her first – and lasting – reaction is to get high. Almost immediately after she discovers the dead child, she tells Renton that she needs a hit and he springs (relatively speaking) into action to provide it (56). Heroin's tendency to produce an intense isolation and inwardness, and to anaesthetize its users against the shocks of social existence is on full display here. The promise of generational renewal is suddenly withdrawn due to heroin, and the pain of that withdrawal in turn dulled by yet more heroin. Dull to her daughter's needs in the first place – to a criminally negligent extent – Lesley now seeks more of the same to dull her pain at the loss of her child.

The confusion and anaesthetic demands of the situation find their parallel in the group's effort to ascertain who Dawn's father was. Though they never actually get beyond platitudes – 'naebody's fault though … cot death n that … wee Dawn … barry wee bairn … fuckin shame … fuckin sin man, ah'm tellin ye' (55) – the junkies seem to intuit that Dawn's death has a larger significance. With it, a curtain falls on the future such that they suddenly discover an interest in the lineage thus interrupted. Spud, Matty and Renton run through a list of possible fathers, before Renton finally figures out from Sick Boy's demeanour that he is the father: 'Wisnae Seeker, Sick Boy shakes his heid. He puts a hand oan the deid bairn's cauld cheek. Tears are fillin in his eyes. Ah'm gaun tae greet n aw. There's a constricting tightness in ma chest. One mystery has been solved. Wee Dawn's dead face looks so obviously like ma mate Simon Williamson's' (54). Sick Boy follows up this revelation by claiming that he is quitting heroin for good now, but Renton quickly gives the lie by illustrating the extent to which heroin has supplanted human contact for this truly lost generation: 'Ah feel thit ah love thum aw. Matty, Spud, Sick Boy and Lesley. Ah want tae tell thum. Ah try, but it comes oot as: – Ah'm cookin. They look at us, fuckin scoobied. – That's me, ah shrug ma shooders, in self-justification' (55). Love is translated into the promise of a hit in the short journey from Renton's heart to his mouth. The question of paternity is solved only in its termination, bringing both Sick Boy's chance to attain a functional mature masculinity and Dawn's potential to present a new future to a sickeningly sterile conclusion. Last stop! Everybody off!

Renton's role as anaesthetist in this situation leads us to consider him next, not as a father of a child, but as a son of a father. Renton's relationship with his father falls into a conventional frame of the traditional father who is disappointed in his child's failures, impatient with his idiosyncrasies (e.g. Renton's vegetarianism), and unable to comprehend the world in which he lives. After his overdose at Swan's, Renton awakes to find himself imprisoned in his old bedroom at his parents' house, subject to his mother's well-meant but cloying care and his father's likewise well-meant but gruff attempt to execute a regime of tough-love. Unable to cross the generational divide to try to understand the nihilism and hopelessness attendant upon being a young man in Thatcher's Britain, Renton's father adopts the conventional line of chastising his son for his failures: 'Mucked up everythin, he accuses, then reads oot the charges: – Apprenticeship. University. That nice wee lassie ye wir seein. Aw the chances ye hud Mark, n ye blew them' (191). Renton's father is a baby boomer, beneficiary of the most prosperous time in history, particularly for young people, and the last generation thus far to be more or less guaranteed of outperforming the previous generation in terms of wealth, comfort, and achievement. His view of the world is shaped by post-war abundance and a clearly defined geopolitical framework in which the Cold War delineations of good versus evil are at least ostensibly clear. Before he decides that it is pointless to argue with his father, Renton informs us that it would be useless in no small part precisely because 'He disnae need tae say aboot how he nivir hud they chances growin up in Govan n leavin school at fifteen n takin an apprenticeship. That's implicit. When ye think aboot it though, it isnae that much different fae growin up in Leith n leaving school at sixteen n takin an apprenticeship. Especially as he nivir grew up in an era ay mass unemployment' (191). A middle-aged Arthur Seaton, Renton's father is unable to comprehend his son's inability to engage with the world as he imagines he would have done. His experience is temporally limited, though, belonging to an earlier moment and irrelevant to the new realities of the post-Cold War world in which Renton is growing up. The gap between his generation and Renton's thus presents as an abyss, one that cannot be bridged, and that only consumes those who try – witness the fate of Renton's brother Billy, who attempts to live up to his father's outdated values and ends up being killed in Northern Ireland by IRA provisional forces while serving in the British Army. In an eloquent eulogy that sums up the generational impasse faced by Renton and his cohort brilliantly, Renton says,

He died a hero they sais. Ah remember that song: 'Billy Don't Be A Hero.' In fact, he died a spare prick in a uniform, walking along a country road wi a rifle in his hand. He died an ignorant victim ay imperialism, understanding fuck all about the myriad circumstances which led tae his death. That wis the biggest crime, he understood fuck all about it. Aw he hud tae guide um through this great adventure in Ireland, which led tae his death, wis a few vaguely formed sectarian sentiments. The cunt died as he lived: completely fuckin scoobied. (210)

The patrilineal line is doomed, it would seem: Billy leaves behind Sharon, his pregnant fiancée. She will receive no supplement from the army because they were not yet married, and her child will grow up fatherless like so many others. Renton only degrades this outcome further when he seduces her at Billy's funeral, sneering at her desperate hope that by having sex with him she can simply substitute one brother for the other and regain the future now vanishing before her eyes (220). If she carries the pregnancy to term, her child will grow up fatherless and foredoomed; it is already falling through the cracks.

If Renton's generation seems hopelessly cut off from both the past and the future, no one better exemplifies that than Begbie. As we have seen, Begbie is the embodiment of working-class Scottish masculinity, a traditional figure working desperately to sustain the values he has imbibed from birth. His isolation, and *Trainspotting*'s bleak view of the sterility of those values, however, manifests unmistakably in his generational isolation. Unlike Sick Boy, Begbie accepts and acknowledges his paternity of his girlfriend June's baby. At the same time, he utterly disavows any responsibility for the baby, and insistently refers to it only as her child. As Spud puts it, recounting one exchange between Begbie and June, 'Jist you fuckin see tae yir fuckin bairn! Begbie snaps. The wey he sais it, it's likesay, it's no his bairn n aw, ken? Ah suppose in a wey he's right, likesay; Franco's no what ye'd really sortay call the parental type' (284). When June provokes Begbie into anger, he has no compunction about hitting her even though she is pregnant, and in making her bear the blame for any injury done to the foetus by his violence, telling Renton, 'that cunt's deid if she's made us hurt that fuckin bairn. Ivir since she's been huvin that bairn, she thinks she kin git fuckin lippy wi us. Nae cunt gits.fuckin lippy wi me, bairn or nae fuckin bairn' (112–113). The trap of Begbie's hard-man masculinity absolutely precludes not only interpersonal tenderness but also generational continuity. Though he appears to care inasmuch as he will perversely punish June if 'she's made [him] hurt' the baby, he also declares, 'Fucked if ah'm gaunnae stey wi that fuckin June eftir the bairn's here' (112), making it abundantly clear that being a father to the child is not on his list of priorities. As with Sharon's bairn, so with June's: It will grow up without a father, unmoored from any sort of usable past and doomed to repeat its father's or mother's mistakes.

As though to drive home this bleak view of generational sterility and hopelessness, *Trainspotting* supplements Begbie's total abdication of paternity with a glimpse into the past/future of that abdication in Begbie's own father. He first appears in a pub entered by Begbie, Renton, et al. after a full night of carousing. At first, he is just an old man at the bar: 'Their entry to the pub is observed by an indeterminately old drunkard who is propped up against the bar. The man's face has been destroyed by the consumption of cheap spirits and overexposure to the frozen wind blasting cruelly from the North Sea' (263). A prototypical hard man, the old drunk has been beaten down by a lifetime of work on the north sea oil rigs or fishing boats, paired with shore time spent drinking, fighting, and carousing. He epitomizes 'manhood Ecosse' just as Begbie does, and in fact recognizes his progeny in the group of young partiers:

> His face strains in vague recognition as the noisy group move up to the bar. One of the young men, perhaps more than one, he sardonically thinks, is his son. He had been responsible for bringing quite a few of them into the world at one time, when a certain type of woman found him attractive. That was before the drink had destroyed his appearance and distorted the output of his cruel, sharp tongue to an incomprehensible growl. He looks at the young man in question and considers saying something, before deciding that he has nothing to say to him. He never had. (263–264)

Recognizing Begbie before Begbie recognizes him, the old man decides to say nothing. Beyond insemination, he has had nothing to do with the youth until now; he has no wisdom to impart and no tenderness to demonstrate. As Begbie's progenitor, he has stamped the mould into which Begbie so comfortably fits. He is also a vision of Begbie's future, the absent father to any number of children who will go on to repeat the cycle. Finally cluing in to who the old drunkard is, Begbie does not let on – he, too, 'has nothing to say to him' – instead surveying the pub and ordering everyone to depart: 'He looks bitterly around the cavernous, nicotine-stained bar, like an arrogant aristocrat finding himself in reduced circumstances. In fact, he has just seen the old drunkard at the bar' (270). The comparison of Begbie to an 'arrogant aristocrat' in 'reduced circumstances' is spot-on: Though he still adheres to the notion of himself as the very embodiment of Scottish masculinity, thus anchored in a long tradition of Scottish manhood and accorded nobility by virtue of sustaining its values, Begbie is nonetheless impoverished in a way that exposes for all to see the vacuity of those values and that tradition. From the novel's perspective, Begbie's self-conception is utterly bankrupt, producing not a strong line of noble men who sire noble sons, but a fractured and compromised line of fatherless sons and sonless fathers. Begbie thus stands as the exemplar of an ever-tightening circle of fatherlessness, repeating itself indefinitely without any hope of escape.

Begbie's father's second appearance only ratifies this conclusion, as he lurches up to Renton and Begbie in the abandoned Leith Central train station, where they have stopped to relieve themselves, and jokingly asks if they are doing a bit of trainspotting:

> An auld drunkard, whom Begbie had been looking at, lurched up tae us, wine boatil in his hand. Loads ay them used this place tae bevvy and crash in.

> – What yis up tae lads? Trainspottin, eh? He sais, laughing uncontrollably at his ain fuckin wit.
> – Aye. That's right, Begbie sais. Then under his breath: – Fuckin auld cunt.
> – Ah well, ah'll leave yis tae it. Keep up the trainspottin mind! He staggered oaf, his rasping, drunkard's cackles filling the desolate barn. Ah noticed that Begbie seemed strangely subdued and uncomfortable. He wis turned away fae us. It wis only then ah realised thit the auld wino wis Begbie's faither. (309)

This exchange gives the novel its title, and establishes the generational divide at a stroke. Trainspotting in Begbie Sr.'s parlance refers to the practice of tracking and noting down trains coming and going along a particular line. In the parlance of Begbie Jr.'s cohort, it refers to the practice of seeking out good veins for injection and/or noting the presence of needle tracks on a user's arm, indicating how heavy his or her habit is. In this exchange, it condenses the worm of generational tension working in the bud of 1990s Scottish working-class community, and clarifies the many ironies in circulation. The novel's total vision of generational sterility and angst manifests in a dense image of hopelessness. There will be no regeneration, no escape from the emptiness and futility of foreclosed paternity. In this sense, we might even revise our thesis: Where we began tracing generational tension with the post-war generation's self-conscious break with its predecessors, we now find no tension at all. There is, instead, only inertia, a near-total stasis against which characters can only either seek anaesthetic comfort or make a last desperate bid for escape.

Trainspotting concludes with Renton trying just that: A desperate escape that will cut him off forever from his past and maybe – just maybe – open up a new vista of potential. In a bid to cut himself loose from the sterile past and to pursue a utopian future of possibility, Renton steals from his mates and flees the country. After he, Begbie, Spud and Sick Boy sell a large quantity of heroin to a dealer in London, Renton makes an irrevocable decision to take the money and run. Doing so is the end of his past: He will never be able to return to Edinburgh or his old friends because Begbie will kill him even if the others do not. Even the thought of running into Begbie as he is leaving the apartment with the money is enough to make him almost collapse with fear (311):

> Ripping off your mates was the highest offence in his book, and he would demand the severest penalty. Renton had used Begbie, used him to burn his boats completely and utterly. It was Begbie who ensured he could never return. He had done what he wanted to do. He could now never go back to Leith, to Edinburgh, even to Scotland, ever again. (344)

This disconnection from Scotland manifests stylistically as well: The chapter is the only one not written in dialect, but in standard written English. The local flavour is gone, and Renton's dislocation from Scottish history, place, rhythms, idioms and values is likewise completed. Renton deposits just over half the money into his bank account and then gets on a ferry to the Netherlands with the rest in cash. On the surface, it's a moment of divine liberation. Noting that in Edinburgh he is trapped – 'There, he could not be anything other than he was' (344) – Renton looks only forward: 'Now, free from them all, for good, he could be what he wanted to be. He'd stand or fall alone. This thought both terrified and excited him as he contemplated life in Amsterdam' (344). Free from his past, from who 'he was', and unable ever to turn back, Renton achieves exit velocity as no one else in the novel has managed to do. Renton has taken the money and headed off for the horizon, a vision of youthful opportunity – of the very future itself on the cusp of its advent.

But wait. Renton is joyous on his way to 'life in' … where? Amsterdam!? The city famous the world over for legalized prostitution and drugs? The same Renton who dropped out of university 'after blowing his grant money on drugs and prostitutes' (147)? As pretty much everyone who has ever written about the novel has pointed out, this is not an auspicious fresh start. As if those facts were not enough to make us suspicious of the novel's apparent optimism, there's the little matter of the port to which Renton is sailing: 'the Hook of Holland' (342). The former junky is on his way to the Hook, taking a bag full of cash to a city where his two chief vices are legal and freely available. As with other endings we have seen that radically undercut the apparent drift of their respective narratives – the relapse into delusion of the Teenager at the end of *Absolute Beginners*, the abdication of free choice in the last chapter of *A Clockwork Orange* – this ending seems to take back everything it has offered. Renton has wagered everything, down to and including the very accent of his narrative, on an incredibly long-shot. Given the back-and-forth nature of the rest of the narrative, with its sections entitled 'Kicking', 'Relapsing', 'Kicking Again', 'Blowing It', 'Exile', 'Home and finally', 'Exit', it is difficult to believe that Renton is in fact finally headed somewhere good. Instead, *Trainspotting* seems at last to fulfil punk's nihilism. To return to Kierkegaard at the last, perhaps Renton's 'Exit' is truly an embrace of the alternative to choosing life, a desperately suicidal final act aimed at achieving something like authenticity and autonomy before they vanish from the scene forever. As Henry Miller put it, writing about the advent of the hipster in 1957,

> If the fate of twentieth century man is to live with death from adolescence to premature senescence, why then the only life-giving answer is to accept the terms of death, to live with death as immediate danger, to divorce

oneself from society, to exist without roots, to set out on that uncharted journey into the rebellious imperatives of the self. (n.p.)

Perhaps, then, Renton is the first of that last breed of youth-cultural adherents, the hipster: 'I chose not to choose life. I chose somethin' else.'

NOTES

1 Angry(-ish) Young(-ish) Men: *Saturday Night and Sunday Morning* and *Absolute Beginners*

1 Though he could hardly be called an anarchist in any rigorous sense, it does bear mentioning that Sillitoe published at least one essay, 'Poor People', in the journal *Anarchy*.
2 In this notorious episode, 17-year-old John Beckley was stabbed to death at Clapham Common by a group of Teds known as the Plough Boys.
3 Nick Bentley has commented on the novel's tendency to exoticize its black characters, though he subordinates this insight to a larger claim about its utopian drift (see Bentley 2003/4, 165).
4 MacInnes articulates much the same point in his non-fiction writing as well: '"the great social revolution of the past fifteen years may not be the one which re-divided wealth among the adults in the Welfare State, but the one that's given teenagers economic power"' (MacInnes, qtd. in Derdiger 62).

2 How Did Burgess Invent the Skinhead? *A Clockwork Orange*

1 A review from 1962 referred to the droogs as '"Teddy Boys in a not-so-distant state"' (qtd. in Darlington 2016, 127) and that seems to have been about it until the film version was released in 1971.
2 Robin Cook, British foreign secretary, in 2001 declared Chicken Tikka Masala the country's national dish: www.guardian.co.uk/world/2001/apr/19/race. britishidentity

WORKS CITED

'Epitaph for the Eighties? "There Is No Such Thing as Society"'. *Women's Own*, 31 Oct. 1987, http://briandeer.com/social/thatcher-society.htm. Accessed 30 May 2016.

'Looking Back at Salman Rushdie's *The Satanic Verses*'. *The Guardian*, 14 Sep. 2012, https://www.theguardian.com/books/2012/sep/14/looking-at-salman-rushdies-satanic-verses. Accessed 21 Dec. 2017.

'Skinhead'. *Oxford English Dictionary* online. Accessed 21 Dec. 2017.

Acheson, James. *The British and Irish Novel since 1960*. Palgrave Macmillan, 1991.

Allen, Richard. *Skinhead*. London: Dean Street Press, 2015. Kindle file.

Amis, Martin. *The Rachel Papers*. Vintage Books, 2003.

Arendt, Hannah. 'Eichmann in Jerusalem'. *The New Yorker*, 16 Feb. 1963, https://www.newyorker.com/magazine/1963/02/16/eichmann-in-jerusalem-i. Accessed 21 Dec. 2017.

Auden, W. H. 1939. 'September 1, 1939'. *poets. org*, https://www.poets.org/poetsorg/poem/september-1-1939. Accessed 21 Dec. 2017.

Ball, John Clement. 'The Semi-Detached Metropolis: Hanif Kureishi's London'. *ARIEL: A Review of International English Literature* 27.4 (1996): 7–27.

Becker, Howard S. *Outsiders: Studies in the Sociology of Deviance*. Free Press, 1997.

Bell, Amy Helen. 'Teddy Boys and Girls as Neo-flâneurs in Postwar London'. *The Literary London Journal* 11.2 (2014): 3–17.

Benjamin, Walter. 'Theses on the Philosophy of History'. *Illuminations: Essays and Reflections*. New York: Schocken Books, 1968.

Bentley, Nick. 'Translating English: Youth, Race and Nation in Colin MacInnes's *City of Spades* and *Absolute Beginners*'. *Connotations* 13.1–2 (2003/2004): 149–69.

Bentley, Nick. '"New Elizabethans': The Representation of Youth Subcultures in 1950s British Fiction'. *Literature and History* 19.1 (2010): 16–33.

Boyle, Danny, director. *Trainspotting*. Channel Four Films, 1996.

Bracewell, Michael. *England Is Mine: Pop Life in Albion from Wilde to Goldie*. Harper Collins, 1997.

Brookes, Ian. '"All the Rest Is Propaganda": Reading the Paratexts of *Saturday Night and Sunday Morning*'. *Adaptation* 2.1 (2009): 17–33.

Burgess, Anthony. *A Clockwork Orange*. W. W. Norton, 1987.

Burgess, Anthony. 'A Clockwork Orange Resucked'. *A Clockwork Orange*. W. W. Norton, 1987, v–xi.

Caserio, Robert L., ed. *The Cambridge Companion to the Twentieth-Century English Novel*. Cambridge UP, 2009.

Clarke, Alan, director. *Made in Britain*. ITV, 1982.

Cohen, Stanley. *Folk Devils and Moral Panics*. Routledge, 2002.

Connor, Steven. *The English Novel in History 1950–1995*. Routledge, 1996.

Cook, Roger. 2013. 'The Changing Face of Youth Unemployment in Scotland 1992–2012'. *The Scotland Institute*, http://www.allofusfirst.org/commonweal/assets/File/youth-unemployment-scotland-institute-may-2013.pdf. Accessed 13 Dec. 2017.

Darlington, Joseph. '*ACO*: The Art of Moral Panic?' *The Cambridge Quarterly* 45.2 (2016): 119–34.

Davis, Thomas S. *The Extinct Scene: Late Modernism and Everyday Life*. Columbia UP, 2016.

Davis, Todd F., and Kenneth Womack. '"O my brothers": Reading the Anti-Ethics of the Pseudo-Family in Anthony Burgess's *A Clockwork Orange*'. *College Literature* 29.2 (2002): 19–36.

Derdiger, Paula. 'To Drag Out a Rough Poetry: Colin MacInnes and the New Brutalism in Postwar Britain'. *MFS: Modern Fiction Studies* 62.1 (2016): 53–69.

Edemariam, Aida, and Kirsty Scott. 'What Happened to the Trainspotting Generation?' *The Guardian*, 15 Aug. 2009, http://www.theguardian.com/society/2009/aug/15/scotland-trainspotting-generation-dying-fact. Accessed 19 May 2016.

English, James F. *A Concise Companion to Contemporary British Fiction*. Wiley-Blackwell, 2006.

Farred, Grant. 2004. 'Wankerdom: Trainspotting as a Rejection of the Postcolonial?' *The South Atlantic Quarterly* 103.1 (2004): 215–26.

Ferrebe, Alice. *Masculinity in Male-Authored Fiction 1950–2000*. Palgrave Macmillan, 2005.

Finney, Brian. *English Fiction Since 1984: Narrating a Nation*. Palgrave Macmillan UK, 2006, doi: 10.1057/9780230207073. Accessed 24 Aug. 2017.

Gasiorek, Andrzej. *Post-War British Fiction: Realism and After*. Hodder Education Publishers, 1995.

Greene, Graham. *Brighton Rock*. Oxford: Blackwell, 1969.

Hall, G. Stanley. *Adolescence: Its Psychology and Its Relations to Physiology, Anthropology, Sociology, Sex, Crime, Religion and Education*. D. Appleton and Company, 1914.

Hans-Jürgen Diller, Erwin Otto, and Gerd Stratmann, eds. *Youth Identities: Teens and Tweens in British Culture*. Universitätsverlag C. Winter, 2000.

Head, Dominic. *The State of the Novel: Britain and Beyond*. Wiley-Blackwell, 2008.

Hebdige, Dick. *Subculture: The Meaning of Style*. Routledge, 2004.

Herbrechter, Stefan. 'From *Trainspotting* to *Filth* – Masculinity and Cultural Politics in Irvine Welsh's Writings'. *Subverting Masculinity: Hegemonic and Alternative Versions of Masculinity in Contemporary Culture*, edited by Russell West and Frank Lay, Rodopi, 2000, pp. 109–27.

Horkheimer, Max, and Theodor Adorno. *Dialectic of Enlightenment*. Stanford UP, 1948.

Huntington, Samuel P. *The Clash of Civilizations and the Remaking of World Order*. Simon and Schuster, 1996.

Ilona, Anthony. 'Hanif Kureishi's *The Buddha of Suburbia*: "A New Way of Being British."' *Contemporary British Fiction*, edited by Richard Lane, Polity, 2003, pp. 87–105.

Jachimiak, Peter Hughes. '"Putting the Boot in": *A Clockwork Orange*, Post-'69 Youth Culture and the Onset of Late Modernity'. *Anthony Burgess and Modernity*, edited by Alan R. Roughely, Manchester UP, 2008, pp. 147–64.

James, David. *Legacies of Modernism: Historicising Postwar and Contemporary Fiction*. Cambridge UP, 2011.

Jenks, Chris. *Subculture: The Fragmentation of the Social*. SAGE, 2004.

Kubrick, Stanley, director. *A Clockwork Orange*. Warner Bros, 1971.

Kureishi, Hanif. *The Buddha of Suburbia*. Penguin Books, 1990.

Leader, Zachary. *On Modern British Fiction*. Oxford UP, 2002.

Letts, Don. "The Story of Skinhead." *YouTube*, uploaded by fortunatehobo, 16 Oct. 2016, https://www.youtube.com/watch?v=reGXa3vgeF4. Accessed 10 Nov. 2017.

Lewis, Daniel. '"Say It, Don't Do It": Male Speech and Male Action in *Saturday Night and Sunday Morning*'. *The Journal of Men's Studies* 20.2 (2012): 91–107.

Lyotard, Jean-Francois. *The Postmodern Condition: A Report on Knowledge*. Theory and History of Literature, Vol. 10. Translated by Geoff Bennington and Brian Massumi, U of Minnesota P, 1978.

MacInnes, Colin. *The London Novels*. London: Allison & Busby, 2005.

MacLeod, Lewis. 'Life Among the Leith Plebs: Of Arseholes, Wankers, and Tourists in Irvine Welsh's *Trainspotting*'. *Studies in the Literary Imagination* 41.1 (2008): 89–106.

Marwick, Arthur. '*Room at the Top*, *Saturday Night and Sunday Morning*, and the "Cultural Revolution" in Britain'. *Journal of Contemporary History* 19 (1984): 127–52. Rpt. in *Contemporary Literary Criticism Select*. Gale, 2008.

McEntee, Joy. 'The End of Family in Kubrick's *A Clockwork Orange*'. *Adaptation* 8.3 (2015): 321–29.

McKay, Marina, and Lyndsey Stonebridge, eds. *British Fiction After Modernism*. Palgrave Macmillan, 2007.

McKay, Marina. *Modernism and World War II*. Cambridge UP, 2003.

McRae, Leanne. 'Writing and Resistance: *Trainspotting*'. *In-between: Essays and Studies in Literary Criticism* 13 (2004): 117–33.

McRobbie, Angela, ed. *Zoot-Suits and Second-Hand Dresses*. Macmillan, 1988.

McRobbie, Angela. 'Shut Up and Dance: Youth Culture and Changing Modes of Femininity'. *Young* 1.2 (1993): 13–31.

McRobbie, Angela. *'Jackie': An Ideology of Adolescent Femininity*. CCCS Stencilled Occasional Papers, 1978.

McRobbie, Angela. *Feminism and Youth Culture*. Palgrave Macmillan, 2000.

McRobbie, Angela. 'TOP GIRLS?' *Cultural Studies* 21.4–5 (2007): 718–37, doi: 10.1080/09502380701279044

National Institute on Drug Abuse. 'Heroin'. https://www.drugabuse.gov/publications/drugfacts/heroin. Accessed 21 Dec. 2017.

Nehring, Neil. *Flowers in the Dustbin. Culture, Anarchy, and Postwar England*. U of Michigan P, 1993.

O'Reilly, Nathanael. 'Embracing Suburbia: Breaking Tradition and Accepting the Self in Hanif Kureishi's *The Buddha of Suburbia*'. *Literary London: Interdisciplinary Studies in Representations of London* 7.2 (2009):

http://www.literarylondon.org/london-journal/september2009/oreilly.html.
    Accessed 14 Dec. 2016.

Pop Culture Correspondent. 2015. 'Ten Iconic Moments that Capture 1960s
    Britain'. *Saga*, 19 Sep. 2015, https://www.saga.co.uk/magazine/entertainment/
    nostalgia/10-iconic-moments-of-the-1960s. Accessed 21 Dec. 2017.

Pountain, Dick, and David Robins. *Cool Rules. Anatomy of an Attitude*. Reaktion
    Books, 2000.

Quabeck, Franziska. 'Shooting Up and Coming Home: Heroin as a Substitute
    for Home in Irvine Welsh's *Trainspotting* and *Porno*'. *Constructions of
    Home: Interdisciplinary Studies in Architecture, Law, and Literature*, AMS
    Studies in Cultural History (Book 9), edited by Klaus Stierstorfer, AMS Press,
    2010, pp. 291–301.

Rabinovitz, Rubin. 'Ethical Values in Anthony Burgess's *A Clockwork Orange*'.
    Studies in the Novel 11.1 (1979): 43–50.

Reynolds, Simon. 'Rave Culture: Living Dream or Living Death?' *The Clubcultures
    Reader. Readings in Popular Cultural Studies*, edited by Steve Redhead, with
    Derek Wynne and Justin O'Connor, Wiley-Blackwell, 1997, pp. 84–93.

Reynolds, Simon. *Generation Ecstasy. Into the World of Techno and Rave Culture*.
    Routledge, 1999.

Rushdie, Salman. *The Satanic Verses*. Penguin, 1988.

Russell, Ken. 1955. 'The Last of the Teddy Girls'. *Tate Modern Online*, 2013.
    http://www.tate.org.uk/art/artworks/russell-the-last-of-the-teddy-girls-p13821.
    Accessed 16 June 2016.

Ryman, Ernest. *Teddy Boy*. Michael Joseph Ltd, 1958.

Saglam, Berkem Gurenci. 'Rocking London: Youth Culture as Commodity
    in *The Buddha of Suburbia*'. *The Journal of Popular Culture* 47.3
    (2014): 554–70.

Saunders, Robert. 'Deadlier than the Male?' *Wikidot*, 15 Sep. 2013, http://
    robertsaunders.wikidot.com/deadlier-than-the-male. Accessed 11 May 2016.

Savage, Jon. *Teenage. The Creation of Youth Culture*. Viking, 2007.

Schlossman, Beryl. 'Burgess/Kubrick/A Clockwork Orange (twenty-to-one)'.
    Anthony Burgess and Modernity, edited by Alan R. Roughely, Manchester UP,
    2008, pp. 270–82.

Selvon, Samuel. *Lonely Londoners*. Longman, 1989.

Shaffer, Brian. *A Companion to The British and Irish Novel 1945–2000*.
    Blackwell, 2005.

Sillitoe, Alan. 'Poor People'. *Anarchy* 38.4 (1964): 124–28.

Sillitoe, Alan. *Saturday Night and Sunday Morning*. Flamingo, 1994.

Simpson, Dave. 'Malcolm McLaren Obituary'. *The Guardian*. 9 Apr. 2010, https://
    www.theguardian.com/music/2010/apr/09/malcolm-mclaren-obituary. Accessed
    21 Dec. 2017.

Stalcup, Scott. '*Trainspotting, High Fidelity*, and the Diction of Addiction'. *Studies
    in Popular Culture* 30.2 (2008): 119–36.

Stevenson, Randall, ed. *The Oxford English Literary History*. Vol. 12, *1960–
    2000: The Last of England?* Oxford UP. 2004.

Storry, Mike and Peter Childs, eds. *British Cultural Identities*. Routledge, 1997.

Temple, Julien, director. *Absolute Beginners*. Goldcrest Films and Virgin Films,
    1986.

Waterhouse, Keith. *Billy Liar*. *Billy Liar and The Loneliness of the Long-Distance Runner*, edited by Keith Waterhouse and Alan Sillitoe, Longman, 1966, pp. 3–157.

Watson, Kimberly. 'The 1960s. The Decade that Shook Britain'. http://www.historic-uk.com/CultureUK/The-1960s-The-Decade-that-Shook-Britain. Accessed 21 Dec. 2017.

Welsh, Irvine. *Trainspotting*. W. W. Norton, 1996.

Welsh, Irvine. *Irvine Welsh*. irvinewelsh.net. Accessed 21 Dec. 2017.

West, Russell, and Frank Lay, eds. *Subverting Masculinity. Hegemonic and Alternative Versions of Masculinity in Contemporary Culture*. Rodopi, 2000.

Wheatle, Alex. *Brixton Rock*. Arcadia Books, Ltd., 1999.

Wheatle, Alex. *East of Acre Lane*. Harper Collins, 2002.

Winkgens, Meinhard. "Cultural Hybridity and Fluid Masculinities in the Postcolonial Metropolis: Individualized Gender Identities in Hanif Kureishi's *The Buddha of Suburbia* and *The Black Album*." *Constructions of Masculinity in British Literature from the Middle Ages to the Present*, edited by Stefan Horlacher, Palgrave Macmillan US, 2011, pp. 229–45.

INDEX

Note: Page numbers in *italic* denote figures and those in **bold** refer to sustained discussions.